STRATFORD
A Town at War
1914–1945

STRATFORD
A Town at War
1914–1945

NICHOLAS FOGG

First published in the United Kingdom in 2008 by Sutton Publishing

Reprinted in 2017 by
The History Press
The Mill, Brimscombe Port,
Stroud, Gloucestershire, GL5 2QG
www.thehistorypress.co.uk

British Library Cataloguing in Publication Data
A catalogue record for this book is available from the British Library.

ISBN 978 0 7509 4891 3

This book is dedicated to Ann Fogg, who had a good war.

Typesetting and origination by
The History Press Limited.
Printed and bound by TJ International Ltd, Padstow, Cornwall

CONTENTS

ACKNOWLEDGEMENTS

Thanks go to the following people: Charlie Baldwin, Bob Bearman, Cyril Bennis, Anthony and Philip Bobroff, Michael Caldwell, Simon Fletcher, Michael Fogg, Angela Hewins, Mairi Macdonald, Matilda Pearce, the late Albert Pearce, Chris Towner, and Jo Wong.

'This Happy Grouping'

'More Tory than the Leader of the Opposition'

In January 1906, hundreds of people braved pouring rain in Stratford-upon-Avon's High Street. A local electrical shop was projecting the results of the General Election onto a screen as they were received by telephone. Deafening cheers greeted the emerging Liberal landslide, with the loudest reserved for the defeat of the Tory Prime Minister, A.J. Balfour. Excitement increased as rumours spread that the local result was very close. Indeed it was! A great roar greeted the news that Captain Malcolm Kincaid-Smith had ended three decades of Tory domination of the constituency by a mere 148 votes.

The new member was a curious choice as Liberal candidate. A professed Imperialist, he had participated in the abortive Jamieson raid whose object was to coerce the Transvaal into the British Empire. He was later decorated for his gallantry in the Boer War. If he had been selected for his appeal in a naturally Tory area, it was a shortsighted strategy. He proved a dubious asset for the Liberals. In his first six months in Parliament, Kincaid-Smith opposed important government policies while developing his own idiosyncratic programme, a form of conscription known as 'Universal Military Training'. Lloyd-George described Stratford's representative as 'one of the freaks of the last election… more Tory then the Leader of the Opposition'. Back in Stratford, the Liberal committee decided to canvass the membership for its views. An emergency meeting resolved that the Executive should find 'a fit Liberal candidate'. This meant that Kincaid-Smith, who was present, had nothing to lose. He announced that he would elicit opinion in the constituency on his proposals. He was as good as his word, visiting 1,500 houses. In parliament, he brought forward his National Training Bill under the Ten Minute Rule. One clause proposed exemption from conscription for 'habitual drunkards, persons of weak intellect and members of both Houses of Parliament'. According to *Punch*, 'a roar of cheers and laughter greeted this happy grouping'.

The MP did not reveal the result of his survey immediately, but he clearly felt that it gave him a mandate for drastic action. April 1909 brought the amazing news that this affable eccentric had resigned his seat and intended to fight a by-election to test opinion on his Bill.

The result, given the government's current unpopularity and the circumstances under which the by-election had been called, was a foregone conclusion. The Tories swept back with a huge majority. Kincaid-Smith polled a mere 479 votes. He may have felt vindicated in his principled stance when the First World War broke out just five years later.

Kincaid-Smith's proposals for conscription into the services were met with derision because they went against the British tradition of an entirely volunteer army.

This did not mean that there were not strong military traditions: far from it. Outside the classroom, the main activity for boys at Stratford's National School was drill. They stomped around the field next to the vicarage garden in companies of four holding staves for rifles, to the barked orders of a former sergeant major. This was regarded as important character training, making 'the lads smart at their work, as well as fine in their appearance, and it will tell on the future by making them grow up stalwart and healthy men'.

Some of these 'stalwart and healthy men' joined the services in 'the other ranks'. Others, like George Hewins, passed into the 2nd Volunteer Battalion of the Royal Warwickshire Regiment. He played the side drum in the fife and drum band. An instructor came over twice a week from the Regimental Headquarters at Budbroke Barracks near Warwick. They trained on the recreation ground or in the Corn Exchange at the top of Sheep Street. Once a year, the band escorted the Mayor to his annual civic service at Holy Trinity Church.

In 1909, the Volunteers were merged with a new force, the Territorial Army. Many of the Stratford contingent did not fancy undertaking this new commitment and quit. The only proviso was that they had to sign a paper saying they were willing to be conscripted if the country needed them. Doubtless, most of them thought little of it at the time.

William Jones, a mechanic at Bolland's Garage in Henley Street, who was considered Stratford's best shot with an air rifle, became a volunteer in a different service. His spirit of adventure led him to join the Naval Reserve, which gave him two weeks' annual training at sea.

The Warwickshire Yeomanry Cavalry was another possible choice for the volunteer. Its 'D' Company was recruited in the Stratford area and its rural character gave it its nickname of 'the Swedeheads'. It had been raised as long ago as 1794, principally as a means of suppressing civil unrest. Each year, the regiment went on a fortnight's exercises at Combe Abbey, which culminated in a grand 'Yeomanry Ball'. The farmers amongst the troop would take along one of their workers as grooms. In the event of a full-scale war, the Yeomanry was liable to be conscripted for overseas service. That had happened during the Boer War when the regiment had served in South Africa with distinction.

Some who had served in the Boer War were still liable to be recalled to the colours. Youngest of these was Robert Lidzy, who was just 14 when the regiment embarked for South Africa in January 1900. On leaving the National School a few weeks before, he had got a job at R.M. Bird's, the wine merchants. He returned to his employer after the war and rose to the position of Head Cellarman. 'A big, fine built man', he was Captain of the Fire Brigade and a leading Baptist layman.

Those joining the services from the King Edward VI Grammar School (KES) were more likely to pass onto an academy for the training of officers. In 1904, an ex-soldier, Sergeant Worrall, was appointed as School Sergeant. A rifle range was opened and soon two-thirds of the boys were learning to shoot.

The Territorial Batteries of the Royal Horse Artillery were organised on a county basis. A number of Stratford men were serving in the Warwickshire Battery that was founded by Lord Brooke, heir to the Earl of Warwick. They mustered light mobile guns that provided firepower in support of the Yeomanry cavalry. Each Battery had six 13lb field guns and an establishment of five officers, 200 men and 228 horses. They were all factotums, skilled as grooms and artillerymen and taking their turns as cooks.

Until shortly before the First World War, the main school in Stratford for those seeking a commission in the forces was Trinity College in Church Street. It had been founded in 1872 by the then vicar, Dr Collis, and had become a 'crammer' dedicated to gaining places for boys at elite public schools or military academies.

Just a few weeks before the outbreak of war, a new Yeomanry headquarters was opened in Broad Street. The troop is seen here in 1914 drawn up ready for inspection.
(Image courtesy of the Shakespeare Birthplace Trust Records Office)

The boys of King Edward's School prepare to do their bit. (Image courtesy of the Shakespeare Birthplace Trust Records Office)

'C' Battery, Warwickshire Royal Horse Artillery. (Image courtesy of the Shakespeare
Birthplace Trust Records Office)

One such young fellow was Bruce Bairnsfather, the elder son of a former Indian
Army officer. Major Thomas Bairnsfather had served in the Bengal Infantry. In the
early 1900s he bought Victoria Lodge, Bishopton. Bruce was a talented artist, but it
was intended that he should follow his father into the military and he was sent to
the United Services College at Westward Ho. Despite the fact that his parents were
themselves artistic – his mother, Amelia, was a painter and his father a musician and
composer, the school was instructed to beat Bruce's artistic leanings out of him. In
this it failed, but the boy suffered a miserable time and eventually, deliberately or
otherwise, failed the entrance exams to Sandhurst, so in 1904, he was sent to Trinity
College as a weekly boarder. Here he flourished, drawing cartoons on the walls of his
attic bedroom. He finally persuaded his father to allow him to attend art classes at the
newly built Technical College. He was greatly encouraged by the headmaster, Thomas
Holte, who recognised his talent. In 1906, he passed his army exam and joined the 3rd
Militia Royal Warwicks on a short-service commission. He found army life boring. He
managed to extricate himself from it (or so he thought at the time), two years later
and enrolled at the John Hassall School of Art at Olympia. After this, he designed
advertisements on a freelance basis. Lipton's Tea and Player's Navy Mixture were
amongst his commissions, but he found that he couldn't get enough work to support
himself, so he joined Spencer's, a firm of electric joiners, back in Stratford. The firm
had been founded by Spencer Flower, a brother of Archie Flower, the chairman of
Flower's Brewery. The two businesses were closely linked.

Bruce Bairnsfather was best known locally for his performances as a female
impersonator, when he would wear his mother's clothes. His friend, Will Howe,
introduced him to strangers as 'Miss Bairnsfather' on several occasions. The popular
novelist, Marie Corelli, who lived in Church Street, was so entranced by his talents
that she recommended him to the great impresario, C.B. Cochran, but Bruce was too
shy to attend the projected interview.

Younger boys joined the local troop of the Baden-Powell Boy Scouts. It was formed
by Robert Smith, a future Freeman of the town, in 1909, within a year of the inaugural
camp on Brownsea Island. William Bailey, aged 16, second son of Mr and Mrs Arthur

Baden-Powell's scouts, c. 1912. (Image courtesy of the Shakespeare Birthplace Trust Records Office)

Scouting for boys: a strenuous exercise on the recreation ground, c. 1912. (Image courtesy of the Shakespeare Birthplace Trust Records Office)

Britain no longer an island: Monsieur Salmet lands on the recreation ground. (Image courtesy of the Shakespeare Birthplace Trust Records Office)

Bailey of Albert Terrace, Great William Street, left the Church Lads Brigade to join the new organisation. On leaving school, he had gone to work for Mr A.B. Smith, the confectioner in Chapel Street. He rose rapidly to become Assistant Scout Master. Another prominent member of the troop was Adrian Barrett of St Gregory's Road. He joined at the age of 13 and acquired every badge for which he could qualify.

In July 1912, Stratford was thrilled at its first sight of an aeroplane. Monsieur Salmet of the *Daily Mail* Flying Corps, landed on the recreation ground and then took off to give a breathtaking exhibition, diving, flying between trees and skimming the river like a bird. No one seems to have realised the implication that Britain was no longer an island and open to aerial bombardment.

The Bensons

Twice a year, Frank and Constance Benson arrived by train with their theatrical company at Stratford to present three-week seasons at the Shakespeare Memorial Theatre. This was a much-awaited event. Crowds gathered at the station to welcome the actors, and the approaches were decorated with flags and banners. In 1910, Benson was made the second only Freeman of Stratford in the Borough's history.

Originally there was just one annual season – in the three weeks around the celebrations of Shakespeare's birthday on 23 April. In 1893, Benson had been due to play Coriolanus, but he had been taken ill and the performance was restaged in August. This had proved such a success that the second season became a permanent feature.

With the occasional break, the company had been coming to Stratford each year since 1886. The staff at the theatre were all locals, most of them working for the

Flower family. One of Bruce Bairnsfather's tasks as an employee of Spencer Flower was to install the electrical wiring at the theatre. Each season, he worked on the lighting rig for 30s a week. For the rest of the year, he worked at Flower's Brewery, or he travelled the country, installing electrical systems at the mansions of the wealthy where he was generally treated as a houseguest.

The townspeople also performed as 'supers', playing walk-on parts. Whenever they appeared on stage, their friends in the gallery shouted their names.

The Bensons participated in the evolving events of Shakespeare's birthday with great enthusiasm. Since 1823, there had been a luncheon to celebrate the great day. In the 1880s, the boys of King Edward VI Grammar School, the poet's old school, had started placing flowers on his grave in Holy Trinity Church. The townsfolk and visitors soon joined them on their pilgrimage.

Another dimension was added to the celebrations in 1907 when the king presented a Union Jack to be unfurled in Bridge Street. In the following year it was joined by the flags of the nations 'to signify the universality of Shakespeare's genius', and after the Austro-Hungarian ambassador unfurled the standard of the Dual Empire in 1910, it became customary to invite the representatives of the nations to perform this task.

The Benson Company held a unique position in the provinces, if only because it seemed to be on a perpetual tour over the length and breadth of the land. The critic, James Agate, once said that the most fitting monument to Frank Benson would be a statue on wheels. The well-connected Bensons were part of a process that would raise the respectability of the theatre. 'It was very much like a public school', recalled the actress, Dorothy Green, 'we were all loyal and enthusiastic supporters of its reputation. Inspired by Mr and Mrs Benson, the company was the servant of our beloved theatre, and of the public. There was no tiresome preaching, but it was understood that we should behave as became members of a great profession.'

In the public school tradition, Benson was usually referred to by his initials: F.R.B. A major part of the distinctive ethos was his love of sport. There was scarcely an activity to which he did not turn his considerable energies, be it football, cricket, hockey, rugby or athletics. Legend had it that he had once sent a telegram to his agent reading 'SEND ME A GOOD FAST BOWLER TO PLAY LAERTES.'

Memory was to exaggerate the extent of Bensonian sporting activity at Stratford. The hectic repertory at the theatre ensured that time was limited, but there would be the opportunity to take on a couple of the local teams.

In this the Stratfordians were more than a match for the Bensonians. In the pre-war years, they achieved exceptional sporting success on land and water. The rowing eight won trophies at many regattas, including Henley; the cricket XI was formidable and the rugby team won the Midlands Cup at Leicester. Patrick Thompson of Greenhill Street stroked the eight and played in the XV. Wing three-quarter Norman Kinman, son of the High Street fishmonger and poulterer, was widely regarded as the finest sportsman that Stratford had ever produced – and this at a time when memory could reach back to the very start of organised games in the town. He was endowed with a magnificent physique, a fine turn of speed and matchless courage. There was no outdoor sport at which he did not excel. As a boy at the Commercial School, his skill at soccer had won the interest of a leading league club, but he preferred the less lucrative game of rugby, 'Stratford's premier sport'. His magnificent defensive play had played a decisive part in the magnificent victory at Leicester. He won a place in the Midlands Counties team that won a heroic victory against Middlesex on Stratford's home ground at Pearcecroft. His type was that of the taciturn sportsman. 'Plain and blunt, modest and retiring, for anything in the nature of a show of fuss was anathema to Norman.'

The Grammar School contributed fine sportsmen to the town's teams. Head boy in 1913 was Gordon Barber, the eldest son of the Congregational minister. He was an

Stratford Rugby XV – winners of the Midland Cup, 1908. Norman Kinman is second from the right in the middle row. (Image courtesy of the Shakespeare Birthplace Trust Records Office)

excellent wicket keeper, Captain of the XV and Secretary of the Debating Society. As a lay preacher, he won 'great acceptance' in the village chapels. He was looking forward to taking up a place to read History at Birmingham University.

Rus in Urbe

The Bensons were enchanted by the idea of a theatre in the small town where Shakespeare had been born. Its physical limits had changed little since the poet's day and the historic town was still densely populated. This was the last era in which the shopkeepers lived over their premises and much of Stratford's poorer population still lived in the alleys and rough terraces that their forebears had occupied for centuries.

Stratford still possessed a rural air. It was but a few years since the centuries-old tradition of servants and farm labourers plying for hire at the annual Mop Fair had ceased. The name was believed to take its name from the symbols of trade worn by those seeking employment. On the Friday week after the 'Big Mop' on 12 October came the 'Runaway Mop' when those dissatisfied with their positions had a second chance to be hired. By the eve of the First World War, however, the fairs were better known for the large number of roasts that took place outside the town's pubs.

Early on Tuesday mornings, poor people took buckets up to the cattle markets at Bridgefoot and by the GWR station to milk the cows. Cattle were driven down the street to be slaughtered in the yards at the back of the butcher's shops. The skins were sent to the tannery beside the Canal Basin. The carpenters and four blacksmiths at Archer's, the wheelwrights, were proud of their ability to build a farm cart from scratch without referring to any plans.

Aromas of activity permeated Stratford. When the wind blew from the north, the lovely malty smells from Flower's Brewery wafted into the town. Numerous bakeries made their contribution, as did the pong of boiling withies from the basket makers. Most unpleasant of all was the reek from the two fellmongers. After sheep were slaughtered, their skins were sent to Birches Skin Yard to be cured before being made into rugs and clothing. The smell was extremely pungent and the rotting flesh became home to thousands of maggots that were placed in great bins and given out free to fishermen.

The withies were brought by punt from the osier beds along the river, unloaded at the jetty by the Shoulder of Mutton pub and taken by horse and cart to Collins', the basket weavers at the top of Tyler Street, which older people still called 'Donkey Lane', to be steamed over open fires.

In June came the pea-picking season. The women from the poorer areas would walk out into the fields to undertake the backbreaking labour, earning 6d for each 40lb 'pot'.

Poor people with big enough back gardens kept livestock – rabbits and chickens, or a couple of pigs in a sty. Each year one pig would be sold at market to pay for its two replacements. The other was at the mercy of the 'pig sticker', who would come round to slaughter it in the yard. In Guild Street, George Holtom's little daughter, Frances, could not bear to hear the sound of the pig's squeals and ran indoors.

In the Victorian era, small suburbs had grown up: working-class ones off Guild Street, and in the area known as the 'West End': more affluent ones around Albany Road and Evesham Place. Yet open country was no further than a ten-minute walk from the centre of town in any direction. Men would go out with their dogs over the surrounding fields to catch rabbits and gut them on the spot, or to put ferrets down the holes. Many poorer families depended on rabbits for their meat. They would get a penny for the skin from Warburton's in the Birmingham Road. Hares were highly prized. One would feed a family for two or three days.

The town was surrounded by the great estates of patrician families: the great Liberal dynasty of the Trevelyans at Welcombe who had married into the vast wealth of a Lancashire mill owner. At Avoncliffe House at Tiddington, another Liberal dynasty, the Hamiltons, presided. The Shottery Manor Estate owned the fields between that village and Stratford and ensured that it remained separate from the town. Most powerful of all was the nouveau wealth of the Flower family, brewers and philanthropists. Charles Flower had founded the Theatre and appointed Benson as the guardian of its Shakespeare season. The current head of the family was his nephew, Archie, eldest of the ten children of Charles' brother, Edgar. One of his brothers, Richard, had been killed while serving with the Yeomanry in the Boer War. Another, Oswald, was a professional soldier.

The best-known resident of Stratford in 1914 was the best-selling novelist, Marie Corelli. She had moved to the town in 1899 with her companion, Bertha Vyver and lived at Mason's Croft, a fine house in Church Street, next to Trinity College. Her star as a popular writer was in decline, but her eccentricities and her capacity to provoke controversy would make her the most talked-about person in Stratford for many years after her death. In the summer of 1905 she had imported a Venetian gondola, complete with gondolier, onto the Avon. The latter was not a success. In the low parlour of the Dirty Duck, he had developed a taste for Flower's Ale and was merry at the helm once too often. He was replaced by Ernest Chandler, a more phlegmatic local, who had been in Marie's service since leaving school.

In 1903, Marie had brought a libel action against George Boyden, the editor of the local newspaper, the *Stratford-upon-Avon Herald* and a prominent local councillor and tradesman, Fred Winter. She later withdrew the writ against Boyden, but the case against Winter proceeded and, in a case which aroused national publicity and much local derision, she won damages of a farthing.

Marie Corelli in her gondola, with Ernest Chandler, her gondolier. (Image courtesy of the Shakespeare Birthplace Trust Records Office)

Even more fury was raised against Marie in 1908. For years she had complained about the boys of Trinity College, their rudeness and their balls coming over her wall. Now she struck back by purchasing the field behind the school that was rented for games. Life under such a landlady would have been intolerable. The school purchased land in Maidenhead and moved there. Local anger was intense – the school had been a good source of income for local traders. Marie's windows were broken by the departing schoolboys. Undaunted, she purchased the school buildings, which were to remain empty for years.

ONE

'THE INFERNO ON THE CONTINENT'

War

On 31 July 1914, the atmosphere for the arrival of the Bensons was different. Britain was on the verge of war and everyone knew it. The local newspaper, the *Stratford-upon-Avon Herald*, which a few years earlier had expressed its admiration for the Kaiser, had become convinced that England's chief potential enemy lay across the 'German Ocean'. In 1913, it noted that pessimists considered war with Germany to be inevitable. Yet in July 1914, it relegated the news of the assassination of the Austrian Archduke below such items as 'The Search for Fertilisers' and 'Municipal Apathy'.

Summer had wound its usual way, although the rumour that the Suffragettes intended to set fire to Holy Trinity caused some alarm. The regulars at the *One Elm* organised an outing to Blackpool. At Hereford Regatta, the Stratford Eight won the West of England Challenge Vase. The GWR announced August bank holiday excursions to south coast resorts and nearer home, to the Kineton Horse Show and a river trip to Cleeve Prior.

Amid this tranquillity, war clouds were gathering. The *Herald* took more seriously the Austrian bombardment of Belgrade. To match the hour, the Picture House showed *The Hundred Days*, culminating in a spectacular portrayal of the Battle of Waterloo. In the dying days of peace, Kathleen Hudson, aged 19, the daughter of a local printer, was married at Holy Trinity to Charles Stoehr, a 27-year-old officer in the Royal Engineers. The bridegroom was stationed in Aden, so the wedding was timed for his extended furlough.

On the evening of their return to Stratford, a reception was held in the Theatre gardens for the Bensonians. Frank Benson made a short speech, recalling that from the same pen that wrote:

Come the three corners of the world in arms,
And we shall shock them. Nought shall make us rue,
If England to itself do rest but true.

had also come 'One touch of nature makes the whole world kin.' He concluded amidst applause that the one thought should not preclude the other in the trials that were to follow. On 4 August, war was declared and there was a special performance of *Henry V* – 'Now all the youth of England are on fire' – with the leading young actor, Basil Rathbone, as the Dauphin. After the curtain fell, the company drilled on stage with halberds and spears. The next day Benson embarked on a recruiting campaign around the local villages.

The Bensonians drilling in Avonbank garden. (Image courtesy of the Shakespeare Birthplace Trust Records Office)

Miss Bertha Gover, whose parents lived in Albany Road, must have watched the slide to war with some anxiety. She was a governess with a wealthy Russian family and must have wondered whether to stay at her post or risk the hazardous journey home.

'D' Company of the Warwickshire Yeomanry was mobilised the day after the declaration and joined the other squadrons at Warwick on 10 August. Among them was Robert Lidzy, now living at 3 Percy Street with his wife and daughter.

Stratford's fine generation of sportsmen was the first to the colours. Patrick Thompson joined the Royal Engineers. Norman Kinman had been persuaded to turn professional with the noted New South Wales Rugby League Club, Balmain Tigers, but he returned shortly before war broke out. He had been a bombardier with his territorial unit, the 1st Warwickshire Battery of the Royal Horse Artillery (WRHA). He was called up on 4 August, but when he reported to the HQ at Leamington Spa, he was told to return the next day. He went back to Stratford by train with another member of the Battery, L-Cpl Harry Fox of 19 Bridge Street. The Stratfordians on the Battery returned the next day in three cars. Almost certainly among them was the Assistant Scoutmaster, William Bailey.

Another scout to the fore in signing up was Adrian Barrett, who joined the Black Watch in the ranks. Charles Stoehr received his recall while on honeymoon. He returned to Aden, where his bride would join him at the first opportunity.

Already food shortages were apparent, popularly blamed on hoarding by unscrupulous middlemen. Despite fears that a prolonged war would produce near-starvation, an intense patriotic surge swept the area. A recruiting station in Sheep Street was swamped with volunteers. In proportion to its size, Stratford was contributing more men to the war effort than any other town in the county. A Roll of Honour of local recruits was displayed from the Town Hall.

A new company of Territorial Rifles, part of the 3rd Service Reserve Battalion, had temporary headquarters lent by the vicar in the parish parlour. First commander was the 26-year-old Lt Bruce Bairnsfather, who was recalled into the Warwicks. He had been on a job for Spencers in Newfoundland. He returned home to Bishopton to find a terse note from his employers: 'Dear Sir, Owing to the outbreak of European war, your services are no longer required.'

The Warwickshire Yeomanry departs for war: eyes right at Marie Corelli's house. (Image courtesy of the Shakespeare Birthplace Trust Records Office)

Farewell to Stratford: the Warwickshire Yeomanry depart. (Image courtesy of the Shakespeare Birthplace Trust Records Office)

Scores of men seek to join up at Stratford Town Hall in 1914. (Authors collection)

A recruiting rally in Bridge Street, early in the war. (Image courtesy of the Shakespeare Birthplace Trust Records Office)

Roger Noakes, who ran a grocer's shop in the High Street, was an altar server at Holy Trinity. He was so keen to enlist that he cycled over 100 miles in an attempt to join the Cycle Corps. His gallant effort was unsuccessful, but in October, he cast in his lot with the Warwicks.

William Jones was called up into the Naval Reserve and joined HMS *Victorious*, which participated in the first victory of the war, the Battle of Heligoland Bight. Later he was engaged in mine-laying on HMS *Paris* in the North Sea and the English Channel.

The Mayor, Cllr Fred Winter, in sentencing a drunk to a month's imprisonment, told him that all Englishmen should be keeping the peace. The Picture House screened the latest news and appeals to 'The Common Cause'. 'Eat no eggs in Easter Week', suggested the *Herald*, 'but give them to the wounded.' The Town Hall became a hospital with forty beds filled by wounded Belgian soldiers. Seventy-six refugees from 'gallant little Belgium' also had to be accommodated – thirty-four of them lived at a hostel at numbers 2–3 Guild Street. They swelled the congregation at St Gregory's Church at High Mass on Sundays and fished along the river during the rest of the week.

Other Belgians had made their own way to Stratford. One young man, Louis Vandeputte, obtained lodgings in Garden Row, Scholar's Lane. A printer by trade, he obtained work with the Shakespeare Head Press in Henley Street. On 25 March 1915 he received a postcard from someone with the Belgian Government-in-Exile, based at Ste Adriesse, near Le Havre. '*Un Bon Salut de Belgique... ou á peu pres*' ('well nearly'). Louis joined the French Army in 1916 and wrote from the front to his old boss, W.H. Bloomfield, who seems to have become a munitions worker to escape the call-up. In his time in England, he had mastered contemporary colloquialisms, using phrases like 'My dear old sport'.

Marie Corelli, whose companion, Bertha, was Belgian, took great interest in these refugees and the wounded Belgian soldiers, throwing a banquet for them at the Riverside restaurant to celebrate King Albert's birthday.

Political differences were put aside. The Tory and Liberal parliamentary candidates addressed a public meeting in support of the war in the Rother Market.

The *Herald* was reduced to six pages, an indignity that may have influenced its view that economics were precluded by a lengthy war – it was later reduced to four

VAD hospital in the Town Hall. (Image courtesy of the Shakespeare Birthplace Trust Records Office)

pages. It was generally expected that the war would be short. Some considered that it would be over by Christmas and the troops home by spring. Contrary to later belief, this was not in expectation of rapid victory, but because it was considered that the modern industrial economy could not sustain a prolonged war – in this the *Herald* reflected the prevailing view. Britain, which possessed the most powerful economy in the world and dominated the oceans, would triumph, albeit at a great cost. Ultimately this proved correct, but it would be many long months before first Russia and then Austria-Hungary and Germany imploded.

Because of this expectation, many men were rejected as unfit for war service. Edgar Cranmer, aged 23, of Shottery, had been a scholarship boy at the Grammar School and had gone on to qualify as a post office clerk. This involved the vital military skill of telegraphy. He could transmit and receive Morse at an impressive speed, but he was turned down because he had suffered from appendicitis – then a serious ailment.

Marie Corelli's gondolier, Ernest Chandler, was also a medical reject, despite his clear ability to propel the exotic craft up and down the Avon. Two others who were turned down were John Bone and Charles Guise. Bone was a 25-year-old assistant at Noakes and Crofts, the High Street grocers. He was 4ft 11in tall and weighed 6st 10lbs, just 26lbs heavier than an infantryman's equipment. Guise, a printer with the firm of Edward Fox, was just 4ft 9in tall.

On 22 August, the 1st Warwickshire Battery of the Royal Horse Artillery entrained to a camp at Barton Mere near Bury St Edmunds. On the first night, Harry Fox was in charge of the guard. At 1.15 a.m., a motor scout arrived with a dispatch rider in his sidecar with orders to mobilise. The bugle was sounded and the Battery turned out in the dark and took an hour to harness up the horses, attach the guns and ride off. A planned rendezvous with the Worcestershire and Gloucestershire Yeomanry Regiments proved chaotic. The Battery returned to camp at 5 a.m., had breakfast and turned in again for a few hours. That evening, the Adjutant read out a letter from the Brigadier congratulating them on their quick turn out which had taken just three minutes. The Worcestershire Yeomanry had taken three hours!

There followed a series of apparently pointless marches around East Anglia. Four days later, the WRHA left Barton Mere at 10 a.m. on what they were told was a route march to the coast. They arrived at Redgrave Park near Diss at 4 p.m. where they slept in the open. Next day they marched fifteen miles to Harleston. Harry Fox was again on all-night guard duty. The next morning they started from camp at 10 a.m. They were told that they were marching to Bungay, but the order was countermanded at the last moment. Instead, they marched the twenty miles to Norwich. En route they rendezvoused with the Warwickshire, Worcestershire and Gloucestershire Yeomanry Regiments, which had been amalgamated with the Battery to form the South Midland Mounted Brigade. With a strength of 2,000, it was an impressive sight.

The next day, Sunday 31 August, at 2.30 a.m., the Brigade embarked by train for Newbury. They arrived at 10 a.m. and camped on the racecourse. Three days later, the members of the Battery were examined by the Medical Officer in preparation for active service. Not surprisingly, all were passed as fit.

There was clearly some debate in military circles as to what to do with the Brigade. Cavalry had proved inefficacious on the Western Front, but gunners were in high demand. It was decided to send the Yeomanry Regiments to the then backwater of Egypt. On 9 September, they were given embarkation leave.

After a brief weekend together, Robert Lidzy's wife and 9-year-old daughter, a pupil at the National School, were among the crowds at Stratford station to see loved ones off. Florrie Lidzy was to remember what a sad day it was for her mother.

After a 48-hour leave back in Stratford, Harry Fox was inoculated by the doctor. He suffered the after-effects and spent the next day in bed in his 'Sadler's Shanty'. The effect was the same when he had another inoculation on 29 September.

Sergeant J.H. Savage of 24 Henley Street, a regular in the South Wales Borderers, had participated in the allied victory at the First Battle of the Marne, which led to the German retreat to the Aisne and the start of trench warfare. During the subsequent battle, which took place between 14 and 27 September, he was struck by shrapnel. He was brought home and died in Bournbrook Military Hospital on 7 October, the first Stratfordian to die in the First World War.

As yet, life in Stratford was not greatly affected by the war. The Mop took place as usual, with five oxen and seven pigs on the spits. The excursion trains arrived as normal, but collections were made for the War Relief Fund and the 'Aunt Sally' stalls offered the chance to pitch at the Kaiser and his High Command.

A new headmaster, the Revd Cecil Knight, took over at King Edward VI Grammar School in September. Among his first acts was to raise a cadet corps and appoint himself its commanding officer. The boys wore puttees and marched and drilled with dummy rifles. Three or four real rifles were carried by the NCOs. Manoeuvres took place on the Welcombe Hills and there were long marches behind a bugle band. Normally the whole business might have seemed 'a bit of a lark', but there was a strong feeling that it could be a preparation for the real thing, so it was taken very seriously.

France

King George V reviewed the Warwickshire Battery of the Royal Horse Artillery on 11 October at a church parade. Five days later, the camp was flooded out by torrential rain. The Battery's fourteen NCOs experienced the luxury of sleeping in an empty house at Thatcham. They were about to enjoy what the *Herald* described as 'the privilege' of being the first Territorial Battery to embark for France. On 30 October, they entrained for Southampton, arriving at 8 a.m. At 1.30 p.m., they embarked for Le Havre aboard *The Victorian*, a ship of the Leyland Line. On arrival, they lay in dock till morning. The ship was unloaded at 8 a.m. and at 4 p.m. they marched the two miles to a camp through crowds of people whose facial expressions Harry Fox found 'rather indifferent'. Doubtlessly the townspeople were accustomed to the sight of disembarking British soldiers.

The next day, they left for the station. They worked hard at loading the guns and horses onto a train. The greys were left behind. It was considered they would be too conspicuous on the battlefield.

They were escorted on their journey by a party of French soldiers. Harry Fox was taken with their colourful red trousers, long blue coats and blue caps. They were given no clue to their destination, but it would not have taken a great deal of imagination to hazard a guess. Harry was entranced by the French countryside, which reminded him of England. He was delighted by the 'very fine' market gardens and found the 'beautiful and green' vegetables 'a grand sight'. He was enchanted as they passed through Rouen with its great cathedral. 'It seemed impossible to realise that the country was at war.'

Early the next morning, they arrived at St Omer and marched to Esquades, about thirty miles from the front line. On the way, they passed 'newly-dug graves where a lot of soldiers had been buried'. They could hear the gunfire and aeroplanes circled overhead continuously. They encamped in a field, but everyone slept in a neighbouring mill.

The next day, Harry Fox was put in charge of issuing weapons. Later he called on the Mayor of the district, with a view to requisitioning three wagons in which to gather supplies. The Mayor was absent, however, owing to the fact that his secretary had been arrested as a German spy!

Harry met the Mayor next day and found him 'a good sort'. The requisition order was duly signed and the wagons sequestered from local farmers. He spent the next week, foraging around local farms for hay and potatoes. He was shocked by the primitive conditions in which the peasants lived. He found one family 'at their dinner, using wooden spoons and flint and steel for lighting'. The weather was dreadful. Day after day, he was soaked to the skin and his boots were in a very bad state. It was having ill effects on the horses: forty were sick and two died – and the Battery had not yet reached the frontline.

On Sunday 15 November, the Mayor came out to the camp and gave the men rum and coffee. At 9 a.m. the news came that the former commander-in-chief, the 82-year-old Field Marshall, Earl Roberts of Kandahar, had died the previous day while on a visit of inspection to St Omer. The Battery was delegated to send a gun carriage to bear his coffin.

The next morning, Harry Fox was deputed to act as a pall-bearer at St Omer before Lord Roberts' body was returned to England. At the last moment the order was postponed until the next day.

The ceremony was an impressive affair. The streets were lined with infantry. Pipers playing a lament preceded the coffin. A body of French cavalry followed, with their blue cloaks, brass helmets with black plumes and lances. Behind came Indian troops representing brigades that Lord Roberts had commanded. The streets were crowded but once again, Harry noted that the spectators seemed 'rather indifferent'. His party carried the coffin into a service at the Town Hall. Afterwards, it was conveyed to Boulogne in a Red Cross car.

Had Lord Roberts survived, he might well have inspected the Battery. The top brass spent a lot of time on such activity. Over the next two months, they were inspected twice by General Monroe and by Lord Brooke, their founder, Sir John French and General Gough. On 2 December, the king and the Prince of Wales inspected the entire division.

On the day after the funeral pomps, the Battery held a full dress rehearsal in preparation for leaving for the front. As was customary, they were issued with tobacco and chocolate.

That night there was a sharp frost. Reveille was at 5.30 a.m. When they were ready to march, the order was countermanded. Another Battery had been sent to the front in their place and they went on a route march instead. In the afternoon, there was a heavy fall of snow. That night, Harry's feet were dry for the first time in a week. This comfort was short-lived. After another early reveille, they moved off towards the front at 10.30 a.m., passing the graves of two German airmen who had been shot down. Travelling was very bad on the icy roads. Each hill had to be strewn with earth and the horses and wagons frequently slid into the ditch. It was dark when they arrived at their destination: a farmhouse where they slept in the barn. The cold was getting to Harry. He only had one blanket. At reveille, his boots were frozen stiff and he found it almost impossible to put them on. The journey the next day was equally difficult. It was bitterly cold. They struggled on to Hazebrouck, where they fed the horses before moving onto a place called Vieux Berguin, where they slept in another barn. While there, Harry met another Stratfordian, Royal Engineer, Pte George Taylor, of 3 Meer Street. He was returning from the trenches and doubtless imparted useful survival tips.

After spending three weeks some seven miles behind the trenches, the Battery left for the front at 10 a.m. on Saturday 12 December. The next morning, at precisely 10.10 a.m., a sergeant in the Right Section fired its first shell of the First World War. At noon they were obliged to pull out after the German gunners, with their heavier ordinance, located their position. When the Battery was not in action, it was withdrawn behind the firing line. For the first time since arriving in France, it was in proper billets.

The artillery was a safer option than the infantry because it was located in the second line of trenches and was generally less exposed. December 15th was spent on digging gun pits, so that the Battery would be less vulnerable to German counter-fire. The next day, Harry Fox took supplies up to the front line with a Sgt Smith and a Trooper Davies. They passed through the village of Doulieu, where, on 15 October, the Germans had held a revolver to the head of a 'prominent inhabitant' and made him set fire to the 'magnificent church'. Harry was appalled by this act of desecration, but paused to admire the remaining stained glass and the carvings. Near the front line, they took a wrong turning and were soon in the thick of the firing, within 20 yards of forty-seven guns with 'Jack Johnsons'[1] and shells bursting all around them. After passing some twelve batteries, all in action, they found their comrades, but were soon compelled to retire. The Germans had found their position again. As they retreated to their billets, they passed through Fleurbeaux, 'rather a large town, but completely ruined, churches in ruins and all shops closed with boards up. Quite a scene of desolation.'

That night, Harry was in charge of the armed guard of twenty-two men. The dark did not bring peace. There was a very heavy cannonade around midnight. A German plane passed overhead and searchlights and star shells lit up the sky.

Harry soon realised the necessities for survival, recording assiduously each time he saw a German aircraft. This was not born of an enthusiasm for plane spotting, but from the knowledge that the plane was engaged on the task of observing gun positions for its own artillery:

When an observer sees a flash of gun fire, a photo is immediately taken, developed at once, then by means of lenses enlarged to same scale as map carried by observer. Placed on map and a pin is then passed through the flash on negative and exact position is marked.

At first ground-fire was the only hazard to patrolling aircraft, but aerial combat soon developed. Before the Battle of Loos in September 1915, Harry watched a 'thrilling duel in mid-air between two Germans and a Frenchman armed with guns and maxims'.

The greatest danger was shrapnel. 'It's the splinters that do the damage', wrote Signalman William Clarke of 36 Broad Street, 'They fly a long way.'

The Warwickshire Lads

Back in Stratford, in December, the Recruiting Office, desperate for men, announced that the minimum height had been reduced to 5ft. Attention turned to the 100 'unwilling and selfish' young men who had not volunteered. One big strong fellow of about 26 caused derision when asked 'Why not enlist?' by replying 'Mother won't let me.' The father of four youths sent them off to London to evade the recruiting officer. The *Herald* suggested that taxpayers should 'give these enlistable men no peace until they do their duty. Failing that, they should give the government no rest until the order is issued for conscription.'

At Christmas, George Hewins was called up into the 7th Battalion of the Royal Warwicks, despite being a married man of 35 with seven children. There were some thirty Stratfordians in his Company. They were sent for a brief spell of training at Danbury Huts, five miles from Chelmsford and marched through the lanes singing:

> We are the Warwickshire lads,
> We know our manners,
> We spend our tanners,
> Marchin' down the Danbury Road,
> Doors an' winders open wide,
> We're the boys of the infantry,
> We don't care for the ASC,
> We are the Warwickshire lads!

A ploy used by the recruiting office was to encourage young men to join up with their pals. In January 1915, Victor Hyatt, the 18-year-old son of a Wood Street saddler and harness maker, enlisted with his friends from the Grammar School, Thomas and Dix. They were to serve together in 'D' Company of the 18th Battalion Royal Fusiliers.

Victor Hyatt. (Image courtesy of the Shakespeare Birthplace Trust Records Office)

The Christmas Truce

Lieutenant Bruce Bairnsfather had transferred to the 1st Battalion of the Royal Warwicks. He had been assigned command of a Maxim gun section serving at the village of St Yvon in the Ploegsteert (Plugstreet) Wood sector in Belgium. He was appalled at the horrors of war and declined the chance of home leave because he felt he would probably be disinclined to return. He had started to submit cartoons to the noted magazine, *The Bystander*. To his delight, they were accepted and he began to send his work on a regular basis.

Bruce witnessed the spontaneous Christmas truce of 1914, which occurred in many places along the line. 'It all felt most curious', he wrote. The Battalion had returned to the line on 23 December after a spell in reserve. On Christmas Eve, on a freezing night, he heard *Stille Nacht* being sung from the German trenches. The response from the British lines was the singing of 'irreverent songs'. A boot flew through the air and landed in his trench. It was filled with sausages and chocolates. He looked round for something to throw back and sent the Germans a Christmas pudding.

Suddenly a 'complete Boche type' appeared on the parapet and looked about:

> This complaint became infectious. It didn't take 'Our Bert' long to be upon the skyline. This was a signal for more Boche anatomy to be disclosed, and this was replied to by all our Alfs and Bills, until, in less time than it takes to tell, half a dozen or so each of the belligerents were outside the trenches and were advancing towards each other in no-man's land....
>
> There were those sausage-eating wretches who had elected to start this infernal European fracas, and in so doing had brought us all into the same muddy pickle as themselves... There was not an atom of hate on either side that day; and yet, on our side that day, not for a moment was the will to war and the will to beat them relaxed.

Later, Bairnsfather was astonished to see one of his Battalion's machine-gunners, a hairdresser in civilian life, cutting the unnaturally long hair of a docile German, who was patiently kneeling on the ground while the automatic clippers crept up the back of his neck.

For his inaction to prevent this Anglo-German fraternisation, Bairnsfather was investigated with a view to a court martial, but it was clearly felt that he was too valuable an officer to lose.

Behind the lines, the 1st Warwickshire Battery of the Royal Horse Artillery saw nothing of the Christmas truce. Harry Fox was on cooking duty. On Christmas Eve, he burnt one of the plum puddings, but he spent the night in the cook house and was able to rustle up enough to serve to the men after their bread and cheese despite being on his sickbed all day himself.

Three days later, 'tired of the rats', Harry and a companion called Brown found an abandoned cottage behind the lines with a bed to sleep in. It was the first time he had undressed in two months. That night he lay in bed and watched the shellfire through the window. In the morning they washed their clothes in the kitchen and left them in the bedroom to dry. They went outside to take the air and found that the latch had broken so they could not get back in and had to break a window.

With the thaw, the countryside became 'a perfect quagmire'. The district was 'like a vast lake, dotted with islands'. The roads were almost impassable. The awful weather was having an even more debilitating effect on the horses than the men. Harry Fox was put in charge of the forty in the 'sick line' and he was allocated extra men to help tend them. On New Year's Eve, six broke loose so he had to saddle up and scour the country for them. Eventually he found them all. On 4 January, the grooms took ten sick horses to the depot of the Royal Army Veterinary Corps. Those that recovered would be sent back to base, the rest would be shot.

On 11 January, the Battery was ordered the four miles back up to the front at La Coutrire. On the march they passed many freshly-dug graves in the fields. On arrival, they put their guns in the second line of trenches and started to dig themselves in, opening fire two days later.

Away from the Trenches

It was a curious feature of trench life that all infantry regiments were played in and out of the line by their regimental bands: bagpipes vied with brass, drum, fife and bugle. It was an odd life for the artillerymen. They could visit villages behind the lines where there was a semblance of normality. It was almost like commuting to work. Harry Fox rode the seven miles into Bailleul to visit the dentist. While there he visited the church, which was so large he thought it was a cathedral. On other occasions he spent an amusing evening of music and dancing with a group of Belgian refugees, went into Hazebrouck to see a 'movie' and heard the band of the 20th Hussars playing ragtime. There were frequent football matches against the other Batteries in the 2nd Division Field Artillery – and, in the summer, cricket matches. There was even a Divisional Football Cup, for which the different regiments competed. The Battery had a star player in Norman Kinman. On 4 April, he received the cup from General Mullions after a 2–0 victory in the final. Each team member received a silver matchbox and 20 francs.

Amazingly, wildlife co-existed with the war. Harry heard his first cuckoo of spring on 28 March 1915 and saw the first swallow on his birthday, 12 April.

Apart from regular soldiers, many of whom had seen much of the world, most of those arriving in France had never been abroad. George Hewins' furthest expedition from Stratford had been an excursion by train to Weston-super-Mare. France was a different world. Harry Fox was amazed by the common practice in Flanders of using dogs as draught animals, writing with astonishment at seeing them employed in churning milk and pulling carts.

Things seemed even more extraordinary during the rest periods away from the front. On 24 January 1915, they marched the thirty-six miles to the village of Dohem between St Omer and Calais. Everyday details gained great significance. Harry saw a train for the first time in two months. He noted the beautiful church at Aire and admired the 'good looking women' they passed and the bearing of the Indian mounted troops 'from Lahore, Merrut and Mysore' who were on the road in great numbers: 'good horses and riders'. They met motor ambulances that were provided from funds raised by the women of America and Canada.

Dohem turned out to be a place with 'plenty of bad smells' and typhoid was raging through the village. Three funerals of victims took place next day. Nevertheless, the men were billeted in the village as arranged. This news must have reached the powers-that-be, for, at 5 a.m., they received orders to return to Vieux Berquin and marched off at 9 a.m. It was a terrible journey: twenty-five miles of tramping through snow in the freezing cold. Once there, the horses and guns were put in a field and the men into different barns. Harry and his friend were fortunate enough to find lodgings in an *estimet* 'with rather good people'. Four days later he was promoted to full corporal.

On 25 February, there was a sharp frost and a heavy fall of snow. Some of the men developed frostbite. Despite the conditions, the entire division was moved to a rest camp back at Dohem. Twelve days later, 25,000 troops were on the move as the division returned along the thirty miles to the front line. On arrival, several of the Battery's cooks reported ill with what turned out to be diphtheria. Six weeks later, seven soldiers, including Norman Kinman, were hospitalised with measles.

Neuve Chapelle

On 10 March 1915, the Battery received a sudden call-up for a major offensive. General Haig planned to capture Aubers Ridge at Neuve Chapelle. Five hundred guns blazed away all day, in the biggest artillery barrage of the war so far. It was directed at smashing the barbed wire and the German trenches before the infantry advanced along a one-and-a-quarter mile front – four British divisions against one German.

The Battery saddled up and awaited orders. At 1 p.m. they marched for six miles. German prisoners were pouring back towards Estaires. Next day, reveille was at 4 a.m. and the Battery rode out again at six. Many wounded – British, Indian and German – were continuously passing to the rear. On the road, Harry Fox met Sgt John Berry, an old school friend, whose parents lived at 36 Henley Street. Like Edgar Cranmer, after leaving the Grammar School, he had trained as a telegrapher at Stratford post office. At the start of the war he was working in Leicester and volunteered for the Leicestershire Yeomanry. He was killed at the Battle of Frezenburg Ridge near Ypres, when his regiment lost two-thirds of its strength, two months later.

The offensive lasted three days. 'Plan not working out as desired', Harry wrote cryptically in his diary. He recorded that British casualties had been 6,000 while German losses were 16,000. This was 'very satisfactory in every way'. He had been misinformed. The offensive was a disaster. A strip 2,000 yards wide and 1,200 yards deep had been won at the cost of 7,000 British and 4,000 Indian casualties. Aubers Ridge had not been taken. The Germans had counter-attacked and, in the process, lost almost as many men as the British.

A new tactic had been tried. The intense artillery bombardment had lasted thirty-five minutes and then the range had been lengthened so that the British infantry, behind a second screen of shells, could overrun the trenches flattened by the first. The scheme failed because a shortage of munitions meant that the second barrage was inadequate and there had been a five-hour delay in launching the assault, enabling the Germans to regroup.

At the end of the month, the Battery participated in exercises and performed their gun drill. A Major attended to 'explain the method of our next advance', which was presumably a briefing on the failed tactics of two weeks before

The Second Battle of Ypres

In April 1915, the war, which had previously been fought between the two sides in a spirit of military discipline, turned nasty. On the 17th, the British blew up the German strong point of Hill 60, a low ridge created by the debris caused when a railway cutting was dug. They had been tunnelling under it for months and followed up the devastation with a charge in which most of the stunned German survivors were bayoneted. On 22 April, the Germans introduced a terrible new weapon. North of Ypres, clouds of chlorine overwhelmed allied forces, mainly French colonial infantry. The defenders fled, leaving a gap in the Allied line, but, like the Allies the month before, the Germans did not press home their advantage.

The 1st Warwicks were in action during this attack and Bruce Bairnsfather was a victim of the gas attack, although he did not leave the line. As he sought refuge on the sloping bank of a gully, he heard a huge rushing swish in the air. It was an old military maxim that, if you heard the crash, you were safe. He didn't hear it:

> All seemed dull and foggy, a sort of silence, worse than all the shelling, surrounded me. I lay in a filthy, stagnant ditch counsel covered with mud and slime from head to foot. I suddenly started to tremble all over. I couldn't grasp where I was...

I lay there some little time, I imagine, with a most peculiar sensation. All fear of shells and explosions had left me. I still heard them dropping about and exploding, but I listened to them and watched them as calmly as one would watch an apple fall off a tree. I couldn't make myself out. Was I all right or all wrong?

I tried to get up and then I knew. The spell was broken. I shook all over, and had to lie still, with tears pouring down my face. I could see my part in this battle was over.

The Warwicks had taken a severe drubbing: 500 other ranks and seventeen officers were listed as killed, wounded or missing. Lieutenant Bairnsfather's wounds were treated at a field station and he was eventually conveyed to King's College Hospital in London, where he was diagnosed as suffering from shell shock.

'I am now a brigade orderly', wrote Pte George Taylor in a letter home to Meer Street, 'and we have got a very tough job, as we are out all hours of the night and day. But we don't mind as long as we get through the night. The snipers are our worst enemies. There are sad sights now where we are...'

The worsening rancour had led to the alleged maltreatment of wounded Canadian prisoners by the Germans. 'Retaliation by British' Harry Fox recorded laconically on 23 April, but gave no details. Three days later, he saw wounded from the battle lying on the pavements in Hazebroeck awaiting entry into hospital. That night, he met some Canadians who had been involved in the battle in an *estimet* and found them 'very hot boys'.

The Battery was transferred up the line into the Ypres salient and wore respirators for the first time. They passed into Belgium at Poperinge, where there were 'heaps of wounded – most of them gassed'. Hill 60, where the Canadians had made their charge, was to the right of their position. Canadian and French rifles were scattered all around.

The remnants of the 1st Warwicks were in the line close to the Battery and Harry walked over to see them. He met Sgt Worrall, who had run the cadet force at the Grammar School and four Stratfordians named Wright (one of four brothers who lived at 53 Birmingham Road), Walton, Neal and Quiney. Given that there were millions of men serving on the Western Front, it is remarkable how often Stratfordians encountered each other. 'Thompson (football) came to see Kinman', he recorded on 15 August 1915. This was probably Lt Patrick Thompson of the Royal Engineers, who had been with Norman in the triumphant Stratford XV. Next month Harry met a man had been a hairdresser at Land's shop in Bridge Street and was now in the Army Service Corps.

The Hampshires

Early in 1915 the 2nd Battalion of the Hampshire Regiment was billeted in Stratford for several weeks, establishing its HQ in the Methodist Chapel. Romances ensued. Private Bartholomew Mullins met Lucy Conway, of 8 Mulberry Street. Fred, her husband, the proud possessor of medals from the Sudan and Afghan Wars, had left her to go to Canada eighteen months before. On the outbreak of war, he joined the Canadian Field Artillery. His military experience ensured that he was at once promoted to Sergeant.

Corporal James Harrington was billeted with the Meadows family in Arden Street and courted Rose Edith, one of the daughters of the house. Private Frederick 'Ben' Hayter was billeted with Agnes Emms, who ran a teashop at 12 Sheep Street with her sister Theresa. The 'policeman' of the regiment, Jack Griffin from Portsmouth, who was 6ft 4in, began to 'walk out' with another local lass, Mary Nichols, while L-Cpl Charles Robinson, who was billeted in Bull Street, was courting Emily Colwell of 3 Welcombe Cottages, Mayfield Road.

Above: *The Hampshire Regiment arrives in Stratford.* (Image courtesy of the Shakespeare Birthplace Trust Records Office)

Left: *Members of the Hampshire Regiment read news from the Front.* (Image courtesy of the Shakespeare Birthplace Trust Records Office)

The Hampshire's practice entrenching. (Image courtesy of the Shakespeare Birthplace Trust Records Office)

The return of the Hampshire's from Gallipoli. (Image courtesy of the Shakespeare Birthplace Trust Records Office)

On 3 February, Pte John Scammell, who was billeted at 2 Alcester Road, married Daisy Harris, his sweetheart from Eastleigh at Holy Trinity. There were to be many marriages like this: a brief period of intense intimacy before the bridegroom was plucked away amidst the uncertainty whether he would ever return. A few days later, the regiment held a church parade at Holy Trinity. Next month they marched to Warwick for a short time before embarking for war. It seemed as if the whole of Stratford turned out to see them off. Agnes Emms waved a sad farewell to Ben Hayter. They had fallen in love and her sister had been walking out with another soldier from the regiment, Pte. Percy Horwood.

On the Sunday afternoon before they embarked, Mary Nichols walked over to Warwick with a young cousin at whose home Jack Griffin and three other soldiers had been billeted. Jack accompanied them halfway back to Stratford. It was the last time they would see him.

In April, the Hampshires participated in the expeditionary force that attempted to breach the Dardenelles at Gallipoli. People back in Stratford were horrified to hear that they had suffered a disaster. Only 150 survived unscathed from a roll call of 1,050. Jack Griffin had been killed instantly by a sniper when he peered over the sandbags in the trenches. James Harrington, Ben Hayter (by now promoted to Sergeant) and Percy Horwood had survived. Ben and Percy had been wounded and were eventually transferred to military hospitals in Britain. On his discharge, Percy was able to transfer to the Warwickshire Yeomanry. On 20 November, Sgt Ben Hayter and Trooper Percy Horwood married their sister sweethearts in a double wedding at Holy Trinity.

The Hampshires had won a place in the hearts of Stratfordians. In April 1916, a Memorial Service at Holy Trinity commemorated the many members of the Regiment who had fallen. Afterwards, the Mayor, Archie Flower, entertained those survivors who had attended the service to lunch.

Frank Benson was back in Stratford in the spring of 1915 with a much-depleted company. Age had prevented him from enlisting despite several attempts, but at least he could boost morale as Henry V. Oscar Asche played Shylock and Genevieve Ward, Queen Margaret, to stalls filled with the convalescent blue of the wounded. The flags were absent on the birthday. A ceremony intended to preach the unity of the nations was deemed inappropriate.

After his discharge from hospital, Bruce Bairnsfather returned to Bishopton to convalesce. When he recovered, he did not rejoin his regiment, but was transferred to Albany Barracks on the Isle of Wight to train recruits. While there that he devised a prime image of the war with his cartoon character, 'Old Bill' of 'Well if you knows a better 'ole, go to it' fame.

More and more wounded were returning from 'the inferno on the continent'. Marie Corelli generously offered Trinity College, which had stood empty for a decade, as a hospital, but through the largesse of the Revd Francis Hodgson, Clopton House was placed at the disposal of the military authorities and a hospital, 'perfect in every essential', erected in the grounds. The patriotic fervour of the Hon. Mrs Hodgson matched her husband's and she undertook its administration. The first invalids arrived on 31 May 1915. The move from battlefield to hospital was rapid. William Walker of the 13th Northumberland Fusiliers, got a machine-gun bullet through his elbow at the Battle of Loos on 26 September 1915. 'First I was taken to Arques, then to Rouen, and from thence to England, where, at Stratford-on-Avon, soft beds and kind hearts awaited me.'

Major Thomas Bairnsfather with his sons, Bruce and Duncan. (Image courtesy of the Shakespeare Birthplace Trust Records Office)

Above left: *One of Bruce Bairnsfather's cartoons.* (Author's collection)

Above right: *'Well if you knows of a better 'ole, go to it.' Bruce Bairnsfather's most famous cartoon.* (Author's collection)

Gallipoli

When the Warwickshire Yeomanry embarked for Egypt, most of the men sailed on the troopship *Saturnia*, but 195 officers embarked on SS *Wayfarer* with 763 horses. She was abandoned when she was torpedoed off the Scillies and the horses left to their fate. The ship did not sink as expected, so a volunteer party returned on board and she was towed to Queenstown in Ireland. Only three horses were lost. Farrier-Sergeant Jones of Stratford was awarded the Meritorious Service Medal for his gallant efforts.

Thus it was not until 24 April 1915 that the regiment assembled at Alexandria in its entirety. The Regimental Quarter Master Sergeant Tippitt was deemed too old to serve and sent home to Stratford. Although he may not have thought so at the time, he was exceedingly fortunate.

Things at Gallipoli were so desperate that the regiment was retrained as infantry. On 14 August, it embarked from Mudros – a cadre remained to look after the horses – landing on 'A' Beach, Sulva Bay, Gallipoli in the early hours of the morning of 18 August. They were soon in trouble. 'The reception we got on landing', wrote brothers Jack and Arthur Fincher with studied understatement, to their parents at Shottery, 'was rather warm, and not altogether to our liking.'

Three days after landing, the Stratford contingent was involved in a chaotic advance from 'Silver' (Sulva) Bay across an open plain in front of the Turkish lines to the trenches they were to occupy on 'Chocolate Hill':

> By jove, it was a terrible ordeal, being our first time really under fire, but the boys kept on and on. Arthur came through all right and also all the other Stratford boys. Jack and twelve others were sent back for ammunition to the bottom of the hill, and on regaining the top with our supplies found the regiment had gone on. Here we lost touch with them, and after spending the whole night in the trenches found our brigade had been withdrawn and gone back to Silver Bay. Towards dark we were making preparations to rejoin when the order came through that the brigade was returning so, of course, we stayed to welcome them.

Corporal Robert Lidzy fell in a 'magnificent charge' (probably a euphemism for a suicidal infantry assault on machine-guns) during an attack on Hill 112. Constance Lidzy was the first woman in Stratford to receive the dreaded telegram: '...regret to say your husband was killed...' Florrie had just won a scholarship to King's High School for Girls at Warwick. Now her teacher, Miss Viveash, told her mother that she wouldn't be able to afford to send her.

The Fincher brothers soon discovered that there were few places of refuge on the restricted front:

> Since that night we have been stationed here (Chocolate Hill) and are living in holes dug out in the earth for shelter.
>
> On one occasion Arthur had a miraculous escape; he was on fatigue with a party for water-carrying, and hearing a whistling through the air of a shell they immediately lay down on the ground for protection. The thing dropped between Arthur and his mate, and though he got off Scot free, the other had a fair piece blown out of his arm and two others were badly wounded.

It was alleged that the Turks had poisoned the waterholes as they retreated. Men and horses had to be held back at gunpoint, so mad were they for a drink. The letter closes on a note of characteristic *sang-froid*:

We are ever under shell fire. Apart from this worry everyone is very cheerful and the food is good and plentiful, so we have little to grumble at on active service, except that our casualties are so large.

In September, Jack Fincher was made regimental quartermaster, a dubious promotion since part of his duty was to take a party down to the beach each morning to draw the stores. The Turks were aware of this and would begin shelling. Every morning someone was 'knocked out'. Jack was beginning to think his life was charmed. One shell fell within five yards of him, killing one soldier and wounding several others. By the end of that month only forty-one of the 308 men who had landed at Sulva Bay remained on duty. Many of the absentees were suffering from dysentery and other illnesses.

At the Borough Police Court, on 17 September, a man was fined £5, or a month's hard labour, for spreading the false report that all the officers in the Warwickshire Yeomanry had been killed or wounded and that 200 men had been put out of action.

A formidable Shottery woman was involved in this campaign. Sister Florence Cattell was a nurse aboard the hospital ship *Formosa* which stood two miles off the coast of the Dardenelles to receive wounded soldiers for transfer to hospitals in Egypt. As the *Herald* put it, 'the experience was one which would have unnerved any lady who had not been accustomed to similar scenes elsewhere.' In the following spring, she was at Salonika aboard the *Formosa* and was extremely scathing about the unsanitary condition of the city.

The Gallipoli campaign was a failure. The Yeomanry were evacuated from the peninsula on 31 October prior to the general evacuation in December. They had lost fifteen killed and ninety-four wounded. They returned to Egypt where they had the satisfaction of regaining their horses. Curiously, during the campaign, a junior officer in the regiment and a future Mayor of Stratford, Lt Robert Smith, had been appointed as a Justice of the Peace despite being hundreds of miles from the Town Hall with no certainty that he would ever return.

'Another Swim'

Exercises were part of the respites from the fighting on the Western Front. After the second Battle of Ypres, the Battery was sent to Morbeque to practice river crossings. On the afternoon of 18 July 1915, the Right Section harnessed up and marched to the nearby canal for 'a trial shot'. One man nearly drowned and the attempt was a failure, although progress was hampered by the traffic on the waterway.

All the NCOs on the Left Section, including Harry Fox, watched the exercise to 'see how to do things' (or in this instance how not to do things). Next morning it was their turn and they were successful, conveying sixty-five horses, fifty men (of whom thirty could not swim), two guns and four wagons containing harness, ammunition and stores, across the canal in two hours. Subsequently, the Right Section made another unsuccessful attempt. In the afternoon, there was a tug-of-war between the two sections, which the jubilant Left Section won.

Next day there was what Harry described as 'another swim' and this time both sections managed the crossing: the Left in one and a half hours, the Right in one hour fifty minutes.

The record time for the canal crossing by a regular Battery was one and a half hours. Next day both sections surpassed this. The Left getting across in an astonishing one hour seventeen minutes and the Right in one hour twenty-nine minutes.

In August, the entire brigade was sent to a rest camp at Mardyk, four miles west of Dunkirk. Harry was impressed by the magnificent sweep of sands and swam in the sea. Later he went to an *estaminet* on the sea front. It was soon drunk out of beer, so the soldiers started on the wine and spirits and soon the entire place was drunk dry. Next day, the officers of the cavalry regiments held horse races on the beach. Next morning at 4 a.m., the entire brigade was called out to drill on the sands – an impressive sight of 3,000 men.

'The Big Push'

In late August, the Battery was transferred to the Loos sector in Artois in preparation for the coming offensive, which was dubbed 'the Big Push'. Harry Fox suffered a cracked rib when a horse rolled over on top of him, so he was excused from a grim party that was obliged to dig through a churchyard at Elredough to create a gun pit. Skeletons and skulls were exposed. 'In one trench a skeleton had to be cut in half to enable the trench to be dug.' Harry inspected their work on 8 September:

> Sand bags all round and on top, iron girders, heavy stones, bricks, earth, etc. Protection to a depth of six feet. Orders conveyed by a rain water pipe laid from telephone dug-out to gun. Trenches connected all guns and dug-outs, going through the cellars of houses, etc.

The soldiers called the trenches 'streets' and each had its own name. The interconnecting system was very complex and it was very easy to get lost.

Two days later Harry had a narrow escape when a fuse from a shell fired at a German aeroplane landed very close to him. Two days later, he was on guard duty at around 9.30 p.m. when two shells crashed down. He and the other guard dived behind some sandbags. They were covered with dirt and pieces of brick, but were unharmed.

Each night, Harry admired 'the beautiful effect' of the red, green and white star shells. These were the prelude to a bombardment that began on 20 September. A quarter of a million shells were fired before the infantry attack began four days later. Initially, there was considerable success. The village of Loos was taken. Thousands of Germans were impounded near the Battery's camp with one guard to 100 prisoners: 'Big men and apparently well fed and well clothed, but very dirty.' Harry was incensed that the prisoners' rations of 'Best bully and biscuit' were drawn from their camp's stores.

'The Big Push' was another disaster. Sir John French had held his reserves too deep to exploit the early gains. There were insufficient shells to enable the artillery to cover the advance and the infantry was mown down by the German machine-guns. The attack was called off on 28 September. With no shells left to fire, the men of the Battery were put onto hospital duty to assist with the wounded.

The carnage was staggering. Private George Sheasby of the Royal Welch Fusiliers, aged 20, became the first Stratfordian to be awarded the Distinguished Conduct Medal as one of only two survivors of the sixteen stretcher-bearers. 'Rumoured losses in attack 7,000' recorded Harry Fox in another massive underestimate. The British had suffered 50,000 casualties and the French, 48,000. Such was the scale of the disaster that the German casualties of 24,000 appear modest. As a result of this debacle, Sir John French was relieved of his command and Asquith's Government fell to be replaced by a coalition.

The Zeppelin Scare

The evening of Sunday, 5 March 1915 brought Stratford's first Zeppelin scare. The news that enemy airships were approaching the East coast sent the more nervous inhabitants into a panic. Many took cover in cellars and shelters. Special constables ordered lights extinguished in houses, motor cars and even on bicycles. The town was in a state of funereal darkness and, not for the last time, walking round the place was more hazardous than any likely effect of enemy action.

The apprehension about air raids is understandable. War, terrible as it was, was always something that had happened beyond the seas. Now it seemed that no one's home was safe. A campaign began to increase awareness. One evening some men fixed a sheet to the window of Miss Bailey's wool shop on Shottery Green and showed lanternslides of all the classes of German aircraft. They told the onlookers that they should make for cover if they saw any of them.

Among the listeners was Thomas Arthur, aged 9. At midnight on New Year's Eve he looked out of his bedroom window, as the full moon was over Bordon Hill:

> I spotted a long cigar with something like a railway carriage lighted up under its belly. This 'thing' was followed by six more heading for Birmingham. I told my parents in the next bedroom and they told me to go to sleep again, as I'd been dreaming.

Next morning the Birmingham papers were full of the first Zeppelin raid on the Midlands. The target had been a munitions factory near Walsall. Many people had been killed and heavy damage caused.

The anti-German propaganda that had prevailed for two years bore fruit. Saturated with stories of Hunnish atrocities against cultural institutions, Stratfordians believed their town would be a prime target. Word of this penetrated to Berlin where the press waxed indignant at the suggestion, declaring that Germans so venerated Shakespeare that they would do nothing to violate the sanctity of his birthplace. This 'touch of nature' was not reciprocated. At the Town Council on 8 February, the Mayor, Archie Flower, said that their priceless historic buildings were sufficient reasons for Germany to pick out Stratford. 'We also have our due compliment of women and children and that is another reason for Germany coming against us.' Blackout orders were introduced. 'Until the war is over', said the *New York Evening Mail*, 'Stratfordians shall go to bed with the chickens or spend their evenings in darkness.' Offenders against the Lighting Orders were fined, including a clergyman and a shopkeeper, Frank Organ.

Some Stratfordians were embarking onwards and upwards. William Jones had transferred to the Royal Naval Air Service and been promoted to Chief Petty Officer. He was drafted to Mitylene, in Greece, flying with No. 2 Wing as bomber and observation officer. He was awarded the Distinguished Service Medal for successfully bombing the main railway to Constantinople. On a subsequent raid, his plane was brought down. He rescued the pilot and burnt the machine and its records before he was captured.

A future Mayor of Stratford, Leigh Dingley, aged 20, of the Worcestershire Regiment, had trained as a pilot with the Royal Flying Corps. He went missing after setting off on a flight with an observer over enemy lines at dusk on 19 October 1916. His plane had been brought down behind enemy lines and he was taken prisoner.

Notes

[1] A nickname for mortar shells. Jack Johnson was the first black man to be Heavyweight Champion of the World. He lost his title that year.

TWO

'JUST THE MAN FOR ONE OF THE TANKS'

'A Good Bed'

The future deployment of the Warwickshire Battery remained in doubt. In November 1915, all the men were examined about their capabilities for retraining as engineers, turners, fitters and other trades. December saw torrential rainfall. The trenches were flooded. They were up to their knees in mud and were issued with waders. One man was up to his waist in water and his heavy greatcoat was dragging him under. It had to be cut in half to save him. Bodies were buried in the mud. It was not long before their hands and legs were sticking out of the quagmire. The men were frenetically repairing their trenches that were in danger of being washed away.

Harry Fox had a stroke of good fortune. 'C' Section had established its night quarters in a cellar, but on 12 December, he was ordered to proceed with Bdr Glover to Haillicourt to take over 'D' Section, which was detailed for ammunition supply duty. They took lodgings in an *estaminet*. It was a great relief after the hell of the trenches. The proprietors were hospitable. They had 'a good bed' and a fire in the bedroom. They drank coffee in the morning and beer in the evening. Even that far back, the war impinged. Eight anti-aircraft guns were mounted on the church tower. The troops heading to the front wore gasmasks and all the locals had been issued with them.

Most days they were engaged in sending ammunition up to the Battery, but Harry celebrated Christmas Day with plenty of champagne. He was so exhausted that he went to bed in the afternoon and retired again at 7 p.m.

On Boxing Day, he heard that a shell had fallen on the cellar occupied by 'C' Section four days before, killing eight men. 'Should have been there myself if I had not been on this job', he wrote thankfully.

One Sunday afternoon, Harry witnessed a spectacle that had been banned in England for over sixty years. Behind the *estaminet* there was a 'proper cockpit'. The cocks were fitted 'with long steel splints'. There were lots of people and a great deal of betting on the three fights. He clearly enjoyed it, going again two weeks later when a cock was killed.

After a month's home leave, Harry had another stroke of good fortune. On 10 June, he was put in charge of wagons carrying parcels for French PoWs in Germany from a chateau at Tigny to the station at Samer, an idyll which lasted for two weeks.

'How should you like to be on Clopton Bridge?'

The Mop Fair of 1915 was a shadow of its former self. The menageries had been 'driven from the road' by lack of fodder. Only two beasts were roasted. There were no incoming excursion trains, but thousands thronged the town, glad of the illusion of relief from the war, although the Recruiting Sergeant mingling with the crowds served as a reminder.

In 1916, it was ordered that no fair should be held that would impede or delay the transport or production of war material. Since many of the visitors to the Mop came from areas associated with munitions production, many assumed that this would cause the fair's suppression. In fact it continued throughout the war, but had to close at 6.30 p.m. It was a reflection of the gathering gloom that few thought that it could ever recover its former jollity, but would reflect a post-war world of sombre austerity. To their credit, the members of the Women's Temperance League kept in touch with the showmen who had been called up and sent them parcels while they were on active service.

The three pals from the Grammar School, Victor, Thomas and Dix, embarked for France in November and were posted to the front line at Plantin. On Sunday, 4 December 1915, they were sitting in their dugout. Victor and Thomas were on the grass, leaning against the inner wall, Dix was lying in the middle. After the winter rains and the disturbance created by shelling, the dugout was in a dodgy state and collapsed on top of them. The weight of the wooden posts and the sandbags they had been supporting crushed Victor and Thomas to death, but Dix had little weight on him and was dug out uninjured.

In the dark days of December 1915, the P&O liner SS *Persia* 'fell victim to the fiendish activities of a German submarine'. Among the 350 'precious souls which were summoned to the Great Audit' was Kathleen Stoehr. She had returned to England in the summer and was on her way to rejoin her husband in Aden.

The second wartime Christmas was anything but a Yuletide. The weather was atrocious. It rained non-stop for several hours, but the main cause of the prevailing gloom was that most people found it impossible to act up to the precept of 'Peace on Earth, goodwill towards men' and be merry when so many homes were in mourning.

The 7th Warwicks got their marching orders for France in May 1916 and were given a week's home leave. On the train home, George Hewins discovered he was 'crummy'. When he got home, the first thing his wife did was to put a hot iron over his uniform:

'I'll get the little buggers', she said. It was the only time I got relief, the war through. 'Pop! Pop! Pop!' they went.

When the time came to embark, Emma said, 'I wish you weren't going' and gave him two bottles of rhubarb wine from the *Oddfellows* and a photograph of his family.

Even then I'd no thoughts of *not* going back. There was a chap in Stratford who'd knocked a saucepan o' water over him and scalded both his feet. He said: 'I'll suffer the agony!' They found another chap hiding in a bunker on the golf course. But *I* hadn't seen, you see, I didn't know. If you'd asked me why I was going to fight I'd have said: 'To save the country'. If the Germans had won we would be slaves!

The Battalion was kept in reserve until 21 May 1916, when it was brought up to the front at Fromelles, a salient in the Somme sector, in camouflaged trucks, George's first sight of the trenches was worse than he had expected. The dugouts were just 6½ft high and it was impossible to stand up in them. They oozed water and were never dry. A piece of wet sacking flapped at the entrance. In places the trenches were only 50 yards from the enemy:

We crawled and we scrabbled and we crouched. We fell asleep crouching. It was bad enough for us and we was mainly on the short side – but the officers.

One thing George never learned to bear was the swarms of rats:

Rats with yella eyes and big fat bellies like old ladies' cats, running all over, after the food. One squeak or a rustle – that was enough for me! I didn't give them a chance to get nearer. I kicked out and they'd hit the roof.

One day George was standing on the firestep, looking through the periscope when he saw what looked like a yellow wave rolling towards him. 'I thought it was water, going to drown us. Then somebody shouts: "GAS!" There was a panic. Those as couldn't get their masks on in time, those as was away from the trenches, it got in their eyes and blinded them.'

Before any offensive the top brass came up to the trenches before returning to GHQ well behind the lines. 'We could sniff them coming', recalled George. '"Ullo", we said, "there's summat coming off"'.

George was touring the trenches with an officer amidst the heavy shelling which was a prelude to an offensive when a voice whispered in his ear: 'Hewins. How should you like to be on Clopton Bridge now?'

'Bleedin' nice.' By the light of a flare, he saw the speaker's face. It was a leading actor in Benson's Company who had played the gravedigger in *Hamlet* and went by the stage name of Harry Caine. Now, as Lt Hawkins, he had reverted to his real name.

Before they went over the top they were issued with a rum ration. They hadn't eaten for two days so they became rapidly tipsy, which was the purpose of the exercise. The first sight George saw in No Man's Land was a headless corpse. There were bodies everywhere. They couldn't be picked up for burial.

Shells from their own side dropped among them as they advanced. The artillery was not lifting its barrage high enough. They used their entrenching tools to dig in a foot deep and when the shelling stopped they ran forward, bayonets fixed. When they got to the opposing trenches most of the enemy had fled. 'They was crafty, the Germans: if you got them cornered they upped their hands in a tick: chucked you their rifles. They didn't make a fight of it.'

After that the Company had five nights so-called 'rest' behind the lines. They were still within the range of the German guns, but at least they were in houses. They slept in their clothes with their blankets round them: five or six together to keep warm.

Later the Company got two weeks rest leave out of the line. George was billeted with a French family. One day, he asked the daughter of the house where her father was. 'Mama too big', she replied. 'She give im money to go to ze brothel. 'E got what you English call cock stand!'

'I reckon I got it an all', said George to his mate. 'Come on!'

They went down the street and saw a long queue. At first they thought it was for a picture palace, but it was for the brothel. They waited and waited and eventually gained admission. They were asked to select a whore from photographs on the wall. George went upstairs. The whores were all naked and didn't look much like the photos. The floor was covered in spittle. He couldn't go through with it and fled. It was a lucky escape. A lot of those who stayed 'got the claps into the bargain'.

Home Leave

The proximity of the Western Front meant that soldiers could return on all-too-brief leave. Often it was only granted at the last minute so families were not aware of

Home leave: Sergeant Taylor and his wife enjoy a moment together in their garden. She is probably knitting a garment for him to take back to the Front. (Image courtesy of the Shakespeare Birthplace Trust Records Office)

the insipient arrival. Around two days of a five-day leave were taken up in travel. Six-year-old Frances Holtom thought how rough her dad's uniform was when she snuggled up to him – even his shirt. After the second Battle of Ypres, Harry Fox left at 4 p.m. on Monday, 31 May and travelled in a cattle truck to Boulogne. He arrived at midnight and slept in a shed, catching the boat at 11 a.m. He got to Victoria Station at 3 p.m. and caught the 4 o'clock train from Paddington that arrived in Stratford at 6.30 p.m. He was at home on the Wednesday and Thursday. 'A good time on leave', he recorded. On the Friday he left home at 8.45 a.m. In London, he met some colleagues from the Battery for lunch before they caught the train. From Boulogne, they travelled in a mail truck as far as Cassel. They were back in the billets at 10 a.m. on the Saturday morning, only to find that they had returned a day early.

Marriages occurred in these snatched moments. On 28 April 1916, Bombardier Norman Kinman, while on a month's leave, married a Stratford girl, Kathleen Adams, at Holy Trinity. The couple cannot have seen much of each other. Norman had been in the army for nearly two years and before that he had been in Australia for three. In the following June, Charles Robinson of the 2nd Hampshires married Emily Colwell at Holy Trinity.

For some the leave was a final farewell. Sergeant James Brebner, a 28-year-old regular in the Royal Field Artillery, spent a few days at his home at 13 Russell Cottages with his wife, Margaret, and three children in June 1917. He was killed in action on 3 August.

The uncertainty of survival led to an intense need for physical relationships – and matches that may not have taken place in peacetime. Richard Kane, a 22-year-old Captain in the Royal Field Artillery from South Ascot in Berkshire, was a patient in the Clopton War Hospital. Gwendolen Webb, who was thirteen years his senior, was probably one of his nurses. The couple were married by special license at Holy Trinity early in 1916 by the Revd Francis Hodgson, with the groom's mother as a witness. In 1918, a convalescent at Stratford's other military hospital, the Whytegate, Pte Reginald Dewing of the Royal Irish Rifles, married Flossie Gibbs from Norfolk. She too may have been a nurse. The couple were only 21 years old, but she was already a widow.

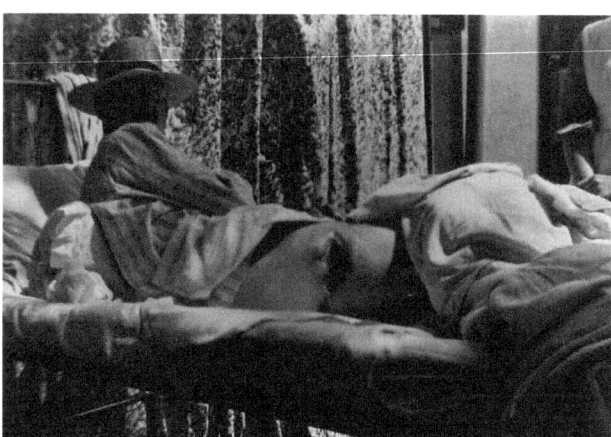

Above: *Nurses and patients at the Clopton War Hospital.* (Author's collection)

Left: *Private Hearne displays his wound at the Clopton War Hospital.* (Image courtesy of the Shakespeare Birthplace Trust Records Office)

The Borough War Tribunal

From July 1915, all men and women aged between 16 and 65 were obliged to register for potential call-up. Already the large numbers of men in the colours was leading to a drastic change in patterns of employment. In nearly every shop and office and even in some of the banks, woman had become the predominant figure. 'And so far', considered the *Herald*, 'she is conducting herself so admirably that the male assistants will have the problem confronting them when they return from the war of what is to be their future position.'

The advent of universal conscription on 1 March 1916 meant that those who had been rejected in 1914 faced a renewed call to arms. Edgar Cranmer was summoned to a medical at Budbrook Barracks and was passed B1. The Post Office could insist that when telegraphists were called up they should serve in the Signals Section of the Royal Engineers, so Edgar was transferred to the special training section at Worcester.

Some were canny enough to anticipate the call-up and obtain work in a reserved occupation – one that was deemed vital to the war effort. Marie Corelli's chauffeur, Leonard Norman, got a job at the Standard Motor Works at Coventry. This led to a furious row with Marie. He took the opportunity offered by his departure to tell her what he thought of her. In an angry letter to his son, she wrote that he 'leaves my service for good this Saturday. I greatly regret that he has spoken with such rudeness.'

Ernest Chandler, the erstwhile gondolier, had also left Marie's employ and was living with his wife and two children on the Evesham road. Now he was summoned to another medical examination and this time he was passed fit for general service. He joined the Royal Warwicks in October 1916.

The Act came into being because the manpower situation was getting desperate. The carnage on the Western Front was absorbing bodies with a reckless heed for neither humanity nor strategy. 'We have not had any trouble', wrote L-Cpl Eric Winter, son of the draper, on garrison duty at Folkestone, to his father, 'bar some of the men who have been in prison in England for desertion, etc. They took into their heads to raid the YMCA this morning and went off with £16 worth of goods.'

The Act brought into being the Borough War Tribunal, consisting of Town Councillors, a representative of the Trades Council and a retired officer representing the military. It heard appeals from those claiming exemption through conscientious objection, because they were in a reserved occupation, or because of 'special financial, business or business obligations'. These had to be registered within three weeks of the receipt of call-up papers.

The Tribunal tried to be fair, but its prime task was to send men to the Army, so it was impossible to be sympathetic or unbiased in too many cases. This was the first time that conscription had been introduced, so conscientious objection to war was an issue for the first time. On 24 February 1916, Henry Bullard, an auctioneer, claimed absolute exemption on grounds of his religious beliefs. Had he been a Quaker, this would have been granted, but he was a Congregationalist. As a denomination they were not pacifists.

Had he sought exemption on the grounds of his trade he may well have succeeded. Another auctioneer, Robert Garrett, was deemed to be doing work of national importance, but had this argument failed in this argument, Bullard would have had no choice but to serve. The Tribunal did not question him on his beliefs, but granted

Lieutenant Eric Winter. (Image courtesy of the Shakespeare Birthplace Trust Records Office)

him non-combatant status, which meant that he was forced into the Army, where he fared badly. He was court-marshalled and twice sentenced to Wormwood Scrubs.

Conscientious objectors, although few in number, were something of an embarrassment to the Government, which appointed the Pelham Committee to place them appropriately. On 10 August, Bullard applied to the Borough Tribunal to be referred to it, but the Army, probably exasperated with him, had already done so.

Later, a similar response was given to a baker's assistant, Charles Handy, who told the Tribunal that going to war would be 'opposed to the example of Jesus Christ'. The only other applicant to claim full exemption, John Ready, described as a 'village evangelist and colporteur' was granted it, but at 40, he was too old for service.

Generally the response to those who claimed exemption on non-conscientious grounds was the same. A short period of grace was given to arrange alternatives in their place of employment: a woman, a boy, or a discharged soldier. Albert Pearce, a Wood Street confectioner, was given a respite to sort out his business affairs, but that night, in the back bar of the 'Windmill', a woman gave him the white feather of cowardice. He promptly enlisted in the Durham Light Infantry, temporarily billeted in Stratford, en route for Salonika. Such was the need for manpower that he was embarked immediately and was not issued with a uniform until he got to Marseilles.

White feathers were the least of the worries for many who had once been keen to go. The tales of horror from the Western Front had diminished their patriotic fervour and now they appealed against conscription. Both John Bone and Charles Guise, the diminutive grocer's assistant and printer, appeared before the Tribunal. Bone had been given a B2 fitness assessment at Budbrook Barracks, but was granted exemption on the grounds of his size. The Mayor could not resist the comment that had he been passed A1 he would have been 'just the man for one of the tanks'. This new fighting vehicle had first seen action on the Western Front just five days before. The increasing pressure for manpower was reflected two months later when Guise was given a mere two-month exemption, despite being two inches shorter than Bone.

The call-up brought genuine difficulties for the self-employed. Thirty-six-year-old Fred Chivers of 2 Garden Row, Scholar's Lane, had a building and carpentry business at Broom to which he travelled on his motorbike. Although he employed eight men, seven were over military age and the eighth was exempted. There was no one who could run the business in his absence. The Tribunal granted him exemption till the end of the year

The Tribunal made no concessions to those who claimed they had already 'done their bit'. Arthur Wright, a bricklayer's labourer, of 53 Birmingham Road stated that his four brothers had all served in the Army and one had died at the Battle of Loos. His widowed mother was unable to work and could not manage on the remittances they sent her. Mr Talbot, the military representative, responded that Mr Wright was an old soldier who had fought in the Boer War. He was very suitable for the Army. Fred Amphlett, aged 37, a Snitterfield postman who lived in Great William Street, said he had an invalid father and was the only son at home. He had two brothers serving in France. The Tribunal decreed that with the allowances he could claim there would be no hardship for the father.

A judgement of Solomon was required in the case of Eborall brothers, William and Frank. They ran the Oddfellow's Arms, Stratford's last home-brew pub. Frank had appealed against conscription, but on 16 May 1917, he told the Tribunal he would withdraw his appeal and go if his brother was excused, but William said that as he was single, he thought he should go and his brother stay at home. A member of the Tribunal, Cllr E.W. Everard, missed the point entirely. 'It is refreshing to see two young men willing to serve. Can't you both go?' It was essential that one brother remain to do the brewing and run the pub, was the reply. Archie Flower looked benignly upon this minor rival establishment to his brewery and Frank Eborall was granted exemption as long as his brother remained in the Army.

At the same hearing, Amos Unitt applied for temporary exemption on domestic grounds and was granted three months' grace. He was the 28-year-old manager of Lennard's, the boot-makers, and lived with his wife over the shop in the High Street. He was also a teacher in the Wesleyan Sunday School, and an 'acceptable' local preacher who sang in the choir.

The necessity to recruit had led to a fall in standards. On the opening day of the Somme battle, Harry Fox thought that the infantry looked 'very young and small.'

The Somme

At 12.45 a.m. on 1 July 1916, the Battery was ordered up into the line and left its quarters at Querriere. At 5 a.m. they arrived in the village of Lavieville about 7km from Albert. The district was full of moving troops. The Somme offensive was about to begin and they were to be part of it. Preparations for the attack had been thorough. All the troops had been issued with closer fitting shrapnel helmets. A railway line had been specially constructed to supply the logistics to support the attack. A tremendous bombardment that had begun on 24 June was continuing.

Dawn brought what Harry Fox described as 'a beautiful fine day'. Quite 'the nicest day for weeks', he added, without a trace of irony. Ever optimistic, he recorded a report that the infantry had 'attacked and done well'. His fortune was still with him. At 6 p.m. came a characteristic change of orders. The cavalry and the horse artillery were to move back to their previous quarters. It had been decided that they were highly-exposed to shellfire if the enemy were to locate their position. His earlier optimism was soon dispelled. It was reported that, although the troops had advanced six miles, the attack had 'hung up', due to the failure to take a village and the lack of water in the front line.

On its way back through the lines, the Battery passed great numbers of wounded. The 8th Division had suffered very heavily. In some Battalions only a few men had survived. A huge train pulling some 100 trucks and wagons had been brought down to the railhead was filled with them. Such was the congestion that on 5 July the horse artillery and cavalry were ordered to move even further back from the railhead.

The Battle of the Somme was another disaster. The lengthy bombardment had given the Germans ample warning of British intentions. There were 58,000 casualties on the opening day – one third killed. It had been expected that the massive bombardment would have wiped the Germans or at least have so numbed them that they lost the will to fight. Harry Fox knew well the reasons for the failure of this strategy:

> German dug-outs very safe and deep – 30ft and sloping towards our lines. Machine-guns in twos and on lifts. While one is being fired, the other is being loaded.

The carnage was particularly great among young officers, who were called upon to lead their men into battle by example. Twenty-year-old 2nd Lt Adrian Barrett had gained a commission and transferred to the 13th (Territorial) Battalion of the Royal Welch Fusiliers which was part of the 38th Welsh Division. The Battalion commander was Lt-Col Oswald Flower, the brother of the brewery Chairman, a retired officer who had re-enlisted at the beginning of the war.

On 7 July the Battalion was engaged in fierce fighting to take Mametz Wood, 500 yards north of the Somme. Three days later Adrian Barrett was killed leading his men in an attack on the German positions. Colonel Flower was also killed in this assault – by the flying splinters from a tree that had been hit by a British shell.

Further up the line, in the Fromelles salient, things were relatively quiet, but the men of the 2/7th Battalion of the Warwicks knew what was coming when jars of rum appeared. On 19 July 1916, three days after the main attack, a decoy feint was

Left: *Lieutenant-Colonel Oswald Flower.* (Image courtesy of the Shakespeare Birthplace Trust Records Office)

Below: *The Royal Welch Fusiliers memorial on the Somme, bearing the names of Lt-Cnl Oswald Flower and Lt Adrian Barret.* (Image courtesy of the Shakespeare Birthplace Trust Records Office)

launched into the German lines. It was intended to divert reinforcements from the main thrust.

It was another lovely summer's day. At 5.30 p.m. they crawled out though a cornfield. At first they made steady progress unseen by the enemy to within 100 yards of his trenches, but the British troops on their flanks spotted them and were given the order to follow, which caused the Germans to open up a barrage. 'It came like chucking gravel out of a cart. It was busting everywhere.' George Hewins stayed close to his officer, Captain Edwards. When they reached the barbed wire those with cutters on the end of their rifles started to carve a way through. George's trousers and puttees were ripped and he thought that if he could get into the German trenches he might have a chance.

It was not to be. A shell burst over them. George felt as if a donkey had kicked him. He was bleeding. It seemed that he had been hit on the hip and Captain Edwards on the knee. He removed one of his puttees, meaning to bind up the officer's leg. A German came at him from behind and Captain Edwards shot him and he fell dead over George, 'but not afore he's stuck his bayonet in my arse.'

George was taken to the dressing station. The bayonet had made a wound 18in long in his thigh, while the shrapnel had caused three wounds in his back, ripped one leg open to the knee 'and blown the top of my privates off'.

It had been a day of slaughter for the 7th. Out of a thousand men, only eighty were left standing, not one an officer. Such was the scale of the disaster that the Battalion was withdrawn for the remainder of the 1916 campaign.

Women's Work

The spectacle of men who had lost limbs at the front was becoming sadly familiar in Stratford, part of 'the boys in blue' – wounded soldiers in convalescent uniform. Harry Fox donned convalescent blue in January 1916. His health was shattered after months of active service. He had developed varicose veins and was regularly in the sickbay. On 6 January, the Medical Officer certified him unfit for active service and he was put on a hospital train to Rouen. He had two more examinations before a fourth doctor confirmed his debility and he was put aboard the hospital ship, *St George*, bound for England.

The Women's Volunteer Reserve: Eleanor Melville is in the middle. (Image courtesy of the Shakespeare Birthplace Trust Records Office)

Sergeant Frederick Conway of the Canadian Field Artillery had been in the thick of the fighting, but did not escape unscathed. He was sent to a base hospital in Liverpool and then to Lincoln Military Hospital where he died of nephritis on 3 March 1916. He was buried in Stratford Cemetery with full military honours in the presence of his widow, who hadn't seen him since he'd left her three years before.

The emancipation of women was becoming a necessity as the acute labour shortages propelled more and more jobs into the female domain. Over a third of the male workforce of around 160 at the Brewery was in the forces. Twenty women had replaced them.

Changed attitudes were having their effects on social norms. Before the war, mixed swimming was discouraged at the Town Council's Bathing Place up the river. Now Cllr Edward Fox noted that it had become prevalent, but was gratified to note that 'there were no unseemly sights'.

For the first time women could join a branch of the services other than nursing. Eleanor Melville, the vicar's wife, formed a local branch of the Women's Volunteer Reserve. After Margery Eliot of 4 Chapel Street joined the newly formed Women's Auxiliary Army Corps (WAAC), she spent 'a fortnight in England "training", but her 'chief occupation was being vaccinated and inoculated for overseas work.'

After the war, the Revd Francis Hodgson expressed gratitude to 'the sons of the Empire' who 'had proven themselves magnificent men'. Such attitudes were not shared by Margery's family and friends, who expressed concern that she would have 'to work alongside native troops'. She could reassure them on this point. 'This *is* so in *some* of our work, but as all native troops work under the eagle eyes of white NCO's and officers I can say from my own experience that no harm or unpleasantness is even possible.'

When twenty-six-year-old Sarah Bull married Driver William Wright of 53 Birmingham Road on 18 October 1918, she became an unwitting first in the parish records. Rather than 'spinster' or 'widow', as women had always been described, she was entered as a Foreman Cook with the WAAC.

Before her husband's death, Constance Lidzy had never worked, but her war widow's pension was only 29s 10d a week, so she was obliged to take menial cleaning jobs to pay the rent and support her daughter. On two mornings a week, she worked for 6d an hour at a house called The Myrtles in Rother Street. There were a lot of patterned tiles so 'it was all scrubbing and cleaning'. When that was finished there was an 'awful lot' of polishing. Her hours were 8 a.m. till noon, but she was so conscientious that she was often going at 7 a.m. and not finishing till one o'clock.

On three other days she went to a big house in Rowley Crescent, the home of a Birmingham dentist. She worked from 8 a.m. till 5 p.m., doing so much scrubbing and cleaning that her hands became chapped and painful and she was obliged to bandage them at night. Fortunately, the household possessed a 'very good, old-fashioned cook'. When Constance got to work, breakfast always awaited her. At 11 a.m. she made her sit down for a quarter of an hour with a piece of cake and a cup of cocoa. At 1 p.m. she sat her down again, saying 'No, you don't, you have an hour for your dinner'. Before she left there would be a cup of tea and a piece of cake.

Bitter Years

A release for Stratfordians from the horrors of war was provided by the knighting of Frank Benson, with characteristic theatricality, by the King in the Royal Box at Drury Lane on 2 May 1916. The news was announced to a delighted Festival audience at the Memorial Theatre and cheers resounded throughout the house. Next day, cheering crowds waited at the station and sheaves of lilies were presented to Lady Benson and a chaplet of bays to Sir Frank, before members of the Company drew them to the Theatre in an open landau.

After Ben Greet brought a depleted Old Vic Company that summer, there were no more Festivals for the duration of the war. Even Benson deserted Stratford. He enlisted in the French Red Cross and was awarded the *Croix de Guerre* for his bravery in rescuing wounded soldiers in the firing line. Constance ran a recreation centre for British troops at Etaples.

Before the war, the famous journalist, W.T. Stead, had told Benson that he could not fully understand Shakespeare unless he learned something of Spiritualism. He recalled this conversation on 16 September 1916. He had retired to his hut someway behind the British lines in Flanders when he saw his son, Eric, a Major in the King's Royal Rifle Corps, standing at the bottom of his bed. He sprang up in surprise, for he knew that his regiment was 100 miles further up the line. In their conversation, Eric told him that death was not the end. Three days later he learnt that his son had been mortally wounded in action, dying just before he had appeared at the bedside.

The censors had learnt their lesson from the Boer War when letters home from disaffected soldiers complaining about the conditions had caused something of a furore. Now news from the front was generalised and sparse. There was a sameness to letters sent by comrades to grieving relatives recounting the circumstances of deaths. All died instantly and without pain. Acts of gallantry the censor did allow past. At Arras on 9 April 1917, while under heavy fire and without no regard to his own safety, Sgt Norman Kinman had continued to serve his gun, although the next gun had received a direct hit, killing ten and wounding five men. On 6 July 1917, he was awarded the Military Medal.

The ex-Scout Master, Gunner William Bailey was killed on 17 July 1917. On 10 August, the Battery came under heavy shellfire on the canal bank at Boesinghehe. Two guns were put out of action and a third set alight. The ammunition started to explode. Sergeant Kinman and two other soldiers worked for twenty minutes under continuous shellfire to extinguish the fires. He was awarded a bar to his Military Medal. On 28 September, he played in a football match behind the lines, as the pivot of his section in a two-goal victory. In October, his old team mate, Lt Patrick Thompson was awarded the Military Cross for his 'devotion to duty in taping out a jumping-off line for an infantry attack under exceptionally difficult and dangerous circumstances.'

George Hewins' troubles were not over. When he had recovered sufficiently to travel, it was decided to send him back to London. He embarked at Boulogne still wearing his tin helmet. 'You won't need that any more', he was told and it was taken from him. When the ship got out into the Channel, there was a sudden shudder and a boom. They'd been torpedoed! George was blown into the sea, strapped to his stretcher. 'Raise yourself up!' somebody shouted as the waves rushed over him. He was picked up by the Navy, but would have drowned had he still been wearing his helmet.

The desperate need for manpower was reflected in the increasing intransigence of the Tribunal. The deal made with William Eborall was forgotten as he received his call-up papers again. As he remarked to the Tribunal, 'The Army had rather placed him in the cart.' His appeal was heard on 26 July. This time he was offered just two months exemption.

In October, Arthur Fletcher, a 21-year-old plumber and painter, was passed fit for general service, but he appealed on the apparently reasonable grounds that he had only one eye! One of the panel, Mr R.G. Savage, thought it 'a scandalous thing to pass a man under such conditions.' 'You make too much of this one-eye business,' retorted Mr Talbot. 'I have practically had the use of only one eye since I was twelve.' Mr Savage asked him if he had ever been in the Army. 'No', he replied, 'but I have been in the Volunteers.' Exemption was refused.

In 1916, in an effort to increase agricultural and industrial production, the Government imposed daylight saving time. The clocks were brought forward by an hour during the summer months. This was observed in every house in Stratford save one. Marie Corelli insisted that her household continued on what she called 'God's time', so that the clocks at Mason's Croft were one hour behind all the others in town during the summer. This caused some confusion to those receiving social invitations from her as to when they should to arrive.

Summertime was to become the least of Marie's troubles. The 1917 Food Hoarding Act made it illegal to hold any more provisions than those required for normal household use. In the case of sugar this was defined as ½lb per head per week. With a household of seven, she was entitled to 32lbs during the period from 5 September to 15 November, but she was holding 183lbs. She had been ordering it from Lipton's in London as well as buying it locally. Someone tipped off the local police and PCs Walton and Hawkes called on her. 'I am a patriot', she told them, 'and would not think of hoarding. I think you police are overstepping your duty to visit my house.' She added the astonishing information that 'Lloyd George will be resigning tomorrow and there will be a revolution in England in less than a week.' This wild prophecy caused great hilarity when it was read out in the Police Court on 2 January. Bertha Vyver stated that the sugar was not for personal use, but was for food production – to make jam from the large quantities of fruit in the garden. The plea was rejected and Marie was fined £50 with 20 guineas costs. This was somewhat unfair, since a similar plea was accepted on other occasions, but perhaps she could not hope for much sympathy from a bench on which sat her old protagonists, George Boyden and Fred Winter.

Early in 1917, Lennards Ltd asked for a further exemption for their manager, Amos Unitt, but this was refused. He joined the Royal Warwicks in February 1917 and embarked for France in December. The company allowed his wife to continue to live over the shop in the High Street. On 1 February, Fred Chivers gained a further exemption for two months, but he was not called up to the 1st Royal Warwicks till July. Such was the carnage among NCOs on the Western Front that he was rapidly promoted to Corporal.

Shortages were compounded by one of the coldest winters on record in 1917. The way through the fields to Shottery was so deep in snow that travellers could not trace the road.

Many were the sad reflections on the emptiness of Stratford during the last two bitter years of the war. The town was devoid of men under 40 years of age and the lengthening casualty lists – something that even the rigorous censorship could not suppress – recorded

The boys of the National School dig for victory, watched over by their teacher Mr Holdsworth. (Image courtesy of the Shakespeare Birthplace Trust Records Office)

those who would not return. On 7 April 1917, Lt Patrick Thompson was killed in action. Out of the 'splendid' eight who had triumphed at Hereford in 1914, only one survived. Sixty-one members of the Boat Club served in the forces and nineteen did not return.

There was no street in Stratford that was not mourning the death of its young men. The three sons of the Beesley family of 44 Great William Street, all joined up. A German sniper killed Henry, aged 20, at dusk on 23 May 1916. Albert, aged 19, was posted missing eight weeks later. Arthur, aged 18, was serving in the Worcester Cycling Corps and survived the war. James and Elizabeth Berry of Swan's Nest Cottage also lost two sons. James, aged 27, was killed in September 1918, while Harold, aged 19, was appointed valet to the vicar in his role as Lt-Col Melville of the Warwickshire Horse Artillery, but he got no further than Worcester, where he died of illness in 1915.

Ernest Chandler had been transferred to the Machine-Gun Corps. He went to France with them in March 1917. He was killed by a shell at Arras on the afternoon of 14 May. It was his first day in the trenches. The explosion also killed his sergeant and another soldier.

The Warwickshire Yeomanry had become part of the Desert Mounted Corps and was back in action against the Turks in Palestine. Private Arthur Fincher's luck did not follow him from Gallipoli. A sniper's bullet hit him in the shoulder on 21 April. The wound was not serious and he went into hospital at El-Arish. Three months later came the abortive First Battle of Gaza. Corporal Eric Barnard, second son of the auctioneer, Walker Barnard, of Old Town House, had shared the experiences of his unit through Gallipoli and beyond, but now he was laid up in hospital with fever. During the battle a shell burst within 3 yards of Lt Robert Smith and shrapnel struck him on the chest and neck. His condition was too serious for an operation in the field hospital, so he was sent on the four-day journey to Alexandria, which, amazingly, he survived. He was invalided out of the service and by November he was back with his parents in Stratford.

The regiment's moment of undying glory came on 7 November 1917 when it participated in the last cavalry charge on guns in the long history of the British army. The Turks were in full retreat towards Beersheba but their rearguard had taken up position on a ridge at Huy, twenty miles north of Gaza, and was inflicting heavy losses on the advancing British. An attack was ordered. Two thousand yards from the ridge B and C (of which Jack Fincher was a member) squadrons of the Warwickshire Yeomanry joined up with a squadron of the Worcestershire Yeomanry and advanced at a trot. The cavalry encountered terrific fire from field guns, machine-guns and rifles before the Colonel gave the order to charge and the enemy was routed. Eric Barnard was back with the regiment. He was awarded the Military Medal for his 'good work on the day of the charge' and promoted to Sergeant. On 9 December, he carried the regimental colours on a white horse as General Allenby entered Jerusalem, a moment that was captured in a photograph that went round the world.

As a Turkish PoW, William Jones was suffering great privations. He made two escape attempts. On the second occasion his companion was shot.

Whereas in the last six months of 1914, only one serving soldier got married at Holy Trinity, during 1917–18, there were 40. Some of the 28 bridegrooms who were not recorded as serving in the forces may already have been discharged, others were in the process of call-up and a number were in reserved occupations – two farmers, a railway fireman and a signalman, an engineer, a dental surgeon and, somewhat surprisingly, a dockyard riveter and a stevedore.

Soldiers from afar made their mark in the registers. In 1916, Sgt Frank Cobb of the 110th Canadian Battalion married Iva Symington of 31 High Street. In 1917, seventy-seven Australian convalescents arrived in town. Within weeks, four had married local girls.

Some 100 German prisoners of war were working on local farms. They did not produce 'the slightest consternation or curiosity' and behaved in 'an exemplary fashion'. To help with their support, they were allowed to trap rabbits, but when it was discovered that they had been selling them to a meat-starved local populace, the privilege was withdrawn. The *Herald* waxed both indignantly and tolerantly:

> Much better to employ men in useful labour than consign them to internment camps, there to waste their time in idleness. All brave men should be well treated, even if they are our enemies…

Edgar Cranmer had joined the Bantam Division as a telegrapher in France in 1917. It was comprised of soldiers who had been originally considered too small for service. In November he contracted trench fever and was hospitalised. When he recovered he was sent up to the 2nd Army Observation Group, immediately behind the lines, a wireless station that monitored German signals.

Bertha Gover, who had decided to remain as a governess in Russia, found herself caught up in the Bolshevik Revolution. The family asked her to take the daughter of the house to safety in Norway. In order to secure the necessary papers, she secured an interview with the Chairman of the Petrograd Soviet, Leon Trotsky. Whether this legendary revolutionary was overawed by a dominant English nanny, or whether he was impressed by her powers of persuasion, is uncertain, but she got the papers.

Sergeant Norman Kinman had become a legend in Stratford. 'Although many times in the thick of the fighting with the Battery he enjoyed a remarkable immunity from the Hun shell and shrapnel', but on 30 November, they suffered further heavy shelling. Norman was digging out some men who had been buried by a shell blast when the Germans sent over some gas canisters. The next thing he knew was when he woke up in hospital in Rouen. By January, he was back in Stratford. He must have made some recovery from his injuries, for, in that month, he impregnated his wife, Kitty. He set up home with her at 77 Clopton Road, In February, he received his discharge from the Army and found a position as a commercial clerk at the brewery.

Hawkes, the policeman, by now promoted to Sergeant, was having a good war. At 6.20 a.m. one morning in February 1918, he asked a young man he met in Chapel Street to identify himself. He immediately confessed that he was an escaped German prisoner called Bernhard Hardt who was trying to make his way to the coast in the hope of boarding a Dutch ship. Flushed with this success, he challenged another young man while on duty at the Market Cross five months later. He turned out to be a deserter from the South Staffordshire Regiment called Alfred Richards.

In the spring of 1918, Leigh Dingley was one of 120 officers who were moved from his PoW camp to Aachen with the prospect of being sent into neutral Holland as part of a prisoner exchange. The usual delay in these proceedings was a mere two or three days, but on this occasion there was a hitch in the negotiations and after a tedious wait of three weeks, the Allied prisoners were moved away to resume their internment. They had travelled in first-class carriages to Aachen, but they left in 3rd and 4th class ones. The journey of 400 miles took several days and included a halt in a siding for fourteen hours. The men had only half a loaf each for the journey and they were too weak to stand when they reached their destination on the Baltic. This treatment, coupled with the disappointment of being baulked at the last moment of the comparative freedom that Holland spelt, proved too much for four of the men who went mad.

Another PoW, 2nd Lt Eric Winter, was suffering similar deprivations. 'You often see officers strolling about picking up cigarette ends to put in their pipes', he wrote in June, 'and there is always a rush for tea leaves to dry and to put in pipes. The tea we get is more of the hedgerow variety and includes grass, straw, etc. ... However they say it smokes pretty well.'

The collapse of Russia had enabled the Germans to transfer divisions to the Western Front, giving them a numerical advantage there for the first time since 1914. On 21 March 1918, they launched their last great offensive. Edgar Cranmer was due to go on leave that day, but instead found himself helping to smash up the huts and cut down the wireless masts before evacuating.

All activity on the home front was now subordinate to the war. Virtually all the iron railings in Stratford went into the melting pot, including those in front of Marie Corelli's house. The rails and sleepers on the old tramway that had run between Stratford and Moreton-in-the-Marsh went the same way. An urgent message came down to the Tribunal that all men listed as Grades 1 and 2 were required. On 10 April, it heard twenty-one cases – mainly reviews of previous exemptions – with 'a result favourable to the National Service department'.

On 23 July, the *Herald* published a letter from L-Cpl Charles Robinson of the 2nd Hampshires:

> I have been reported as killed in action on 28th April. I should like my friends to know that I am still alive and that I was only wounded, and that, on the 4th June. The injury was to my right hand and I am now ready for active duty again.

Sadly, Charles Robinson, who had been promoted to Sergeant, was killed in action a few days after this affirmation that he was still alive.

Sir Frank Benson made a brief return to Stratford to address a packed 'patriotic meeting' at the Theatre on the Birthday in 1918. It is indicative of the times that he shared the stage with a Miss Peers, the travelling inspector for the Food Production Department. A branch of the 'National Kitchen' was opened in Stratford in May. It provided cheap and nutritious meals. On its first day, it served 633 portions.

On 10 August, a recruiting rally was held for the WAAC. A contingent of girls from Budbrook Barracks 'who had answered the call' joined Mrs Melville's Women's Volunteer Reserve in a march through the town. The women were desperately needed. On 16 August, the *Herald* announced that the age limit for conscription had been increased to fifty.

Ada Chivers did not like her daughter Dorothy playing in the street, so she found the funds from her limited budget to pay for dancing lessons with Leah Hanman, the Old Bensonian actress who had established a dance school at the bottom of Bridge Street. Her husband, serving with the 1st Royal Warwicks was awarded the Military Medal when he continued to work the gun he commanded for several hours after the other seven

Members of the Heavy Lorry Section: Edgar Cranmer is in the middle of the back row. (Image courtesy of the Shakespeare Birthplace Trust Records Office)

soldiers were killed. In September, she received a letter from the Captain of the number 1 casualty clearing station. Fred had been dangerously wounded in the neck. A letter followed from her husband from Number 16 General Hospital at Le Treport, saying that he felt a little better. On 18 September, she was told that she could go and see him. This rare occurrence was probably achieved through the good offices of the Salvation Army, whose barracks were opposite her house. She packed hastily and left that evening in the red dress she was wearing. Except for the occasional holiday, she'd never been out of Stratford and she'd never been on the sea before, which was very rough. When she arrived at the hospital late on Thursday night she was told that her husband had died earlier in the day. Two days later she attended his funeral in the red dress – the only one she had with her – and was always distressed that she had not worn black.

After his undignified retreat, Edgar Cranmer was relieved to be seconded to the wireless section of the British Army GHQ, partly located in railway carriages at Bertincourt near Arras. The engine of a lorry powered his transmitter. Each morning at 6am, the driver switched it on and the clerk on duty exchanged signals with the various sections of the front line to check the code, which changed each day.

After the German offensive was stemmed, the British counter-offensive began with a series of spectacular victories and GHQ moved forward to Ghoury for about five weeks. The wireless operators were sending out messages every night, abandoning the use of code as they told the troops 'how many prisoners we had captured, how many guns and all the rest of it. Then we moved from Ghoury to Verticorn, still doing it. Well, we knew Gerry had had it.'

A muted optimism began to prevail. 'All the lads here are looking for the end', wrote William Clarke from the trenches. 'Everybody seems "fed up."'

Back home, people were looking beyond the war. Local discussions were taking place about the desirability of ending the workhouse system once peace was declared.

The transatlantic reinforcements were tipping the balance in favour of the Allies. At least one Stratfordian was serving with the American forces. Private Sidney Townsend's mother, Mrs Mary Townsend of 11 Guild Street, enabled him to keep in touch with his hometown by sending him copies of the *Herald*. She was not aware that he had embarked for France with American Expeditionary Force because she wrote to him in the United States on 22 April. He did not get her letter until 20 June.

Private Townsend's attitudes to the war are not dissimilar to those felt by his contemporaries at home in 1914, but they also reflect renewed certainties. 'We came 3,000 miles to do our bit' he wrote to her, 'and God knows America will never take her boys back until the Allies have gained a certain victory (it is coming soon). America has millions of men if needed'.

Yet the vision was being tempered by realism. 'I have seen some awful sights and the noise is awful. I hope we can finish it by Xmas, wouldn't that be fine.'

> Mother dear if anything happens to me, don't worry. I will have done my duty like a man. I know you will miss me but you will feel proud of me... but Mother, God is over all and if it is His will no harm will come to me.

If the worst happened Private Townsend's mother was provided for. He had taken out a life insurance policy in her name, 'but I know you would rather have me than all the money in the world', he added. He closed with a request that she send him a dozen blades for a Gem razor. 'I can't get them in France.' His war finished late next month. 'The Huns have got me at last', he wrote to his mother on 4 August in a letter which reveals that he had not lost the old Warwickshire speech pattern of combining the first person singular with the second person plural. 'I was wounded rather badly on 31 July, shot through the right thigh. Have been operated on and are getting along nicely.'

The Stratfordians were delighted to greet the arriving Americans. In September 1918, sixty officers and men of the US Air Force were entertained in the town. Teams from two of the Flying Squadrons – the Red Sox and the White Sox – played baseball on the cricket ground. Marie Corelli entertained a group of officers at a weekend gathering at Mason's Croft. She was so touched by their enthusiasm for the beauties of Stratford that she offered Trinity College, free of rent, as a hostel – 'The American Inn'. Forty bedrooms would be available to officers from all the Allied armies, but the Americans would take precedence. The American YMCA would put up the considerable sum needed to convert the building and agreed to run it. Marie was waxing mellow, for she even offered the free use of the extensive paddock.

Spanish 'flu

In the autumn Stratford was struck by an epidemic whish cost more lives worldwide than the Great War. Part of the horror of 'Spanish 'flu' was that it struck younger people rather than old. The prolonged wartime shortages ensured that people's ability to cope with this dreaded infection was reduced. Winter was coming and there was a deficiency of fuel, food and warm clothing. The *Herald* purveyed obvious advice to sufferers:

> If every person who is suffering from influenza or catarrh recognises that he is a likely source of infection to others, that some of the persons infected by him may die as a result of this infection, and took all possible precautions, the present disability and mortality from catarrhal epidemics would be materially reduced.

Spirits were much in demand to allay the effects of the disease, but such was the scarcity that doctors were driven to issuing certificates to retailers directing them to supply small quantities to applicants. The great majority of these were not honoured 'not because of an unwillingness or a fear of breaking the law, but because the purveyors had no stocks in hand.'

The *Herald* blamed the Food Department 'for not liberating the large stock reported to be in bond.' Crowds of sufferers overwhelmed the doctors' surgeries. In many of them half the staff had been stricken. Entire households were struck down and were unable to obtain any assistance. The schools were closed and an entertainment at the theatre cancelled. In the last week of October, funerals reached record levels. At the Workhouse, there were nine deaths in a month. At the worst extreme, two or three members of a family were lying dead at one time. The Meadows family in Arden Street lost two of their children. After three years of waiting, Rose Meadows had been due at last to wed Cpl James Harrington, but the marriage was postponed for another month and then must have been a muted affair.

Norman and Kitty Kinman were prostrated by the disease. She gave birth to a son on 27 October, but died the next day. She was 29. Norman fought hard against the malady, but his constitution had been badly undermined by his privations and the shock of his bereavement. He died on 5 November. Kitty's sister, Mrs Ernest Horton, took in the baby. On 6 December, he was christened Paul Norman Kinman.

'That is All'

The last wartime Mop was a month before the Armistice. The new atmosphere of hope brought large numbers of people, many from the surrounding villages, determined to enjoy the shows and stalls, which the *Herald* described as 'meagre and dowdy'. Two roundabouts constituted the sole amusement for children and the fair proprietors had 'caught the infection of putting up prices and charged double for whatever they retailed.' There were no 'sacrificial beasts or pigs' since meat was rationed and no pubs opened 'to obtain the wherewithal for making merry.' The subsequent Runaway Mop was 'a very poor affair, just a few swing boats and ordinary booths'. Wounded soldiers worked energetically to relieve people of their coppers to create a mile of pennies for charity.

The last meeting of the Tribunal took place on 23 October, when two exemptions were granted for 46-year-olds until 1 April. The clear imminence of the end of the war may have made this a rare jocular gesture from the panel.

Germany was disintegrating. On 8 November, German soldiers entered the PoW camp where Leigh Dingley was incarcerated and removed the officers' swords. Within a month he was home.

On 22 October, Edgar Cranmer was on duty at the wireless control centre. At 6 a.m., the driver started the engine of his lorry and sat down beside him. Edgar called up the Cavalry Corps and was about to call up another division when he realised that the German Headquarters at Spa was offering him a message. He did not understand German, but 'of course, it was all in Morse so it didn't matter two hoots what language it was in.' 'Here, Germany calling,' he told the driver. 'Go and fetch Sergeant.'

'What's Cranny had in his cocoa this morning?' was the Sergeant's response when the driver woke him up, but he realised the importance of the situation and went straight over to the wireless station where Edgar was still receiving the message, which neither of them understood. The Sergeant took it to the train, which was just round the corner, and found the Intelligence Officer. He read it and said 'Well, Sergeant, in a few words, it's Gerry asking for an armistice!'

It was obviously vital to convey the news to Marshall Foch, the Allied Supreme Commander, but his headquarters were in the Vosges mountains beyond their wireless range, so they communicated with the Eiffel Tower, which retransmitted the message. Two days later, Foch and the British C-in-C, General Douglas Hague, arrived by car.

After the Armistice was signed on 11 November, the wireless operators were instructed to have a bath and a change of clothes and to re-equip anything they wanted at the station in preparation to move up to take over the German wireless systems at Spa.

In Stratford, the war effort continued to the end. The town claimed to have contributed more per head to the National War Savings Fund than any other borough in the country. It was asked to raise £250,000 in 1918, but in the event the astonishing total of

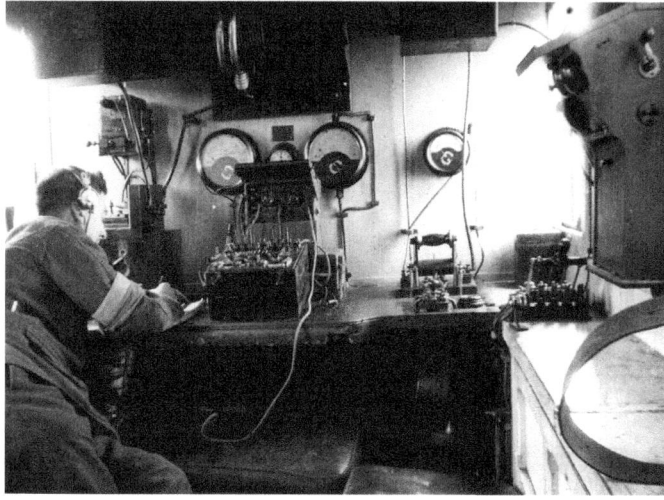

*Edgar Cranmer at
his wireless station.*
(Image courtesy of the
Shakespeare Birthplace
Trust Records Office)

*Gunweek: not the
'Ponderous Tank'.*
(Image courtesy of the
Shakespeare Birthplace
Trust Records Office)

£318,000 was provided. On 4 November, a captured German howitzer and 'that greater destructive agent, the ponderous tank', recently built in Birmingham and probably intended to trundle its way to the Western Front, were placed at the top of Bridge Street. From this platform appeals were made for contributions to the War Loan.

The first intimation of the good tidings was the hooting of train whistles just before 11 a.m. Within minutes, flags were flying all over the town. That afternoon the Mayor and Corporation and a large number of wounded soldiers processed to a service of thanksgiving at Holy Trinity. Hundreds were unable to gain admittance and stood in the porch or avenues. Elation at the victory was muted by reflection on the scores of fallen which the *Herald* had poignantly recorded throughout the war. The vicar, the Revd Canon Melville, caught the sombre note in a short address:

> What for four long weary years we have struggled for has been achieved. That is all. We have prayed, worked, denied ourselves, fought and some have paid the extreme sacrifice. Many have given their all freely in the cause of truth, honour, and liberty. So we shall sing our *Te Deum* of thankfulness, go back to our little world, think it over and wonder what is coming. We are paying our vows; we are mindful of the death of those who have saved us. Let us see to it that it be not said of us 'These people honoured me with their lips, but their hearts were far from me.'

THREE

'GERMANY DOES NOT ADMIT DEFEAT'

Aftermath

The news of the last Stratfordian to fall in action, Pte Frederick Boyne of the 2-8th Worcestershire Regiment, was almost simultaneous with the news of the Armistice. He lived in Greenhill Street and had embarked across the Channel as recently as Easter Monday. Before he was conscripted he worked in the bottling plant at the Brewery.

With the ending of the war, censorship was relaxed and the *Herald* could report that the super dreadnaught, HMS *Audacious*, had sunk after striking a mine off the Irish coast on 27 October 1914. It handled the announcement with a touch of irony. 'Now that hostilities have ceased the Admiralty lets the world know (or rather that part of it that had not discovered the secret for themselves) that the war had only been in progress for ten weeks when we lost one of the finest ships of our Navy.'

In an effort to raise the spirits of the Stratfordians 'to a pitch of exuberance' to celebrate the Victory, a torchlight procession was held on 16 November. Although some people put out bunting, the sombre mood prevailed. The *Herald* was not surprised that the town had no heart for excessive rejoicing. 'It remembers the fallen, those who have made the supreme sacrifice; the maimed and suffering; the widows and orphans; the parents left without well-loved sons.'

On 13 December 1918, Marie Corelli's 'American Inn' opened, too late to receive combatants, but the US Army was still in full force in Europe. Marie herself had supervised the arrangements. At the opening ceremony, the American General Biddle demonstrated that he had learnt in a few minutes what many Stratfordians had failed to grasp in two decades – that flattery was the key to Marie's heart. 'They felt', he said, 'that one of the greatest pleasures American officers could have in coming there would be to see Miss Corelli.'

The *Herald*, which in recent years cannot have featured on Marie's list of friends, was delighted by this development, seeing it as contributing to the economic regeneration of the town. Once peace came large numbers of the Americans serving on the continent would visit England before returning home and Stratford was sure to receive their attention. Nevertheless, the American Inn was a short-lived facility. Lack of funds forced its closure in April.

Anti-German feeling and rhetoric continued to prevail, which, given the scale of the slaughter which had occurred, is understandable. The most outspoken statements tended to come from older non-combatants and could border on absurdity. At a mass meeting at the Theatre to commemorate the Armistice, the Mayor, Archie Flower, referred to the ex-Kaiser as a 'blasphemous felon'. The phrase was taken up by Alderman Edward Fox. He had visited a church at Upper Dovercourt, near Harwich and was shocked to find that it contained a stained-glass window that had been presented by the German Emperor. He demanded that the vicar and churchwardens expel this 'vain-glorious memorial of a debased and treacherous foe'. The vicar replied that Mr Fox had 'a confused idea' of the King's English:

> One cannot solemnly inform a window that it is 'expelled with ignominy' or otherwise. If E. Fox will pay for a fresh window, I think facilities will be afforded him to heave a brick through the offending glass. This is, perhaps, a more effective way than 'killing the Kaiser with his mouth'.

The anti-German sentiments even had their effects on small children. Paul Morgan remembered suffering 'from an ingrained terror of "Huns" due to the propaganda of the day'. On a journey on GWR in 1919 when he was four, the knowledge that there were two coaches of German PoWs attached to the train kept him terrified for the entire trip.

The flags of the defeated Central Powers were excluded from the Birthday Celebrations until 1927. Another emblem was added to the list of *refuses* with the exclusion of the Soviet flag after the Bolshevik Revolution. The hammer and sickle was flown for the first time in 1926, but, because of local protests over its presence, the mast bore no shield to indicate its nationality. Since the other sixty-two masts all bore one, this made it the most conspicuous flag in town. Next year, it was dropped again altogether.

As the first peacetime Christmas approached, the shortages eased slightly, but not to the general benefit. 'Fruit can actually be seen and tasted this year', the *Herald* noted with great satisfaction, but, although the food shops 'certainly seemed replete with everything essential to the Christmas table', prices had soared to place the goods 'utterly beyond the purses of ordinary people.'

The New Year was rung in by the full peal at Holy Trinity: a sound that the townspeople had not heard for two years.

'Fed up to the Teeth with Saluting'

The trickle of men returning from the battlefront began, each scarred by the bitter experience. News of fresh tragedies prevented any feeling of jubilance. On 13 December, the *Herald* carried the sad news of the death at the age of 25 of Gunner William Turvey of 41 Ely Street. He had joined up in 1914 and come through the fighting at Mons, Loos and Ypres without a scratch. On his way home, he had succumbed to the 'flu epidemic and died of bronchial pneumonia at Boulogne.

Edgar Cranmer and the wireless crew got to Spa on 17 December. The place was crawling with British officers. As he came out of a photographic shop where he had been getting some film developed, two officers in the Military Police passed him. One turned round and shouted 'Cranmer!'

'Hello, Duncan', he replied.

'Don't you reckon to salute officers?'

'I'm fed up to the teeth with saluting.'

'There are a lot more soldiers than officers', he was told, with the implication that saluting was an unequal two-way process. The officer was Major Duncan Bairnsfather, younger brother of the cartoonist.

Demob

Demobilisation was proving exceedingly slow. Among the first to return to Stratford was a group who had been prisoners of war in Germany. A subscription was raised and each man was presented with a silver-mounted pipe and fifty cigarettes at a 'sumptuous' dinner held at the Shakespeare. Among the party was Sgt George Tadman, aged 36, of the 3rd Battalion of the Sussex Regiment, who had been captured during the retreat from Mons. His sweetheart, Amelia Lee, aged 38, of 7 Guild Street, had waited for him and they were married at Holy Trinity on 22 February.

It was not until June 1919 that the wife of Amos Unitt was finally notified of his death, which was 'supposed to have taken place in the fierce fighting of March of last year'.

A number of war widows married returning soldiers soon after the war. Among them was Lucy Conway, who wed Bartholomew Mullins, once of the Hampshire Regiment, now working as a packer in Stratford, at Holy Trinity on 30 August 1919.

Moves were afoot to commemorate those who had made the 'supreme sacrifice'. The first memorial in Stratford was unveiled at the Scouts' Hall on 25 January 1919. A Roll of Honour commemorated 120 members of the 1st Stratford Troop who had served in the war of whom sixteen had fallen. If the recorded dead were proportionate to the survivors, some 1,800 local men had served in the war. The population recorded in the 1911 census was 8,532. Something under half would have been males. Excluding those too young and too old, those with disabilities and those in reserved occupations, it is clear that virtually every eligible man had served. The War Tribunal had done its job with great efficiency.

One of the names on the memorial was that of 2nd Lt Adrian Barrett. In April 1920, his mother, Mrs Wilson Barrett visited the place where he had fallen at Mametz Wood:

> I wanted to see the French wood, the scenery last looked upon by the blue eyes of an English boy – and that boy, my son.

She took forget-me-knots and pansies with her from 'the garden my boy had known' at their home on St Gregory's Road.

Her first sight of the battlefield was highly traumatic. It was still dominated by the burnt-out stumps of trees 'all bare and ghostly'. Many British helmets were scattered about and ammunition cases half full of live grenades posed a threat to life and limb. The dugouts and gun shelters of the trenches were still intact and field telephone wires intersected the lines.

Yet a process of regeneration was apparent. In the eighteen months since the Armistice, Nature had 'done her best to soften the hard marks the war has made'. In places the undergrowth was quite high.

A large brown wooden cross had been erected to commemorate the soldiers of the 13th Battalion who had fallen in the offensive of 10 July 1916. Mrs Barrett planted her flowers there:

> The sun came out after a heavy shower and brightened all the wood. There was a lark singing just near me. No one could believe that once in this lovely spot, there had been so much dreadful battle fire and our dear men had given their lives so bravely...

In the post-war years such trips to the battlefields were frequent. The Stratford branch of the British Legion was formed in 1922. It was inspected by the Prince of Wales, on a flying visit to Stratford, a year later. In 1928, the veterans went on a pilgrimage to France and Belgium. Despite the solemnity of the occasion, a 'holiday atmosphere' prevailed, doubtless in part borne of a sense of euphoria at survival.

At Ypres, the party joined with other old soldiers to march past the Prince of Wales at the huge war memorial at the Menin Gate. When their banner appeared, the crowd shouted 'Good old Stratford!' and 'Good old Bill – where have you put him?' (a reference to Bruce Bairnsfather's comic creation) and 'What price Flower's Ale?'

Members of the British Legion on parade, 1922. (Image courtesy of the Shakespeare Birthplace Trust Records Office)

'The Supreme Sacrifice'

At the Town Council meeting on 7 April 1919, the Mayor invited suggestions for a permanent reminder of the war and the lives that had been sacrificed. Amongst ideas forthcoming were a boulevard on the Warwick Road, a new bridge, public baths, a promenade along the river and an endowment fund for the hospital. The District Labour Council proposed building 'war memorial houses' for disabled soldiers, or for the aged parents of the fallen. Mr H.C. Lacey said that he was more concerned with 'the flesh and blood of those who had made the supreme sacrifice – the fatherless children'. Their families had lost their breadwinner and the people of Stratford were now the guardians of these little ones. He wanted to see a trust fund established, 'to give them a fair chance when they were launched out into life'.

These suggestions were all rejected on the grounds that they were projects that should be paid for from the rates. A proposal from Cllr. Winter won the day: a memorial on an island site at the top of Bridge Street. He estimated it would cost no more than £600. His suggestion of a statue of a British Tommy, was later changed to a cross of Hornton Stone quarried locally and designed by the local architect. Guy Pemberton.

By February 1921, fine memorials had been erected in all the neighbouring villages, but there was no sign of one in Stratford. The reason for the delay was an argument about whether the names of the fallen should be placed on the memorial or on the walls of the Council Chamber, where it was pointed out that most people seeing them would be those before the Magistrate's Court! The issue was resolved in favour of the memorial.

Canon Melville was also active in the cause of commemorating the dead, commissioning designs for a memorial oak screen and reredos in St Peter's Chapel at Holy Trinity. The names of the fallen would be engraved on copper plates 'as a perpetual reminder of their sacrifice for the Empire'. Those who had lost

The unveiling of the war memorial, 1922. (Image courtesy of the Shakespeare Birthplace Trust Records Office)

relatives in the war were asked to send in their names, rank and regiment. Yet his frequent financial appeals to his parishioners were disappointingly unproductive. By March 1920, a month before the dedication, only £200 of the £420 costs had been subscribed. The Canon's wealthy wife must have made up the shortfall. The memorial to 237 men who had fallen was dedicated after the Shakespeare sermon on 24 April.

Three old soldiers finally unveiled the war memorial on 17 February 1922. It was a dignified ceremony, attended by those who had lost loved ones, who were dressed in mourning clothes. While most of the names on the Memorial were genuine Stratfordians, the fact that their presence depended on the response of friends and relatives, led to some curious anomalies. Whereas Sgt James Brebner of Russell Cottages' name does not appear, that of Pte Walter Garner of the Queen's Royal West Surrey Regiment features on both the memorial screen and the war memorial. He was born in Chile, lived in South Kensington and enlisted in Wood Green. He has no discernable link with Stratford.

The war memorial was not to remain at the top of Bridge Street for long. In 1926, a lorry ran out of control and toppled it and it was decided to move it to the Bancroft Gardens.

'The Worn Out Symbols of War'

It was easier to honour dead heroes than live ones. By 31 March 1919, only 291 Stratfordians had been demobbed, but complaints were rising that the streets were filled 'with youngsters who seem more disposed to obstruct our pavements and indulge in horse play than do any work that will help the general well-being'. It was supposed that the services would 'first liberate' those who had employment, but the experience in Stratford was that 'the more useful are kept behind to do work which is not only humiliating, but which needs no sort of technical skill or ability'.

A correspondent to the *Herald*, signing himself 'A DISCHARGED SOLDIER' tried to explain the 'Unemployment Mystery'. Like 'a great many other Government schemes', it had been badly handled. Each discharged serviceman was entitled to a weekly allowance of 29s whether he was married or single. The result was that the bachelor had no incentive to work and was tempted 'to take a holiday, while the married man who had the responsibility of a home found it difficult to live on the government allowance and thought it unfair that he was getting so little'. If the recipient found work, he was liable to lose all or part of his allowance. The writer knew of three unemployed men, all discharged soldiers, who had been offered work at the 'local rate' by a builder. When they asked what that was, they were told it was 27s a week. 'Can you wonder, then,' the correspondent concludes, 'that employers cannot get men?'

'Since hostilities ceased, it has been nothing but killing time', wrote Signalman William Clarke. Before the war he had worked for F.W. Winter the draper and had become Managing Director of a small toy factory that the firm had established shortly before the conflict. An audit, conducted after he had joined up, revealed discrepancies in the books. In February 1917, he had written from France to Fred Winter, offering to make up the difference.

In response to criticism of the slow demobilisation process, the army announced that it was prepared to discharge all men with a job to go to, but an extraordinary piece of bureaucracy complicated the situation. The job had to be the same one that the soldier was doing when he enlisted. Winter's toy factory had closed during the war and William Clarke's job had ceased to exist. Fred Winter appears to have been reluctant to apply for his return, which left him stymied. 'I am down in the army records as "Toy Manufacturer" and as far as I can see, must be applied for as such', he wrote to his old boss from the camp at Autigny in December 1918. If the Directors made an application for him, he could get a rapid release. 'I hope they will see my point and do so, the question of my resuming my position as Managing Director does not interfere with the application.

'During the twelve years I was in your employ', he added plaintively, 'I don't think we ever had a cross word.'

Clarke's plea had its effect. 'I have just received yours of 1 January', he wrote on 5 January 1919, 'and thank both you and the company for making application for me.' His release came in the nick of time. 'The men out here are very restless', he wrote two weeks later, 'and there has been several riots at the base.'

Another less fortunate former employee was a soldier called McCullough who wrote from the General Reinforcement Camp at Boulogne on 3 April 1919:

> I will admit I have been a very scilly [*sic*] fellow and caused my poor father and mother and sisters a lot of troubles.

As is often the case, McCullough blamed his unspecified bad behaviour on a woman, but this was now remedied:

> But dear sir my wife is now gone and I do not mind what salary I get so I can get a start and you can rely I will work hard.

This plea produced a curt response:

> Mr Winter has no vacancy for Mr McCullough and any reference from him would not do Mr McCullough any good.

It was difficult for civilians to realise that many who had served in the war were permanently scarred by the experience. George Hewins had got a job as a night watchman at the military hospital at Clopton House, where the last contingent of wounded was received on 28 March 1919[1]. He was given a wooden sentry box and told to demand the password from convalescents who were returning from an evening in town:

> In that coffin up Clopton Lane I started to have dreams. I fancied I was still in the trenches, with the rats running all over: swarms o' rats with yella eyes and big fat bellies. You could a-told me it was only the branches of a tree a-squeaking and a-scratching across the top o' the box – it wouldn't a-made no difference. I used to get off the seat and crouch underneath it, eyes shut, hands over my eyes.

When the Medical Board discovered that George was earning 25s a week, £1 was docked off his pension.

George Holtom suffered from lumbago as a result of his time in the trenches. His wife would cover his back with brown paper; he would bend over the table and she would iron it to relieve the pain. One of the four sons of Alderman Fox who had served was crippled with rheumaticism. William Jones died in 1926. It was considered that his premature end had been brought about by the privations he had suffered as a Turkish PoW. He left a wife and three children.

The shell-shocked were a familiar sight around Stratford for the next half-century. Men like 'Larley' Dale and 'Colonel' Franklin were cruelly teased by children who knew or cared nothing of what they had been through.

The return of the 'heroes' brought another scourge from afar. In May, Warwickshire County Council advertised free treatment for 'all persons who are suffering from diseases such as Syphilis or Gonorrhoea at special treatment centres'. Strict privacy would be observed and no hospital ticket was necessary. The affliction was clearly a speciality of quack medicine for it was pointed out that the Venereal Diseases Act of 1917 made it 'illegal for anyone, other than a duly qualified medical practitioner, for reward, either direct or indirect, to treat any person for Venereal Disease, or prescribe any remedy for such disease, or give advice in connection with the treatment thereof.'

A positive result of the return of the young men was the revival of organised games. The golf club was the first back, but, since fewer of its members had fought in the war than those in sporting clubs for younger men, this was hardly surprising. The suspension of activity had taken its toll. The cricket ground and pavilion were in a very neglected state and it would take a considerable sum to restore them, but it was not too late to organise a crash programme of winter games. The draw was made for the Stratford Football Cup with the first round played on Easter Saturday. The first rugby match took place two days later.

The tank and gun that had arrived in the last days of the war were becoming victims of changing attitudes. Once they had represented patriotic fervour and the will to win at all costs. Now the *Herald* dismissed the tank as 'the battered, dirty, disreputable piece of ordnance now disfiguring the top of Bridge Street.'

The fact was that people were still war-weary. 'What need we,' asked the *Herald*, 'of an object of this kind to daily remind us of a costly war, involving the destruction of thousands of precious lives and the mutilation of some of our finest specimens of humanity?'

Celebratory lunch to mark the signing of the Peace Treaty, 1919. (Image courtesy of the Shakespeare Birthplace Trust Records Office)

These 'worn-out symbols of war' were now used by small boys who became as grubby as the tank itself as they showed off their dexterity in climbing. The Town Council was at a loss to know what to do with its trophies. In May it was proposed that a base for the tank should be built at the junction of the Warwick Road and Guild Street. In the meantime, it was moved to the Bancroft Gardens and the gun to the Fountain. The *Herald* took up a suggestion made by the Mayor of Stamford. 'Use it for levelling some of the squalid houses condemned by the Medical Officer of Health, and then send it to some engineering works to be consigned to the melting pot.' Failing this, it should be placed at 'the rear of the adjacent fellmongery. The pungent odours would not in the least affect it and it would be in the company of other tanks'.

The Peace Treaty with Germany was signed on 28 June. At closing time that night, the fate of the gun was sealed. A large band of young men, many recently demobbed, who had imbibed freely, sallied forth and made for the Fountain. They broke the chain holding the gun and dragged it towards the river. On the way, they were joined by hundreds of other 'exuberant spirits'. A police sergeant on Waterside made a futile attempt to stop the procession. The gun was pushed into the river at the Wash in Southern Lane, but the water was not deep enough to cover it. As it was being dragged out part of the wall of a landing stage was knocked down, but, nothing daunted, the mob hurtled the gun towards Clopton Bridge. After Herculean efforts, 'the huge mass of wood and iron' was pushed over the parapet into the river. The bridge was damaged, but this was of no matter to the boisterous crowd. In this 'humiliating position', the gun collected many more sightseers than it had in Rother Street. 'The only thing to be done', suggested the *Herald*, 'is to rescue it from its present position, and, to prevent further indignity, a free gift should be made of it to one of our local ironfounders.'

A potentially more sinister demonstration occurred next evening when some young men decided to visit a farmer who was employing a few German prisoners of war, but a considerable force of police was waiting and 'nothing unseemly occurred.'

On 18 July, the Peace Treaty was celebrated in appropriate fashion. Six hundred 'gallant fellows, the pick of the town, swung off in procession' to the cricket ground.

With prophetic discernment, one person at least was uneasy about the turn of events. A correspondent to the *Herald* signing himself 'H.J.A.' expressed a concern that would be heard with increasing frequency over the next two decades:

Unveiling of the Boat Club memorial, 1922. (Image courtesy of the Shakespeare Birthplace Trust Records Office)

Stratford-on-Avon Boat Club War Memorial. Unveiled, May 21st 1921

A very large part of the civil population of Germany does not now believe that Germany is beaten, for the simple reason that they see no evidence of the fact... I may claim victory but Germany does not admit defeat.

The captain of the Boat Club, Eddie Thompson, the only member of the Eight to survive the War, expressed a similar view. 'I am not so optimistic', he declared at the unveiling of the Boat Club memorial, 'as to believe that the late war is the end of wars.'

Despite such ultimately justified pessimism, an attempt to build a new world order was reflected in Stratford at the close of 1919. The bellicose Edward Fox was an unlikely League of Nations man, but, as Mayor, he fulfilled his duty by presiding at the inaugural branch of the local association.

On 6 February 1920, the Military Medal awarded to her husband was presented to Ada Chivers in Birmingham by Major General Walker, KCB, KCMG, DSO. Her daughters both became teachers.

The problem of providing work for the war veterans remained. In 1920, the County Council established a centre on a 117-acre site at Shottery, which possessed excellent farm buildings. Its purpose was 'to give a thoroughly sound training in agriculture, market gardening, poultry-keeping and dairy work to those disabled men who were qualified in the eyes of the committee to earn a living on the land'. Twenty-five men would be housed in army huts and it was hoped to expand the number to fifty. A Principal was appointed and a lecture series planned.

The centre did not thrive: 117 acres was hardly sufficient to support twenty-five men, let alone fifty. By February 1921, the County Council was already making moves to close it. The *Herald* waxed angry at such egregious blundering. 'The ex-serviceman is being so scandalously treated... something should be done to save him from a condition bordering on starvation.'

Exit Benson

In the early days of the peace, it was felt imperative to revive the Festival in the following April. As the *Herald* put it:

If nothing had been attempted there would have been general disappointment. People were weary of the War – weary of the peace negotiations dragging themselves so languidly along – and they wanted something that would take them out of the morbid state into which they were rapidly drifting. It was felt that amusement was the best cure to effect this object.

On 23 December, Frank Benson made a flying visit to Stratford to discuss plans. In early February, the Memorial Governors announced that there would be a festival and that it would be conducted 'as of yore' by Sir Frank Benson. He faced huge difficulties. Many Bensonians had signed up in the early days of the war. Many had not yet been demobbed. Others would never return. As late as 7 March, he still could not determine which plays his limited resource of actors would enable him to present. In the event, a scratch cast presented an abridged season.

The Chairman of the Governors, Archie Flower, realised that the war had changed so much that the style of the Bensons run its course. That summer, a new, young director, W. Bridges-Adams presented his first season, employing many Old Bensonians. Murray Carrington had played Romeo in 1914 and Basil Rathbone in 1915. Now the drama critic of the *Herald* was moved to contemplation as he watched the Company rehearse:

> Surely that is not the same slim youth rehearsing Romeo, not changed at all, yet in between the Festivals he has been a Captain and won the military cross. Is that Murray striding across the boards, hardly changed, perhaps a little older? Absurd. Majors are old and peppery, or were before the great upheaval. Captains, Lieutenants, Sergeants, and humble privates back here once more at the shrine of the Stratford Mummers again.

In the summer of 1925, Sir Frank Benson returned to see Dame Ellen Terry silently unveil a window in the Theatre Gallery to the Bensonians who had been lost in the war. The principal figure of St George bears the features of his son, Eric. Three months later, Sir Johnstone Forbes-Robertson unveiled the 'Players Memorial' in Holy Trinity, with an inscription by Rudyard Kipling:

> We counterfeited once for your disport Men's joy and sorrow; but our day has passed. We pray your pardon all where we fell short, seeing we were your servants to this last.

On 26 March 1926, the Shakespeare Memorial Theatre was engulfed by fire. For six years, the festival took refuge in the Picture House, while a larger and grander theatre was built.

Intimations of War

The Birthday was becoming more an international than a local institution, attended by more and more representatives of the nations. Time seemed to be healing the wounds of war. In 1931, ex-Crown Prince Ruprecht of Bavaria paid a private visit to Stratford. He had been a leading German general in the war, but he was shown around the town with great courtesy. In the evening, he was entertained at The Hill by Archie Flower, who had mellowed beyond his previous anti-German rhetoric.

The respite from animosity was brief. Ruprecht's visit occurred in the midst of the Great Slump. Hunger marchers, passing through Stratford on their way to petition Parliament, became a familiar sight. The same slump was precipitating the Nazis to power. After 1933 the presence of the swastika at the Birthday Celebrations presaged another war that manifested itself in the skies over Stratford. On 15 April 1934, a rabbi from Birmingham, Dr A. Cohen, spoke to the local religious meeting known as

Hitler's dream: the Nazi flag flies over
Stratford on Shakespeare's birthday, 23 April
1934. (Image courtesy of the Shakespeare
Birthplace Trust Records Office)

the Brotherhood on the persecution of the Jews in Germany. Next month, a meeting of the blackshirts of the British Union of Fascists at the Hippodrome in Wood Street ended in a riot. It was addressed by A.K. Chesterton, who had written theatrical criticism for the *Herald* over the years.

In 1935, Dennis Wickstead left the Grammar School to train as an officer in the Merchant Navy. He was the son of the actor, Kenneth Wickstead, who had first appeared at the theatre in 1901 at the age of 17. He settled in Stratford, combining his seasons there with work under Barry Jackson at the Birmingham Rep. He had acted at the old theatre, the temporary home in the cinema and the new theatre, as well as participating in the North American tour of 1928. From 1919 onwards he appeared in a record twenty-two consecutive seasons. It was said he had played more roles at Stratford than any other actor.

The glamour of the RAF was irresistible to many young men of the new generation. When Elliot Roberts of 118 Shottery Road, the son of the GWR stationmaster, left the Central School at the age of 15 in 1935, he joined up as a 'boy' and trained as a ground crewman. Later he volunteered for the Fleet Air Arm.

The flying craze was affecting the boys at the Grammar School. Quite a number joined the RAF when they left school. Alan Woodward of 7 Glencoe, who had played in the 1st XV and the 1st XI, gained his pilot's license at the Worcestershire Flying School and later entered the RAF Air Navigation School. Such was the passion of Philip Tyler of 211 Evesham Road, to join the Air Force that he gladly underwent surgery at the Stratford and Birmingham General hospitals to enable him to qualify as a wireless operator and later as an air gunner.

Bruce Organ, who lived in Maidenhead Road, shared the same passion, but when he left the Grammar School, he took the safer option and went to work at the National Farmers Union (NFU). The life soon palled, so, by way of contrast, he toured Ireland with the actors company managed by Mr Anew McMaster, who had played Bolingbrooke, Coriolanus, Hamlet and Petruchio at the Theatre in the season of 1933.

It was difficult for scholarship boys from working-class backgrounds to stay on beyond the school-leaving age. Alan Sutton of Albany Place, left the Grammar School in 1926 at the age of 14 to work in the Borough Treasurer's Office. His father had died and his family needed his support. A fine rugby footballer, he established his place in the Stratford XV at the age of 17.

When Ronald Lysons of 26 Sanctus Street, left the Grammar School in 1936, he followed the path blazed by Edgar Cranmer years before, training at Stratford post office as a telegrapher. In the same year, 15-year-old Jack Hall of 44 Albany Place, achieved over 90 per cent in each of his school maths exams, but family circumstances obliged his parents to take him away from the Grammar School to take up a position as a Junior Clerk at the GWR station. It was his job to work out the guards' timesheets and produce the wages audit.

Wilfred Rookes who played football for the Working Men's Club and cricket for the Stratford 2nd XI left the Grammar School in 1937 and helped his brother Chris in his wine merchants business in Union Street before joining the Royal Engineers as a Sapper at the age of 17 in 1938. When clergyman's son, J.O. Passey, left the Grammar School in 1939, he joined the Merchant Navy as an apprentice.

Brigadier and Mrs Stokes-Roberts were in India, where he was serving with the Hampshire Regiment, so their two sons, Lawrence and his younger brother, Dickie, spent their holidays from Malvern College with their grandparents, Sir Whitworth and Lady Wallis at Red Walls, Rowley Crescent. Sir Whitworth was the former keeper of the Birmingham Art Gallery and a Governor of the Shakespeare Memorial Theatre.

War clouds were gathering. In 1937, the Secretary of the local branch of the League of Nations Union, Mr R. Cross, sensed the gloom caused by 'the seemingly inevitable catastrophe'. The nation was beginning to be placed on a war footing. Members of the Surveyor's staff undertook training in Rural District Council Yard in Tyler Street, disposing of a 'bomb' that was thrown off an adjoining roof.

The crisis attained a local dimension in February 1938. Anthony Eden, by now Foreign Secretary, resigned in protest against Neville Chamberlain's policy of appeasement. That autumn came the Munich crisis. 'On all sides faces were grave and voices low. Hearts sank lower and lower until... even the optimists began to lose hope.' Fevered preparations were made for what seemed the inevitable. The Mayor, Cllr Tommy Waldron, toured the streets appealing for volunteers to help build air-raid shelters. Among the willing helpers were boys from the Grammar School. The seventy unemployed men who were dragooned into service may have been less enthusiastic.

Ten shelters were soon under construction around the town. A trench 190ft long, 5ft wide and 7ft deep was covered with corrugated iron and then with soil. The walls were lined with wood and benches ranged on each side. When complete the shelters could hold 1,500 people. There were designs available at the Town Hall for those wishing to build their own versions.

Two large shelters were erected in Rother Street next to the Congregational Church. Obviously it had to be a policy that the doors were never locked, so they became notorious as places where there were 'all sorts of "goings on"'.

Shops selling provisions were advised to issue their customers with no more than their usual requirements and contingency arrangements for issuing ration cards were announced. Families willing to accommodate evacuee children were recruited.

The newly formed corps of air-raid wardens was making a long round of visits to measure people for gas masks. It was announced that air-raid warnings would be given by a two minute warbling signal from the fire station and a series of blasts on the brewery hooter. On hearing these signals, people were advised to go indoors until the all-clear sounded. If hostilities broke out, the schools would close for a week and the possibilities of providing them with their own air-raid shelters were being examined. The *Herald* conceded that the prospect of Stratford suffering an air raid was extremely remote, 'but the need for being prepared for the worst is obvious.'

Early recruits to 'Waldron's Warriors' on parade at the grammar school, 1939. (Image courtesy of the Shakespeare Birthplace Trust Records Office)

Teenager Margaret Dickinson, the daughter of the scenic artist at the Theatre, who was working in a local solicitor's office, joined the Red Cross. After attending a training camp, she became the anti-gas officer for the Stratford detachment. She instructed Civil Defence personnel and air-raid wardens and visited local factories and shops to train people in the use of gas masks.

One man who may have felt that he was escaping the worst was Sapper Wilfred Rookes. Shortly after playing soccer for the Royal Engineers in the final of the Services Cup, he was posted to Malaya, a place that would not long remain on the sidelines.

In September 1938, Miss Gillian Forster of 79 Clopton Road, a handloom weaver at the Web in Shottery, responded to the first appeal for National Service Volunteers by registering for the newly-formed Women's Land Army. Apart from being a keen gardener, she had no experience of agriculture.

On the afternoon of 28 September, news came that the Prime Minister was to meet the leaders of Germany, France and Italy in an eleventh-hour attempt to avert war. Immediately tensions were relaxed and hopes ran high. The Munich agreement brought a rapturous response. A more palpable effect than the Service of Thanksgiving at Holy Trinity came when twelve Czech refugees who had been expelled from the Sudetenland arrived in Stratford. They were accommodated in the Youth Hostel.

With the apparent easing of the crisis, preparations for war were neglected. The trenches that had been so hurriedly dug, were filled in or became waterlogged.

Whatever the rights or wrongs of the Munich Agreement, it undoubtedly gave the nation time to prepare for war. The local Yeomanry Cavalry, in theory an armoured car unit, received thirty-one new recruits and by May were at war strength. What they lacked in experience they made up for in enthusiasm. On 10 March, the Mayor appealed for help in forming a local Territorial unit of infantry. More than 100 volunteers enrolled when 'D' Company of the 7th Battalion of the Warwickshire Regiment was inaugurated at the Hippodrome on 3 May. The new Company was nicknamed Waldron's Warriors.

An early recruit was Robert Lysons, the brother of the post office telegrapher. He had joined the NFU on leaving the Grammar School. He played rugby for the town's 2nd XV, was the popular secretary of the local Toc H and a server at Holy Trinity.

Another joining on inception was F.J.O. Spender, one of three sons of Mr F.O. Spender of Banbury Road. He was secretary of the Grammar School Old Boys Rugby Club. His father was the manager of the agricultural suppliers, Warwickshire Farmers Ltd. On leaving school he had joined his father in the business.

The image of 'square pegs in round holes' was bucked by the volunteers. Robert Lyson's desk experience made him an obvious choice as Company Clerk. E.G. Evans of Banbury Road, an accountant, was made Warrant Officer, while Harold Dornborough, who worked for the bus company, Stratford Blue Motors, became an armoured car driver with the Warwickshire Yeomanry. Since the regiment was still mounted, he was transferred to a regiment that was equipped with armoured cars on the outbreak of war. Another from the 'Stratford Blue' in the first batch of volunteers was the 22-year-old bus conductor, William Colwell of 3 Welcombe Cottages, Mayfield Avenue.

An Auxiliary Fire Service was formed, based at the fire station in Guild Street. It was singularly ill-equipped. When war broke out the volunteers possessed only a tin helmet and an axe each. They had no fire engines, only some old cars. To supplement their transport, a well-wisher presented them with a big old car which they nicknamed 'The Flying Bedstead'.

The volunteer firemen made up a song about their paltry weekly wage:

> We are firemen, maybe in a week
> We only get three pound.
> The more we do, the more we weigh
> Makes no difference to our pay.

Women too had a conspicuous role. In the same week that the T.A. Battalion was formed, an enlistment depot for the Civil Nursing Reserve was opened in Bridge Street.

Early in 1939, local authorities were instructed to ascertain the amount of available accommodation if mass evacuation from the cities became necessary. In Stratford, Henry Tompkins, the Borough Chamberlain, estimated that nearly 5,000 extra people could be accommodated.

Despite later claims to the contrary, the horrors being perpetrated in Nazi Germany were an open secret. Whatever they had heard about concentration camps was likely to be true, Mrs F.M. McNeille told a Workers Educational Association meeting at the Town Hall in March. She had personal evidence of people being killed or maimed and of diabolical cruelty. People were made to stare into the sun until they were blinded. The legal system had disappeared. A perfectly innocent act might cause a man to be sent to a concentration camp.

Early in 1939, Miss Gertrude Bliss, whose family lived at 60 Kendall Avenue, took up the position of companion housekeeper to a couple that lived in a chateau in France between Amiens and Abbeville. The husband was English and the wife French. On leaving school, Gertrude had worked in the Greenhill Street laundry before becoming manageress of a laundry in Luton for nine years.

With the German annexation of the remnants of Czechoslovakia, Anthony Eden saw the exoneration of his stance against Munich. 'Out of all this week's tragic events', he told a meeting at Alveston House on 22 March, 'I think there is one gain. We all have no more comfortable illusions… Some of us have been called harsh names – even warmongers – during the past year because we were unable to accept these optimistic forecasts. Henceforth I hope we shall all realise what confronts us…'

War fears increased dramatically. In the fields next to its aluminium foundry and canning factory on the Birmingham Road, Messrs N.C. Joseph Ltd erected nine air-raid shelters to accommodate all 450 of their employees. The long function room

Stratford youngsters try on some gas masks for size. (Image courtesy of the Shakespeare Birthplace Trust Records Office)

at the Unicorn pub was stacked high with boxes as a team of volunteers worked to provide gas masks for the whole of South Warwickshire. An average of thirty people worked on an assembly line throughout that fatal week, turning out 1,000 respirators an hour. Excellent service was rendered by the Czech refugees. To relieve the monotony, the local electrical suppliers, Messrs Hanson, provided a radio.

The world crisis was affecting the Shakespeare industry. The number of visitors to the Birthplace was down by 11,000. The destruction of so many nations by Axis aggression presented the Birthday Celebrations Committee with dilemmas. The Austrian flag had been withdrawn following the *Anschlus* with Germany in the previous year and the Ethiopian flag disappeared after that nation's conquest by Italy. With war seeming increasingly inevitable, it was decided to retain the flags of Albania (another of Mussolini's recent conquests) and Czechoslovakia. After the Nationalist victory in the Spanish Civil War, the Duke of Alba, Ambassador for the new regime, presented the Committee with a new flag, but the thorny question of which nations to invite to the Birthday Luncheon was resolved when only the Peruvian Ambassador accepted the invitation. In the event, the twelve Czech refugees were invited to unfurl their national flag. Soon afterwards they emigrated to Canada.

As if the complications of diplomatic niceties were not enough, special precautions had to be taken because the IRA had embarked on a considerable campaign of terrorism on the British mainland.

By May, 500 beds had been provided at the hospital, of which 400 were intended for war casualties. Long huts, each taking 150 beds, were erected in the grounds. At the Public Assistance Institution – the old Workhouse – the number of hospital beds was increased from 187 to 300. An emergency rations store was established at the GWR goods yard.

In June, conscription was inaugurated locally when 127 men in the 20 to 21 age group were ordered to register for military training at the Employment Exchange on the Birmingham Road. Three days later, the ninety-strong Territorial Company drilled for the first time on the Grammar School quadrangle.

That summer's Grammar School eight were regarded as the most successful crew the school had ever put on the water. Its star rower, Rogers Miller, younger son of Mr and Mrs C.J. Miller of Alveston Pastures won the Brickwood Skulls for the third year running, but returned the trophy he was entitled to keep. During his school career he had won sixteen cups and eight medals. On leaving school in July, he joined his elder brother, John, in the RAF.

Even as a small boy, young Raymond Timms of Rother Street had a passion for the Navy. While still at Broad Street School he had pestered his parents to allow him to join up, but they had prevailed against it, so, on leaving school he went to work at N.C. Joseph's. Finally, in June, they relented and allowed him to join the Royal Naval Volunteer Reserve as a Boy Seaman.

The Great Black-Out

On 14 July, a blackout was ordered over seventeen counties to enable the RAF to test the night defences. Householders were asked to screen all lights, street lamps were turned off and the traffic lights hooded.

In Stratford, the sirens sounded at midnight and, for the next two hours, hundreds of volunteers in full 'war kit' worked under simulated emergency conditions. An ARP Centre was established in the basement of the Public Library. It had been reinforced with steel pillars that the volunteers found a great inconvenience. A battery of telephones had been installed – three for inward and three for outward calls, with direct lines to the police and fire stations. The supposed dropping of bombs and the resultant provision of services were marked by coloured pins on a large-scale map of the town on the wall.

The calls originated with Air-Raid Wardens on duty throughout the town. Once a telephonist took the call, a complicated procedure was set in motion. After a glance from the message supervisor, a messenger boy rushed it to the plotting clerk, who briefly asked the chart writer whether it was a new call and then scribbled an order for the required services. This was passed to a report clerk who wrote out an order that a messenger rushed to a telephonist for an outward call phone. Ambulances, lorries, fire engines and private cars driven by women volunteers then moved through streets of inky blackness – the kerbstones had been painted white – on ARP service to the points where the supposed dropping of a bomb had brought injury and destruction.

The first call came at 12.25 a.m. when a rescue party was summoned to Meer Street, where three 'bodies' were trapped in a fallen building. The dummies were rapidly rescued and members of the St John's Ambulance Brigade, bearing labels describing their injuries, were substituted. After on-the-spot treatment by a first-aid party they were dispatched to the 'hospital'.

At 12.50 a.m., 'mustard gas' was reported in Union Street. The decontamination squad from the Corporation Yard was rapidly on the scene and after decontaminating the street and buildings, they erected 'Danger Gas' signs and roped off the area. Twenty minutes later, an 'incendiary bomb' set 13 Cherry Street ablaze. The auxiliary fire brigade raced to the scene and coupled the engine to a hydrant.

Around thirty calls were dealt with in less than two hours. As part of the exercise the phone lines were broken and senior boys from the Grammar School acted as messengers to bring vital news to the control centre.

Another extensive exercise took place on 11 August. Previously, all messages had been prearranged, but this time the wardens were told to use their imaginations so no less than forty-eight messages passed through the centre in less than two hours. The most spectacular effort was in Hutchings coal yard where a high-explosive 'bomb' had trapped several people in a building. The rescue party climbed ladders, got through the windows, safely evacuated the 'casualties' and handed them over to the first-aid party. Once again the dummies carried labels giving particulars of their injuries. Volunteers were substituted, the injuries dressed on the spot and the 'patients' removed by car to the first-aid post in Arden Street by car or ambulance according to the seriousness of their 'injuries'.

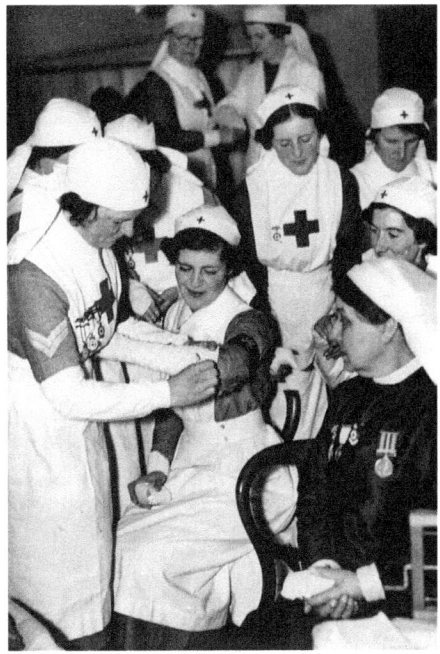

Nurses practice first aid during air-raid practice. (Image courtesy of the Shakespeare Birthplace Trust Records Office)

'A Great Lark'

In 1914, life had gone on as normal while the world slid almost absentmindedly to disaster, but in August 1939, the question was not 'If?' but 'When?' By the last week of the month, as the Polish crisis moved inexorably forward, the prospect of war had become the sole topic of conversation. Yet morale was high. When the theatre orchestra struck up the National Anthem before the performance of *Much Ado about Nothing* on 31 August, the audience rose as one and sang with great fervour.

After 23 August, the telephone services at the General Hospital were staffed twenty-four hours a day. The ARP control centre was to be manned 24 hours a day for the next five years. The air-raid shelters in Arden Street were completed in reinforced concrete and other trenches were being dug around the town. In the sandpits on the Banbury Road, the Corporation workmen, assisted by a squad of King Edward VI Grammar School boys and other volunteers were filling sandbags to place around public buildings. The inevitable problem of hoarding arose again with heavy purchases of food, especially sugar and tinned goods.

On 31 August, Miss Haydon, the Matron of the nursing home in Rother Street, received an order to turn it into a maternity home for expectant mothers who were to be evacuated from Birmingham next day. She immediately got busy. Within half an hour, men were working on the gas and electricity supplies. A squad of policemen undertook the work of setting up beds and removing furniture and lumber. Arrangements were made to transfer the existing patients to establishments in Birmingham and Walsall. No one appears to have observed that these were precisely the areas from which the evacuees would arrive.

Next day, all railway excursions from Stratford were cancelled because 750 evacuee children and their teachers were expected to arrive from the poorest areas of Birmingham. In the event only 420 turned up. Many had clearly adopted a 'wait and see' policy in relation to the war.

On arrival, the Catholic children were escorted to St Gregory's School in Henley Street and the rest to the Alcester Road School. Toddlers struggled under the weight

of suitcases, haversacks, innumerable paper bags and gas masks. Some of the suitcases were as big as the children and it seemed improbable that they would reach their destinations. Most were remarkably cheerful and treated the whole business as 'a great lark.' The Mayoress, Mrs F.N. Waldron, greeted them at the station and many of the children chatted happily with her, their faces wreathed in smiles. Some of the smaller ones looked bewildered. A few sobbed bitterly and were comforted by elder sisters and friends.

Passing the Thatch Tavern on her way to the Catholic school, one little girl got very excited and told her friend that it was the first time she had seen a house with a straw hat on. At the schools, each child was given rations for two days, which included sweetened and unsweetened condensed milk and tins of corned beef. They were then distributed to families that had offered them board. This represented something of a culture clash. Some of the children had never slept in beds above floor level before and quite a few had never eaten a boiled egg and did not know how to tackle one. It was even reported that some youngsters had to learn the nature of stinging nettles from personal experience.

Next day, 600 expectant mothers and their children were due to arrive, but only 90 women and 100 children turned up. They were sent in the first instance to three maternity homes that were still being prepared. One woman arrived just in the nick of time. Stratford's first evacuee baby, a boy, was born that night at the newly-converted maternity home. The conditions were somewhat makeshift. The conversion work wasn't completed until the following Tuesday. A lady doctor was appointed to take charge of the maternity cases and she was soon engaged on her antenatal work with the hall and gardens of the home full of expectant mothers.

Inevitably there were serious mismatches in the pairing of evacuees and their hosts. The office of Mr H.A. Tompkins, the somewhat pompous Borough Chamberlain who had organised the placements, was invaded by both categories to such an extent that he was obliged to lock his door.

Opposite: *The arrival of evacuee children, 1939.*
(Image courtesy of the Shakespeare Birthplace
Trust Records Office)

Right: *Land Army girl, Gillian Foster.* (Image
courtesy of the Shakespeare Birthplace Trust
Records Office)

Mobilisation

On 1 September, reservists were called up. The young brewer, Dennis Flower, was
drafted into the Royal Corps of Signals. At the annual meeting of the Theatre
Governors, he had succeeded his father, who had died earlier that year, as a member
of the Executive Council.

Arthur Sanders of 10 Kerns Terrace, who was well known in the area as a scout
with the Automobile Association, was posted to the motorcycle section of the Military
Police. Mr T. White had previously served in the army and was now working for the
local dairyman, Clyde Higgs. His experience ensured that he immediately achieved
the rank of Sergeant in the Royal Berkshire Regiment. He left behind a sweetheart,
Lily Tandy, who was a neighbour in College Lane. Arthur North of 22 Church Street
was working with an insurance company in Birmingham. Now he joined the army.
At the Grammar School, he had played in the 1st XV and rowed. Postman S.G. 'Fred'
Ryman, of Clopton Road, was called up into the Royal Artillery.

Young Raymond Timms achieved his ambition to serve in the Royal Navy. Postman
S.G. Ryman of 11 Shipston Road, another old Grammar School boy, was called up
into the Royal Artillery while Gillian Forster was sent to Studley College for a month's
training before joining the Women's Land Army (WLA).

The 114 members of the local Territorials were called up as a company. They
were enhanced by an intake of six officers from other units to give a nucleus of
administration.

Eighteen-year-old Norman Watson, who worked at the NFU, found himself called
up within days of joining up. He had played rugby for the Grammar School and the
Old Edwardians. He was a promising soldier. As early as February 1940, he received
a commission.

Arthur Walton, a Somerset man, had moved to Stratford in April to take up a
position as Works Engineer at Stratford Produce Canners. He was a Territorial with

the Royal Engineers, so, on the outbreak of war, he had to report back to his regiment at Frome. It was a statutory obligation that his firm keep his job open, but it would be seven years before he returned.

While the changed nature of warfare meant that there was not the same drive for volunteers as in 1914, many were forthcoming. Among them were 21-year-old Harry Goode of 7 Mulberry Street, a lorry driver with the corn and coal merchants, the Walker Co., who was drafted into the Royal Warwicks; Leonard Millin of 21 Evesham Place, a well-known local rugby player, joined the Royal Engineers, and Herbert Gully of 12 Clopton Road was drafted into the Royal Army Service Corps as a driver. He had worked as a salesman for Messrs F.A. Burchell, the electrical suppliers, for ten years, As the firm's window dresser, he had gained an award in a national competition.

Two staunch members of the St John's Ambulance Brigade, Dennis Hirons, aged 20, the younger son of Mr and Mrs W.R. Hirons, of 1 Arden's Terrace and S.J. Lively, only son of Mr and Mrs Lively of 20 Ely Street, achieved long-held ambitions by volunteering to become sick berth attendants in the Royal Navy. Dennis was a van driver with the tobacconists, Messrs A. Preedy & Sons, a choirboy at St James' Church and a keen member of Stratford Cycling Club. S.J. Lively, who worked at Vincent Nurseries, was an assistant scoutmaster.

Another well-known member of the St John's Ambulance Brigade was Wally Brooks of 27 Great William Street. Before joining the Royal Army Medical Corps, he served as a part-time member of the Civil Defence Ambulance Service.

Age was not a barrier to those with specialist skills. Retired Lt-Col J.M. Crawford of Shottery Road, volunteered to rejoin the Royal Army Medical Corps and was seconded to the Merchant Marine. At the other end of the age-scale, two employees of the local builders, Kirk & Kirk, lied about their ages to sign up for the Royal Marines. Don Clark was 16 and Joe Pitts, 17. They wanted to 'join the Marines because they were the best. It was our adventure…'

Despite the comparative lack of need for mass manpower, something of the hysteria of the Great War persisted. When somebody asked Ted Eborall, the landlord of the Garrick, why he wasn't in the army like everybody else, he went and joined up, despite being too old for automatic service.

As war approached, people clustered around their radios to listen to the news bulletins. Rumours were circulating that, once it broke out, Parliament would be evacuated from London and convene in the Conference Hall. The rumours were exacerbated when a large number of extra phone lines were installed at the Theatre.

The *Herald* pooh-poohed talk of the theatre's imminent closure while doing its best to imply that it was party to the scheme. It managed to reveal the extensive anti-aircraft preparations without contravening the newly-imposed restrictions on reporting matters relating to national security:

> It is true that many large buildings in all parts of the country will be used for various purposes in case of war, but details, of course, cannot appear in the Press. Similarly, publicity about the location of searchlights anti-aircraft guns, listening posts, &c, is undesirable.

In London, the projected move was such an open secret that the Parliamentary Press Gallery Committee sent a posse down to scout round Stratford's pubs and recommend a suitable watering hole as a 'Club House' for the hacks.

Miss Bertha Gover was working in Warsaw as English governess to the family of the Princess Radziwill. She sent a postcard to her widowed mother in Stratford early in August before going to the country to visit the estate of a former pupil. As war clouds gathered, her hostess asked her to take her two boys to Rumania, but it was too late. On 1 September, Germany invaded Poland.

FOUR

'THE SHOW WILL GO ON'

Phoney War

On 3 September, Great Britain and France declared war on Germany. The Shakespeare Festival had two weeks to run, but all theatres and cinemas were ordered to close immediately. The Picture House at Stratford reopened within a fortnight and was packed out every evening.

The closure cost the theatre £4,500 in lost revenue, partly because the Governors honourably decided to pay the actors their remaining wages. By now, Kenneth Wickstead had appeared in thirty-two different Shakespeare plays and played over 200 roles. When war was declared he was playing his usual gamut of character parts. Despite being in his 50s, he managed to join the RAF and achieved the rank of Flying Officer.

Two Stratfordians were soon in action. LAC Philip Tyler was a crew member of a Wellington bomber that raided the Kiel Canal the day after war was declared. Flt Sgt Alan Woodward took part in the first patrols over the Heligoland Bight.

By contrast, 20-year-old gunner Tom Barr, who had joined the Royal Horse Artillery a year before, found himself posted to the comparative backwater of Egypt.

The initial stages of the war did not prove hazardous for the heroes of Waldron's Warriors, who were mobilised on 1 September. Each day they marched through the town to lunch at the Old Red Lion. On route marches someone would be sent on ahead to a pub to order fifty pints of beer, which were duly lined up on the counter.

Tony Hawkins got his call-up papers early in the war, joining the Royal Engineers at Aldershot. Aged 21, he had trained as an electrician at Messrs F.R. Burchell after leaving the Grammar School. A skilled oarsman, he had rowed for the school in the coxless fours at Henley. For two and a half years he had been walking out with 19-year-old Vera Dyson, who lived with her parents at 22 Broad Street, and worked as an assistant at the shoe shop, Freeman, Hardy and Willis.

The Town Council's first act of war was to set aside land in the cemetery for service burials. It appointed a Food Control Committee. Five of the fifteen members represented retail traders and ten, consumers, but only two of these were women. The Borough treasures – Gainsborough's portraits of Shakespeare and Garrick, the maces and the charter – were removed from the Town Hall and taken to the Flower residence at Ilmington Manor.

Just before 8 a.m. on Wednesday, 6 September, the air-raid sirens sounded in earnest for the first time. Every day, Richard Mullins, aged 8, walked up Clopton Road with the postman to the gates of Clopton House. They had got as far as Kitty Holtom's shop at number 37 when the alarm sounded from the nearby brewery. Richard was scared so the postman told him to run home as quickly as possible.

The public reaction to the alarm disappointed the organisers of the painstaking ARP exercises. These had taken place at night. The populace was unprepared for the more likely event of a daytime raid. Many Stratfordians adopted a casual attitude to the sirens, simply going outside and looking up into the air to see what was going on. Even before the all-clear, many people were going about their business as usual. A better example was set at N.C. Joseph's, where the alarm came between two shifts. Nevertheless, the entire workforce was accommodated in the nearby air-raid shelters.

The situation was not helped by the fact that the sirens were not heard in many areas of the town, although, strangely, they were heard four miles away at Wilmcote.

The reality of war hit home a little more on 15 September, when petrol rationing was to be introduced. Long lines of cars besieged garages, but for some reason the rationing was postponed for a week when the queues duly reappeared.

The lighting regulations were another cause for concern. Many people simply ignored them. On 6 September, officers visited the most obvious offenders and warned that proceedings would be taken against them if they persisted. The Chief Constable said that such people could be aiding enemy aircraft and endangering their lives and those of many others. Examples were made *pour encourager les autres*. Miss Hilda Copsey, the manageress of a shop in Henley Street, was fined 5/- for failing to screen lights at the premises on an October evening.

Yet in this period of 'phoney war' there were simply no enemy aircraft about so it was difficult to take the regulations seriously – a view shared by many of the evacuee women who could not bear the loneliness of life 'in the country' and went home. The regulations were actually a greater danger to life and limb than the Luftwaffe. Many were the mishaps caused by the blackout. On 7 October, a motorcyclist was killed when he collided with a stationary van on the Banbury road. The coroner had little doubt that the accident had been caused by the reduced lighting.

On the evening of 25 October, an RAF officer's car broke down outside the Red Lion at Bridgefoot. James Moore of 101 Loxley Road, a night watchman at the nearby telephone exchange, was passing on his way to work and helped give a push. A passing car hit him from behind and he was pinned between the two vehicles, dying later in hospital.

'If it was a foggy night', recalled Rosemary McAteer, one of the new intake of lady 'clippies' on Stratford Blue Motors, 'you could get in at any time because there was no lights on the buses:

> The headlights were covered and there was just three little slots and then the sidelights were covered in. There was just about an inch round circle... and there were no white lines on the roads and no kerbs. It was just a grass verge. Particularly on the Cheltenham run, coming back all round the villages, you used to walk in front of the bus to keep it on the road if it was a very foggy night, with either a newspaper or a handkerchief, so the driver knew where he was.

By contrast, the writer H.V. Morton, on a visit to Stratford in the first weeks of the war, was enchanted by the effects of the blackout, regarding it as 'something never to be forgotten,

> The darkness obliterates everything that is vulgar; it makes everything harmonise. The roofline becomes important; the most commonplace objects become almost operatic; and in fancy every approaching footfall or dark figure shares in the air of mystery.

The Nation's Capital?

The validity of the rumour that there were contingency plans for the Government and Civil Service to move to Stratford was confirmed on 7 September when the Ministry of Works requisitioned most of the town's hotels and boarding houses as a prelude to possible departmental evacuation.

At the Shakespeare, the fourteen permanent guests were given twenty-four hours to leave. On hearing that they could only stay one more night, two settled their bills and left immediately. Five other residents moved to the Swan's Nest, one of the town's few remaining hotels, next morning. The man from the Ministry 'advised' the manager, Mr J.C. Higgins, to give the staff a week's notice.

Documents released under the fifty-year rule reveal the scale of the plans. The Conference Hall was to become the Chamber of the House of Lords. The Commons would be housed in the auditorium, with the Press Gallery on the stage. Three small rooms at the Theatre were to be divided up as private offices for the Lord Chancellor, the Party Leaders, Black Rod, the Whips and Clerks. The Museum and Library were to be partitioned as offices for the press, doorkeepers, parliamentary reporters and the Printed Paper Office.

Private rooms for senior ministers were to be provided at the Shakespeare, which would also house the Parliament Office, the Lord Chancellor's Department and the official shorthand writers. Peers of the Realm were to be billeted in the relatively salubrious setting of the Falcon, while mere MPs were to lodge in small hotels and guesthouses.

On his visit to Stratford, H.V. Morton picked up the fact that the Government had taken over the Shakespeare 'in the first moments of war, when it was believed that London had only a few hours to live, and the inhabitants were given about twenty-four hours to get out:

> Since then nothing has been heard from the Government, and the hotel remains closed, just as it was requisitioned, with the chairs and tables piled up in the lounge, as you can see through the windows. It would be pleasant to think of Treasury officials operating from a room called 'Much Ado about Nothing', or members of the Inland Revenue sending out their forms from one called 'As You Like It', for all the bedrooms in this hotel bear the title of a Shakespearean play.

'The Common Cause of Freedom'

The idyll of 'D' Company ceased some three weeks into the war. The 7th Battalion, with its companies from Stratford, Warwick, Leamington and Coventry was sent off to train near Swindon. One day in November, they were lined up and told that anyone over the age of 19 should raise his hand. They would embark for France in the near future. It was Colin Hughes' 19th birthday, but he kept his hand down. A 'friend' in the company said, 'Colin, you're 19, put your hand up', so he was forced to raise it. The Battalion eventually embarked on 16 January 1940.

After the momentous events of early September, most people had returned as nearly as possible to normal living. An estimated 700 Stratfordians were serving in the forces, at least thirty of them in the Royal Navy, but their progress did not arouse the interest in the *Herald* that it had in the previous war, although censorship would have had something to do with that.

The trained reservists joined active units with great rapidity. Less than three weeks after his call-up, Sergeant White was stationed on the Belgian border. Lance Corporal Arthur Sanders had also been moved rapidly to France. He saw incendiary bombs

*The Territorials
march off to war.*
(Image courtesy of the
Shakespeare Birthplace
Trust Records Office)

dropped on Arras in the first of the German air raids. His nerves were shattered and he was hospitalised for three weeks.

The chateau at which Gertrude Bliss was working became a second home for the Tommies stationed nearby. 'D' Company received a warm welcome from the locals at Raches, a small French village near the Belgian border. Jack Hall and his friends, Will Troughton and Don Holmes, used to go to a little café for egg and chips and beer and wine. They got quite friendly with the daughter of the house who was aged about 17 and tried to teach her English.

The German conquest of Poland took little less than a month. The estate on which Bertha Gover was staying was taken over by German officers, but the family and servants were allowed to remain. She spoke Polish and German, so the Germans did not realise that she was British. For months her mother heard nothing from her, but in April she was able to smuggle a message saying she was safe to the American Ambassador in Warsaw, who conveyed the good news to Mrs Gover in Stratford.

Once again, the uncertainties of war precipitated whirlwind romance, but nuptials were more prosaic. From the earliest days of the war, brides had ceased to wear white. Clothes rationing had made wedding dresses an impossible luxury. On his first home leave, Sergeant White married his Lily. On 21 October, his 21st birthday, Dennis Hirons, RN married Violet Wales, a Durham miner's daughter. She was four years older than he and worked in a factory that had been converted to produce munitions. As they could not get a house, they lived with her sister at 11 Kendall Avenue.

Leonard Millin had been posted to France: not to the Belgian border, but to Rennes, in Brittany to the No 1 Engineers Stores Base Depot. There he fell on love with a young French lady with the splendid name of Mlle Marcelle Rita Jacqueline Marie Mèliès. She was extremely well connected. Her family were legendary pioneers of the film industry and she had been born in New York. Her grandfather and great uncle had made the first-ever science fiction film, *Le Voyage dans La Lune* in 1902.

Elliot Roberts, by now a fully-fledged mechanic, was aboard the carrier HMS *Kenton* on the China station when war broke out. His ship was diverted to the search for the German raider, *Admiral Graf Spee*, but she was not present at the Battle of the River Plate in December.

The Warwickshire Yeomanry was mobilised with great rapidity and embarked for the relative quiet of the Middle East in December. Its complement was similar to that of 1914, for it was still a genuine cavalry regiment. Eight hundred of the finest horses

Trooper Paul Morgan of the Warwickshire Yeomanry. (Image courtesy of the Shakespeare Birthplace Trust Records Office)

in the county were requisitioned. Only £60 per horse was paid to the owners. It would be 1944 before the regiment saw home again.

In January, the regiment was stationed at Tiberius in Galilee, close to its triumphs of 1917–18. Amazingly, lots of the former owners sent parcels to their horses in the distant land and letters enquiring after them.

During 1939, twenty-eight people were prosecuted for drunkenness: a big increase on previous years. The Mayor suggested that, since only eight were Stratfordians, it indicated that the evacuees were responsible for the rise. In fact, most of those remaining were women and children and only six of the drunks were women. A more likely cause was the men in uniform who were crowding the streets. Colonel N.C. Joseph, home for weekend leave from his unit in the North of England, was disturbed by the numbers aimlessly wandering around or hanging about on corners.

On 6 October, the Old Bensonian actor, Gerald Jay Laurier, opened a weekly dance-entertainment club in the Conference Hall. It was intended, in the words of the Mayor, Cllr Tommy Waldron, 'to banish those black-out blues'. Jane Trotman, a self-confessed 'naughty girl' was a regular attendee with her friend:

> It cost a shilling to go in... My mother and Dorothy's mother let us go if each of us went to each other's homes in turn to stay the night because we had to go home together – at least they thought we went home together!

Three days later, the theatre reopened with Ian Hay's comedy, *Little Ladyship*. Things were very different from just five weeks before. No one was admitted without a gasmask, which had to be kept on the lap throughout the performance. The Theatre Manager would inform the audience immediately of an air-raid warning. 'In this event, keep calm', they were instructed with admirable *sang-froid*. 'THE SHOW WILL GO ON.' Somewhat surprisingly, the authorities considered that, in such circumstances, the audience would be safer in the theatre than in the street. If anyone decided to leave, they should do so quietly.

Despite the appearance of Phyllis Neilson-Terry, an old Stratford favourite, in *The Corn is Green*, the short season of touring plays was not a success. Much of the theatre's support came from outside Stratford and petrol rationing restricted access. On 3 November, it was announced that the theatre was closing again.

Under the circumstances, the announcement by the Theatre Governors that there would be a Festival in 1940 was courageous. The Mop occurred as usual on

The Mop Fair of 1939 – it was to be the last held in the street for five years. It was obliged to close early due to lighting regulations. (Image courtesy of the Shakespeare Birthplace Trust Records Office)

12 October, but it was a shadow of its former self, taking place on the Bridgefoot car park. There were no roasts. The fair had to close at dusk and 'all instruments capable of making a noise' were banned. With the petrol restrictions, the call-up of many of their men and the commandeering of many of their vehicles for the war effort, the showmen were hard pushed to put on any kind of fair.

In 1941, the authorities conceded that the Mop could keep going until 10.30 p.m. in the large cattle shed, but the lack of manpower ensured that this was the last one until the end of the war. To maintain continuity and to preserve their historic rights, the Showmen ensured that a solitary roundabout appeared each year.

On 20 October 1940, local government elections were suspended, so Stratford was stuck with its Town Council 'for the duration.'

After her training with the Women's Land Army, Gillian Forster was sent to work at Baraset Farm at Alveston. When she started she had never loosed or tied up a cow. 'I was a bit afraid of the bull, but I had to fetch it every day and I had to put up with it.' She was living at home, but a hostel for other Land Army girls – the only one in the Midlands – was opened on the Clopton road.

The New Year brought news of the death, on the last day of 1939, of Stratford's freeman, Sir Frank Benson, at the age of 80. At a memorial service in Holy Trinity, the actor Randle Ayrton quoted the toast at the annual Bensonian dinner. 'To the health of those that are present and to the memory of those that are away.' It was hoped that Benson's ashes might be scattered in Stratford, but Constance, perhaps mindful of his treatment in 1919, decreed it should be over his beloved Sussex Downs.

The Town Council appointed a committee to consider a public memorial to Stratford's favourite son, but despite the enthusiasm of its members it was clearly not the hour for it. It was not till 1959 that a memorial window to 'FRB' was unveiled at the theatre.

No Stratfordian was killed on war service in 1939. On 25 January 1940, Pte Frederick Townsend, aged 26, of 55 Birmingham Road, was laid to rest at the cemetery. He had joined the Royal Army Veterinary Corps three weeks before. He contracted a chill. His parents were summoned to his bedside, but to no avail.

On 20 March, 19-year-old Flt Sgt Alan Woodward lost control of his Hampden bomber on a night flight and crashed near Scunthorpe. The three-man crew was killed, but no details of the accident were revealed. Alan was buried with full military honours at Stratford Cemetery.

That month another Grammar School sportsman joined the RAF. Jeffrey Longford, aged 18, had won the school steeplechase four years in a row.

Right: *Land Army girls.* (Image courtesy of the Shakespeare Birthplace Trust Records Office)

Below: *Land Army girls on parade.* (Image courtesy of the Shakespeare Birthplace Trust Records Office)

The rigid censorship even extended to the weather. It was forbidden to publish any account of it for two weeks, presumably to prevent the Luftwaffe gaining knowledge of flying conditions. Doubtless they had other sources of information on the British climate than the *Herald*. The German airmen must have been aware that mid-January brought the coldest weather for nearly half a century, as skaters enjoyed themselves on the frozen Avon.

On 22 February, the legendary Irish tenor, Count John McCormick, came out of retirement to give a recital at the theatre 'to help the common cause of freedom'. His accompanist was Gerald Moore. Soon after, the 1940 Festival Company went into rehearsal in London. The Old Bensonian favourite, Baliol Holloway, was to play Shylock.

The Festival opened on the Birthday with *Measure for Measure*. There were no flags or representatives of the nations and no official luncheon. A shortened procession wound its way to the church with its floral tributes.

The Government was introducing limited conscription, calling up some young men and requiring others to register. Many former servicemen were called back. Norman Bennet, who lived on the Alcester Road with his wife and two young children, had served in the RAF. It was perhaps his profession of engineer that made him more useful to the Royal Navy.

This time the Tribunal for those seeking deferment was based in Birmingham. It was almost inevitable that a member of the Bullard family would be summoned. Henry 'Bob' Bullard of 7 Henley Street, appeared in court on 24 April. He was the son of the man who had defied Boer War rioters and refused conscription in the Great War. Although the family's moral integrity is admirable, the Bullards were certainly imbued with a strong measure of contrariness. It had been suggested to the father that he declare himself a Quaker to escape the rigours of the First World War Tribunals. This he had refused to do, but he became one after the war. Bob Bullard had registered as a conscientious objector, but had not revealed he was a Quaker, which would have given him automatic exemption. 'I am not prepared to answer', he replied when he was asked what he did for a living. 'My conscience has no connection with my occupation.' He based his objection on his Christian beliefs.

The Tribunal only wanted the information in order to find an alternative to military service. It showed a much greater breadth of sympathy than its predecessor of 1916. Judge Longton said they were satisfied that Bullard had a conscientious objection. He would therefore be given two months to find work of national importance: that his objection extended to doing *anything* towards the war effort was overlooked. Inevitably he was summoned again. On 24 July, the Tribunal ordered him to be removed from the register of conscientious objectors and placed on the register of men called up for non-combatant duties. On 23 November, he was summoned to attend a medical examination. He failed to appear and was fined £5 or twenty-one days in prison. He failed to pay and was sent to HMP Winson Green on 12 February.

Although the Bullards were pacifists, their employees were not. Fred Scruby had been with the auctioneers since leaving the Alcester Road School, but left to join the RAF, at the age of 17, in 1940.

As in the previous war, women took over the work of men called to the colours. Most of the girls at the Cannery had no previous experience of factory work. During the course of the war they would dispatch 40 million cans of fruit, vegetables, soups and jams to the forces – and, through the Red Cross, to British PoWs. Drawing on the vast supply of displaced people, each summer the company organised camps to pick and prepare fruit.

At the town's two railways stations, there were women in the offices, women porters and even women in the loco maintenance sheds. Several of the drivers and garage hands at Stratford Blue Motors were called up on the outbreak of war. In July 1940, the company appointed its first bus conductress, Mrs Malpass of Bordon Place, who was still zipping up and down the gangways at the end of the war. It was the start of a trend. Within weeks, five more ladies were employed.

Dunkirk

On 6 April 1940, the Germans escalated the war by invading Denmark and Norway. On 30 April, LAC Philip Tyler's Wellington bomber went missing over Stavenger. He was to have married Betty Noble from Leicester in June. Four months later his parents were told that all efforts to trace him had proved unavailing. The notification concluded with the stark and dreaded words:

> Although formal action to presume death for official purposes will not be taken until a further period has elapsed, it is feared that all hope of finding him alive must be abandoned.

Philip had made his mother promise that in the event of his death, she would divide his savings between the Stratford Hospital and the Birmingham General Hospital, where he had undergone the surgery that had enabled him to fly. Like so many in the same situation, his parents and his fiancé resolved not to abandon hope until the last British serviceman was out of Norway.

Sergeant Observer Arthur North had also got engaged: to Marjorie Winwood of Evesham Road. Two weeks later he was reported missing. It was not until September 1941 that his mother and fiancé were informed that he had been shot down near Bergen and was buried in the Hankeland Cemetery.

May 8 1940 was a doubly significant day for Leonard Millin. He was promoted to Quarter-Master Sergeant and his civil wedding to Marcelle was fixed for 29 May. The necessary documentation would have to be produced: the somewhat misnomered *Cerificat de Certificat de Célibat* (in reality, a declaration that the couple were eligible to marry), birth certificates and a *Certificat d'examen medical prenuptial*. Two days later Hitler launched his *Blitzkrieg* through Belgium and Holland. All leave was cancelled. On 14 May, the Germans broke through the French defences at Sedan.

The B.E.F. moved up into Belgium. On 10 May, Waldron's Warriors were at Anderlecht, a suburb of Brussels and home of a famous football team. In Stratford, news was anxiously awaited. Private Harry Goode was in the thick of it. 'Jerry doesn't like it when we fix our bayonets and charge', he wrote to his mother in terms redolent of previous campaigns. 'They don't stop to fight when they see our bayonets shining in the sun.'

Nothing was allowed to stand in the way of the *Blitzkrieg*. The light tank in which 20-year-old Trooper Bernard Hudson, of 208 Loxley Road, was a wireless operator, encountered a heavier German version while on patrol. He and two other crew members were killed in the unequal contest. Sergeant White was horrified to see civilians mown down. In a bombing raid, he sought to help a Belgian woman and her baby to safety. The woman and child were killed and he was wounded in the back, leg and thigh. He was cut off from his unit for several days, but was rescued after his companion, another wounded man, crawled two miles to get an ambulance.

Harry Goode was struck by shrapnel when his convoy was bombed and suffered an ear wound. 'We were shelled all day and bombed all night', recalled Arthur Sanders. 'It is not so bad being shelled because you do not know where they are coming from.'

Bombs were dropped on either side of the platoon's billet and every window was blown out:

When Leopold surrendered it was hopeless. We had to get away as best we could. We were in a hovel on a farm and all the protection we had was afforded by the carts.

For a fortnight we had no rations except biscuits and what we bought. At one farm we bought some tame rabbits and potatoes and cooked them for dinner. That was the best feed we had.

On 24 May, the villagers rushed to the chateau where Gertrude Bliss was working. 'Pack up and get away as soon as you can', they urged, 'the Germans are coming.' They feverishly packed what valuables and clothes they could carry onto a car and farm wagon. Leaving the house open, they went to the village to report to the Mayor. The villagers had loaded whatever belongings they could onto every conceivable type of vehicle, including cycles and handcarts. The road was jammed, but eventually they began to move. Progress was slow and at frequent intervals they had to dive into ditches as they were strafed by German planes.

By nightfall the column had arrived at the next village, only to find it occupied by the Germans. French soldiers were being disarmed and the refugees were ordered home. Miss Bliss and her employers returned to the chateau. Next day, German guards marched hundreds of French prisoners past the gates. She was confined to the chateau for several days until she was ordered to report to the German Commandant's office, several miles away. This became a weekly ritual and she also had to report to the local police.

'D' Company was part of the chaotic retreat. Private Jack Hall was sitting in the front of a lorry with the driver when the convoy stopped for a break. It wasn't until an officer came along and had a go at them that they realised that the other lorries had left while they were asleep.

'We didn't realise what was happening till near the end', he recalled.

You keep moving and you don't really know whether you're moving sideways, forwards or backwards because of course the Germans were both sides of us, so we didn't realise.

He only realised the true seriousness of the situation when he heard Duff Cooper, the Minister of Information, declare on the wireless that the BEF was in a terrible plight.

Driver Harold Dornborough rescued members of the regimental nursing staff and drove his armoured car night and day to get to the coast. He was rescued, but the ordeal had its effects. He spent six weeks in hospital suffering from temporary blindness and shock.

Arthur Sander's narrowest escape came when he and two other motorcyclists were sent out to make forward contact with the enemy. They had stopped at a crossroads when forty German planes came from three different directions. They dropped their motorbikes and dived into the nearest ditch, seconds before a bomb exploded on the other side of the hedge. When they returned to their machines, there were huge pieces of shrapnel lying about.

Tony Hawkins had become a Bridging Engineer with the Royal Marines. He was ordered to drive his bridging wagon as fast as he could 'to somewhere called Dunkirk'. He had never heard of the place. He was not supposed to pick anybody up, but if anyone climbed aboard his wagon, 'I didn't say get off'. He took intense risks to get there, making rapid progress when the columns of refugees fled into the ditches as machine-gunning Stukas dived on them. 'If there weren't too many carts and horses and things abandoned in the middle of the road, we could drive a bit.'

After a long retreat, Arthur North's platoon reached Dunkirk at 4 a.m.:

Every man on the beach who had a gun was blazing away at Jerry and I saw one plane crash. As it hit the beach there was a tremendous explosion and it was just one big flame.

Naval guns were continuously shelling the Germans and the explosions shook the houses. At 10 p.m. they were ordered to embark. They stood with water up to their shoulders for some time, waiting for captured German airmen to go on board, who were given priority for obvious reasons. They then swam out to the ship, which got away at 4 a.m. 'The fellows on that minesweeper that brought us home were marvellous. They found us dry clothes and gave us cocoa, cigarettes and rum.'

Arthur was able to speak to the German airmen, who were aged between 18 and 20. While some 'were "Hitler crazy", others were very decent.' Many could speak English. One had been prevented from going to Cambridge University by the outbreak of war. Arthur saw the irony of the situation. 'He has come to this country, but not to the university!'

When Tony Hawkins arrived at De Panne, the Belgian seaside resort on the outskirts of Dunkirk, he was instructed to trash his bridging wagon. This upset him. It was a fine piece of machinery, but he had no choice, so he slashed the tyres and punctured the tanks. On the crowded beach he found a large rowing boat belonging to inshore fishermen. He suggested to the officer that they use it to ferry troops to the waiting ships. 'Well, I don't know', he replied. 'Rowing is rowing.'

'I have rowed at Henley', said Tony. 'I only want one other man who will do what I say.'

It was harder to row with clothes on, so he stripped down to just a vest. For twelve hours they rowed men out to the ships – eight at a time. He felt safer on the sea than on the beach, where they were waiting for the Stukas to strafe. When he was too exhausted to row any more, it was decided that it was his turn to go, so he found another man to take over the rowing. Just before they reached the ship, a German plane dropped a bomb down the funnel and up it went, so they had to go back to the beach, but eventually he made it to a ship. When he got on board, he was wearing nothing but his wet vest. 'So they're stripping you as well now, are they?' asked his rescuers. They didn't know he'd been rowing, but he was found an officer's greatcoat and that was all he was wearing when he arrived in England.

After two air-raid warnings on the way across the Channel, which came to nothing, Arthur North arrived back at Kerns Terrace on 10 June. 'I don't think I have any nerves now', he said, recalling his ordeal at Arras with a grin. 'It won't be the same next time', he added. 'Jerry has not heard the last of the BEF!'

Miraculously, 'D' Company had only lost two killed in the retreat: 19-year-old Charles Harrington of 2 Vincent Avenue and Harry Smith. An ex-KES boy, Harry had volunteered for the TA on the Mayor's first appeal. He had got engaged to Jean Stratford of Greenhill Street and the couple intended to get married on his next leave.

In common with the rest of the BEF, the Company abandoned its lorries and heavy equipment. They were among the last British troops to leave Dunkirk on 3 June as the French were left to hold the perimeter. Jack Hall recalled the scene as they were assembled on the mole to await evacuation:

They set the oil tanks on fire and the smoke drifted over us which protected us to a certain extent. The night was dark and the mackerel were coming in. I don't know whether you've seen the sea when the mackerel come in, but there's a kind of luminous light on top, so that when the boats came in you couldn't see the boats, but you could see the 'V' shape... in this luminosity.

Private Will Troughton said 'Move over', to a man lying on the mole under a large blanket, and climbed under with him. Next morning he realised he had slept with a corpse.

Eventually they were embarked aboard a very old destroyer, HMS *Malcolm*. They were put in the ship's magazine and given pint mugs of tea. Jack Hall was so exhausted that he fell asleep while reaching for his mug. The ship was bombed on her passage to Dover, but Jack slept through the whole business. The only thing to be damaged was the toilet.

The destroyer on which S.J. Lively was serving as a sick-berth attendant was in the thick of things. She was under fire for ten days and was the last ship to leave Dunkirk.

In the chaos of retreat, many men got cut off from their units and were posted missing. Their anxious families waited to hear whether they had been killed or captured – and clung to the hope that they might have, against all the odds, made their way back to England. Dennis Flower was reported missing in late June. His anxious mother telegraphed a Swiss lady who he knew in Geneva to lobby the headquarters of the International Red Cross for news of his whereabouts.

Harry Goode's mother had heard nothing from him for a month, but on 1 June, the War Office notified her that he had been admitted to a military hospital in Britain. His slight wound had not affected his hearing.

Sergeant White was lying in a hospital on the South coast, where his wife, mother and mother-in-law went to see him. The friend who had rescued him had had to have his leg amputated.

When they disembarked at Dover, the men of 'D' Company were put on a train to an un-revealed destination. Eventually it stopped in Swindon and they got out. They thought they were returning to their old billets, but they were told that they could each send a telegram home to say that they were OK before proceeding. They were taken down to Pembroke to await the regrouping of the Battalions.

Private Robert Lysons had also been evacuated with the Warwicks. Like many another, the experience of Dunkirk and the treatment he had seen meted out to civilians by the Germans made him determined to see things through. On returning from extensive leave in the following January, his anger motivated him to volunteer for a special services Battalion of the regiment which was about to join General Wavell's desert army which was about to fight the Italians. Another who went out to the desert having survived Dunkirk was Gunner Fred Ryman.

As part of the Royal Engineers stores depot, Leonard Millin would have remained in Rennes. Preparations would have been made to destroy the vital military equipment in the event of an evacuation. On 29 May, as the net closed around Dunkirk and a French counter-attack at Abbéville was beaten back, the couple made the bold (and perhaps rash) decision to proceed with their wedding ceremony at the Mairie. The smiles on the faces of the happy couple give no indication of the gathering crisis. He had obtained leave and they intended to spend their honeymoon in England, but this was now out of the question. All leave had been cancelled. There were no ferries across the Channel, but at least the bridegroom was on the spot.

Just a few days after the wedding, Leonard Millin went to his wife's house. Shortly after he arrived, her father rushed in to say that the defences of the Weygand Line had collapsed and the Germans were advancing rapidly into France. Dashing out of the house, he hailed a passing taxi and gave all his money to the driver to take him back to his unit. He arrived just as they were marching away. They were bombed incessantly, but got away from Le Havre on the last boat to leave.

Back in her family home, Marcelle made the bold decision to try to rejoin her husband. Her mother took her to St Malo to enquire about getting a ship to England, but everywhere they were told it was impossible. They could not return home because the German advance had cut them off. The mother had only the clothes she was

The wedding of Leonard Millin
and Marcelle Melies, 29 May 1940.
(Courtesy of Philippe Bobroff)

wearing. Food was difficult to obtain. The situation seemed hopeless. After Marcelle
burst into tears in a café, a sympathetic waitress told them that she had heard that
a small Dutch boat was about to leave for England. The mother had been intending
to return home to her husband, but now she had no choice but to rush to the docks
with Marcelle. A French ship and a 35m Dutch coastal steamer were waiting. They
boarded the smaller vessel, which was normally used for carrying coke, but were told
that they could not be given a passage. They were to have been put ashore, but the
Germans had overrun the port and the Royal Navy blew up the docks. The harbour
was blocked by debris and the two ships appeared trapped. It seemed that they would
fall into the hands of the enemy, but the French ship rammed the barrier formed by
the wreckage and broke through, the smaller ship following in her wake. Her thirty
passengers were the last to leave the port.
    Marcelle was seasick throughout the thirty-hour voyage. Off the British coast the
ship missed a mine by inches. She reached port on 20 June. After securing a place for
her mother in a refuge in London, Marcelle could not contact her husband in Stratford
for three days, but when at last they were reunited he must have been heartily surprised
and delighted. It was probably in the summer of 1940; Marcelle had her picture taken
at a photographic studio in Leamington. This beautiful woman has her hand placed
upon her heart in a dramatic and enigmatic gesture. When Leonard returned to active
service, Marcelle and her mother could not stay with his family who were intending
to leave Stratford. J.H. Davies, the affable Billeting Officer, allocated the two French
ladies lodgings with the Steele family in Shottery, near Anne Hathaway's Cottage, and
Marcelle found work as an auxiliary nurse at Stratford Hospital.

Marcelle Melies, c. 1940.
(Courtesy of Philippe Bobroff)

Alec Maltby of Tiddington Road was among the last members of the BEF to escape from France. His unit had been unable to join the retreat on Dunkirk and he was among the thousands of troops who crowded the roads as they retreated westwards towards the Atlantic port of St Nazaire where there were nineteen ships of varying types and sizes waiting to convey them to England. On 16 June they joined the five-mile queue that was edging its way towards the harbour. Embarkation continued all night. Next day they were conveyed by tender aboard the 16,000-ton Cunard liner *Lancastria*, which was lying offshore. RAF personnel and refugees, mainly women and children, were also on board. It may have been fear of proceeding without an escort that caused her Captain to delay departure despite the clear presence of German reconnaissance aircraft. At 3.48 p.m., minutes before she was due to weigh anchor, a Ju88 twin-engined bomber attacked. The ship received three direct hits and was sunk by a bomb, which went down the funnel. As she went down, the survivors sang *Roll out the Barrel*. Hundreds of people were clinging to the top of her. At 4.15 p.m., she finally turned over.

Alec suffered a broken shoulder, but was able to cling to a piece of wreckage. The German plane returned to machine-gun the struggling mass of people in the water. Many of those who had managed to escape the sinking ship were engulfed by oil leaking from the ship's burst fuel tanks, on which the Germans dropped flares.

After Alec had been in the sea for about two hours, he was picked up by the trawler *Cambridgeshire* which transferred him to another ship. He was too dazed to recall its name when he reached England, but thought it was either the *Oronsay* or the *Andora Star*.

Because there was no record of who was on board, it is not known how many died aboard the *Lancastria*. The most authoritative estimate is that over 2,000 people perished: 2,823 were rescued. It was the worst single disaster in British maritime history, claiming more lives than the *Titanic* and the *Lusitania* combined. Fearing the effect on public morale, Winston Churchill issued a D-notice forbidding publication of the news.

'I won't believe that he is dead'

The circumstance under which the dreaded telegram arrived could be doubly cruel. Violet Hirons had found a house in Kendall Avenue two doors away from her sister's. She had furnished it and kept it neat and clean, ready to welcome her husband into the home he had never seen. On the morning of 6 July, she got a letter from him, saying that he would be home later that day. Violet rushed round to tell her sister, who was just leaving for work. Shortly after her return home, a telegram arrived to notify her that her husband was missing, believed killed in action. Violet went round to her sister's workplace. 'He has come, has he?' she asked. Violet shook her head and gave her the telegram. 'I still keep on hoping', she said, 'I won't believe that he is dead.'

Dennis Hirons had joined the crew of HMS *Foylebank* in Belfast in early June. She was a 5,582-ton merchantman that had been converted at Harland & Wolff's shipyards into an anti-aircraft gunship. On 6 June, she departed for fitting at Portland, arriving there on 9 June. With the advance of German forces to the English Channel, the south coast was under threat from the Luftwaffe and German reconnaissance had already spotted the *Foylebank*, a potential threat to their attempt to destroy Britain's vital coastal shipping.

On the evening of 3 July, Dennis posted his letter home. Next morning, while most of the crew were at breakfast, unidentified aircraft were reported to the south. They were initially believed to be friendly planes returning to base, but it was soon realised that they were a squadron of 26 Ju87 dive-bombers intent on getting the *Foylebank*. The crew was at action stations by the time they launched their screaming attack, but, with no air cover, the ship was doomed. Two, possibly three, of the Stukas were shot down, but twenty-two bombs found their mark and her guns were put out of action. Fires raged, electricity failed and the stricken ship listed to port, shrouded in smoke. She sank the next day. During the mere eight minutes that the action had lasted, 176 of the 300 crew members were killed. Dennis Hirons was one of them.

In late August 1940, S.J. Lively and a shipboard friend were sent for by the Captain. Doubtless they felt some trepidation, but when they arrived at his cabin all the officers were there. They were told that they had been awarded the Distinguished Conduct Medal for their gallantry during the Dunkirk evacuation. Lively was the first Stratfordian to be decorated in the war. 'After that we had to shake hands with all the other officers', he recalled, 'I was glad when it was all over'. He confessed to some nervousness at receiving the award from the King.

In the aftermath of Dunkirk, more young men were called up. Charlie Baldwin, aged 26, a keen tennis player who was born in Church Lane, Shottery, the Assistant Manager of Walker's Stores in Henley Street, had to travel to Liverpool to enlist in the 4th Battalion King's Shropshire Light Infantry. He had got married at Alderminster Church just five days before. The day after he signed up, his Company was transferred to train at Warrenpoint in Northern Ireland. It would be a year before Rene, his new bride, would see him again.

Rumour

In the wake of Dunkirk rumour abounded. The more exotic the story was, the more likely it was to be believed. The rigid censorship, with its denial of basic information to the public, must have contributed to this.

A letter to the *Herald*, signed 'A GUNNER' said that, on two days running in the previous week, his family had heard conflicting rumours of his whereabouts and existence. He had not yet been out of England, or even seen an enemy plane, but that had not stopped people from reporting to his mother that he had been wounded:

In these times it is a pity that the gossips cannot find a better outlet for their energies. Those left at home by men and women in the forces have sufficient worry and anxiety without these disciples of Lord Haw Haw adding to their cares.

The latter reference was to a rumour that the Nazi broadcaster had threatened that Clopton Bridge would be blown up.

The most extravagant gossip concerned the fifth column scare. After Dunkirk, suspected collaborators and Nazi sympathisers were rounded up. The *Herald* professed itself astonished at the number of fifth-columnists 'popular imagination' had arrested in the district including retired police officers, business men and even innocent housewives. That the subjects of the gossip continued to appear in public did not deter 'the chatterbugs from finding new victims to take the place of those whose incarceration has been visibly disproved.'

With the addition of Italy to Britain's list of enemies, anyone with a swarthy complexion was liable to be labelled Italian. The Mayor made an appeal to people not to repeat rumours or distort facts. He had good cause for concern. At the next meeting of the Town Council he rose to refute a 'ridiculous and malicious' rumour that he was a German! 'I cannot speak German. Neither have I any friends in Germany.'

Councillors would best serve the town by reporting anyone they heard repeating this lie, but the *Herald* considered that the Mayor had brought it upon himself by his close-cropped haircut. 'Long before the war... visitors to the town have in all innocence jumped to the wrong conclusion through precisely this reason.'

The gossip could be cruel. In late July, rumours were circulating that Dennis Hirons was a prisoner of war. With the veil of secrecy surrounding the war, the gossips would not have known he had been killed in Portland Harbour.

Such rumours were fuelled by the fact that a number of those posted missing were turning up as PoWs. On 13 August, Dennis Flower's mother heard the good news that he was a German prisoner from the Red Cross at Geneva. That night she received a telegram from his Swiss friend. 'Dennis prisoner: safe: sends love: letter follows.' In fact his seemingly interminable journey into captivity had included a night spent in an open field in the pouring rain. In his first PoW camp Dennis began what he described as 'the dreary monotonous existence' that for most prisoners lasted for the rest of the war.

Around the same time, Warrant Officer E.G. Evans' wife received the news that he had been captured on the retreat to Dunkirk. Private Edward Howell of Park Road was also a prisoner. After the fall of Paris, the Germans displayed big posters in his PoW camp of their plans for the invasion of Britain and told the prisoners they would soon be home. They had even arranged weekend excursions to London.

After the collapse of France, the Government decided to move people from the south and east coasts. They were simply given train tickets and billeting certificates for towns where they claimed to have friends or relations. Anyone who had a spare room was obliged to make it available. Because her husband was in the Auxiliary Fire Brigade, Beatrice Morgan was allocated the safe option of a policeman and his wife, but the room became free again after he was called up into the Navy. Soon after, a man in RAF uniform knocked on the door. He was stationed at Wellesbourne. If he could find a room, he could obtain a sleeping-out pass for himself and his wife. Beatrice agreed. They arrived carrying a piece of wedding cake. They had just got married.

In West Street, the Summerton family put up Land Army girls in the front room. 'Mum was more concerned than father', recalled Peter Summerson, 'because of the front window opening all the time and the chaps coming in and going out. So mum soon put a stop to that.'

A London schoolgirl, Daphne Tizzard, was sent to Stratford to live with her Auntie Maud, a railwayman's wife, in Bordon Place:

Eventually my mother came to Stratford, but not till 1943, so for two years I lived with my aunt and went to Broad Street School. Things were not so easy for me to begin with as I must have seemed strange to the local kids, speaking with a strong Cockney accent. I was very unhappy staying with my aunt. I don't think she wanted to be bothered with me and, afterwards, when I was older, I understood why. Her son, Sid, was in the RAF and was captured by the Germans at the beginning of 1941 and was in a prisoner-of-war camp until the end of the war. This must have made things very difficult for her and she cried a lot.

Other refugees simply came to Stratford and begged Mr J.H. Davies, the kindly Billeting Officer, to find them accommodation. There was a fair amount available because so many of the evacuees from Birmingham had returned home. When he interviewed an evacuee, he would try to visualise the homes they had left and find them a billet that would suit them, although he confessed that he sometimes made mistakes.

In at least one case, the evacuation was a return home. The wife of Chief Petty Officer Telegraphist Hugh Dale, who was living in Dovercourt, was the daughter of Mrs Hirons of Cherry Street. Now she moved to 33 Brookvale Road with her two sons, aged 10 and 4. Her husband had joined the navy when he was 15 and had served on many ships.

Look, Duck and Vanish

The fear of imminent invasion was real. As a result of a clarion call broadcast by Anthony Eden, now the Secretary for War, on 14 May, the Local Defence Volunteers were formed. Its nickname of the 'Look, Duck and Vanish' was short-lived. It was renamed the Home Guard by Winston Churchill. The local volunteers became 'C' Company of the 4th Battalion Royal Warwickshire Regiment. There was a rush to join what the *Herald* encouragingly described as 'a suicide squad… ready to fight in the fields and in the streets with whatever weapons came to hand.' In all 2,000 men volunteered, of whom 1,800 were accepted. The epithet 'Dad's Army' was not inappropriate. Charles 'Chuck' Taylor from Tiddington, a bricklayer with the firm of Price Brothers, who had just turned 18, was atypical. His father, a veteran of the Great War, was more characteristic of the intake. Many other volunteers had seen service in the previous conflict, including Edgar Cranmer, who joined at the inception at the age of 48. Most of them were promoted to sergeant because of their experience of service life. The most remarkable recruit was 71-year-old William Bawcutt of 3 Evenlode Close, who had seen service in the Matabele Campaign and the Boer War.

'C' Company had its headquarters in the police station. Its initial armament to combat an invasion by the victorious panzers was twenty rifles and 270 rounds of ammunition. Five of the precious rounds went missing within days of the inception. Three days later, the commander, Colonel Bryant, phoned up to ask 'Why the hell?' the loss had not been reported and was told that the missing bullets were in the pocket of a man who worked in Coventry and only came home every four days.

The volunteers acquired a gun off a 'Q' ship[1] named *Pelican*. It was mounted on wheels and a makeshift carriage and fired six-inch armour-piercing shells. They dubbed themselves the Stratford Anti-tank Company.

The church bells were again silenced. This time their ringing would announce the arrival of the Germans. A brief exception was made during the induction of the new vicar, Canon Noel Prentice, who was allowed to toll one bell three times.

Obstructions were placed in any field deemed a likely landing spot for an ambitious Luftwaffe pilot. The Grammar School playing fields positively bristled with them, while suitable steps were taken by the Town Council to render the Recreation Ground unattractive to any airman seeking a clandestine landing ground.

The Home Guard on parade. (Image courtesy of the Shakespeare Birthplace Trust Records Office)

The scare led to the removal of road signs and other indicators of whereabouts. This undoubtedly caused more havoc among the native population than any assistance it could have rendered to invading paratroopers. The job was not done with any great logic or efficiency. The word 'Alveston' was removed from the sign at the Alveston Manor Estate, but retained for the one for the Alveston Manor Hotel. The proprietors of the Bridgetown Filling Station had to remove their offending name that was retained on the Bridgetown Stores over the road.

The fifth column scare led to the establishment of roadblocks at such strategic locations as Clopton Bridge, the gas works and the pumping stations. On one occasion, a roadblock was established at the Evesham Road level crossing. Armed with just one bayonet between them, the volunteers stopped everybody and asked for their identity cards. When a driver tried to dodge up Shottery Road, Private Alf 'Doc' Phipps stuck the bayonet into his wheel: out got a tall Italian who explained that he was in the Theatre Orchestra. As he knew they were looking for fifth columnists, he didn't fancy his chances.

Another duty of 'C' Company was to guard the German officers' PoW Camp that had been established on the racecourse. The first inmates were mainly captured U-boat crews who invested a lot of energy on escape attempts. One even got as far as Liverpool Docks. Later, the camp was expanded to house Italians captured in the desert war.

The biggest scare came with the news that the Germans had made an airborne landing on Snitterfield Aerodrome. There was no panic at the Drill Hill in New Broad Street. Everything was very calm, right up to the moment when they were preparing to counter-attack. Three platoons moved off within twenty-five minutes of the first alert, but it turned out to be a 'try-out' to test the efficiency and response of the Home Guard.

In the aftermath of Dunkirk, Stratford became the centre of a makeshift 'International Brigade' consisting of the remnants of armies that had escaped Hitler's clutches. The Czechs were billeted at Walton Hall and the Poles and Free French at Long Marston.

Italian prisoners of war working on the land. (Image courtesy of the Shakespeare Birthplace Trust Records Office)

Aerodromes for the defence of the great industrial centres were being constructed at a frenetic pace in a ring around the town. Wellington bombers arrived at Wellesbourne Mountford after twelve months of hectic work by John Laing & Co. Other airfields were established at Long Marston, Snitterfield and Atherstone. Wimpeys and other contractors brought labourers over from Ireland. In the evenings they came into Stratford to spend their money. With all the allied soldiers doing the same, the place acquired the atmosphere of a frontier town.

Pots and Pans

With the fall of France, the Axis powers controlled nearly half the world's supply of bauxite, the raw material from which aluminium is made. People were asked to hand in all aluminium artefacts, to be transformed into the aeroplanes which would beat Hitler. In Stratford, the collection was undertaken by the Women's Voluntary Service. In the first twenty-four hours, thousands of articles were received at their HQ in Henley Street. Volunteers were busy packing them into sacks and boxes, ready for transport to the factories.

The collection included pots and pans, coffee pots and percolators, egg poachers, hot water bottles, jugs, a vacuum cleaner, eggcups, teapots, electric torches, frying pans, colanders, shoetrees, thermos flasks, moulds, knitting needles and a clock. A piece from the first Zeppelin to be shot down over England arrived. The owner had decided that this was no time for souvenirs.

Even children played their part, showing exemplary personal sacrifice by handing in aluminium dolls' tea sets, although how many it would take to build one Spitfire was not revealed. Not everyone maintained his resolve. One small boy brought in his treasured mug, but, at the moment of handover, he burst into tears and took it away again.

After the war, doubts were cast on the genuineness of the exercise. Whether the metal raised really went for the ostensible purpose, or whether it was an attempt to boost civilian involvement in the war effort and, thereby, the general morale, is uncertain. One man, at least, shared this cynical view at the time. Arriving with a jug, which he said was a wedding present, he announced that he did not mind it going to Hitler as part of a plane, but he did not mean anyone else to use it as a jug, so he proceeded to buckle it beyond usefulness.

Whatever ironwork had not been requisitioned in the Great War was now seconded. Surprisingly, there were still as many as 1,400 sets of railings to be earmarked for appropriation. The selection was arbitrary. The only grounds for appeal were on artistic or historic interest. Yet even this was not a guaranteed defence. There were complaints when the Georgian railings complete with their lamp brackets at numbers 7 and 8 Rother Street were whisked off.

The Show goes on

At the theatre, audiences increased as the summer of 1940 progressed. Although 80,000 people attended the twenty-week season, the inevitable loss of £5,500 was borne by the extensive reserves. To offset this, the company agreed to take a salary cut in 1941.

No sooner had the curtain come down than the company embarked on a tour with ENSA, performing condensed versions of *Twelfth Night* and *Merry Wives of Windsor*. The cup of fine acting overflowed that winter. Alec Guinness made his sole appearance there in *Thunder Rock*. At the close of the Friday performance he appeared before the curtain to apologise to the audience. They had been unable to do justice to the play because of the noise from the gallery. Later the Old Bensonian Oscar winner, Robert Donat, appeared in *The Devil's Disciple*, with Roger Livesey, Rosamund John and the future company director Milton Rosmer.

The Birthday celebrations of 1941 followed the restricted form of the previous year, except that the Mayor symbolically unfurled the Union Jack at the top of Bridge Street. That afternoon the guests at a mayoral reception in the Town Hall were addressed by Margaretta Scott, who was playing Beatrice that evening, and T.C. Kemp, the drama critic of the *Birmingham Post*.

Despite difficulties with transport, audiences were making their way to Stratford again and the twenty-two week Festival Season in 1941 was attended by 140,700 people: a huge increase on the previous year. Takings totalled £20,000, so, to their great delight, the actors had their salaries made up. So many talented actors were serving in the forces that casting was again a problem. The lack of alternatives led to the veteran Bensonian, Baliol Holloway playing Henry V in 1943. 'But he doesn't *look* sixty, you know', said the Festival Director, Milton Rosmer. As T.C. Kemp put it: 'The young actor who should have played Henry was flying, sailing or marching elsewhere on Britain's wartime business. Yet the breach was filled at Stratford.' Holloway's experience made up for his lack of youth and he created a splendid Henry.

Notes
[1] decoy ships intended to attack U-boats

FIVE

'HERE COME THE BLOODY INTERLOPERS'

'The Cheeky Bugger!'

The truth of Churchill's famous prediction – 'The Battle of France is over: the Battle of Britain is about to begin' was soon realised as German air raids intensified across the Midlands. People learned to distinguish between the sound of RAF planes and the higher pitched noise of German ones. 'You could always tell the German planes when they came', recalled local resident, Jane Pearson. As anxiety increased, fines for infringing the blackout regulations were increased to 10s.

Sightings were frequent. Emma Hewins, the caretaker's wife at the Church of England school, was feeding her chickens while the children were playing in the next-door playground when a German plane flew over:

> I never seen a sight like it! 'e waved! To the kiddies – and me! The cheeky devil! The cheeky bugger! 'e 'ad the nerve to wave!

'But she was laughing as she remembered it', her daughter, Mary, recalled.

On 12 August, Pilot Officer John Miller was killed while flying his Wellington bomber on active service. He had got engaged to Miss Vera Purchase of Moseley only a few days before. His younger brother, the 20-year-old Pilot Officer Rogers Miller, was becoming a local hero, shooting down two Heinkel bombers and a Dornier. On 27 September, at the height of the Battle of Britain, he was on patrol over the West Country. At 11.45 a.m. his Spitfire was in a head-on collision with a Beaufighter, exploding over Cheselburne. Whatever was left of him was found later. He was posthumously mentioned in dispatches. People in Stratford remembered the schoolboy he had been only a year before. He was cremated at Perry Barr crematorium on 3 October. The Mayor of Stratford attended the service.

Refugees

The bombing of London in August brought many more people to Stratford. As the indiscriminate bombing of British cities increased, the evacuees arrived in numbers beyond the town's capacity to absorb. During the course of the war, the population increased by 50 per cent.

The situation was exacerbated by the large amount of accommodation still held by the Government. An appeal for the rooms to be released was rejected. In October, the first stages of the plans to evacuate the Civil Service were put in hand when the Treasury Office was transferred to the Welcombe Hotel. Lillian Grace was a shorthand typist in the Treasury Solicitor's Office. At the age of 31, she was on top-scale and was put in charge of the other twenty-five girls in her section, who were to be transferred to new offices in the dining room of the White Swan.

Lillian was living at Wandsworth Common and got a lift to Paddington station. They had got no further than Clapham Junction when a German daylight raid started. 'They were dropping everything all around us.' They jumped out of the car and lay in the gutter. At Paddington, the train couldn't leave because of the air raid. The girls intended to stop in Leamington for lunch, but they didn't arrive there till after three. When they finally got to Stratford they walked to the White Swan, where they were given a cup of tea and a fairy cake: the only food they had all day.

On the corner of Grove Road there was a little group of people. 'Here come the bloody interlopers', one grumbled. The remark was unfortunate and ill-mannered, but it reflected the resentment of the locals at enforced billeting. 'The officials came round and said, "We're sending you two Treasury people." They didn't say "Can You?" They simply had to take whoever was assigned to them into their houses and there was very little money in it.'

Lillian found romance through her enforced move. She started to walk out with Tommy Booker, a member of a well-known local family of undertakers, although he wasn't in that trade himself.

Blitz

The increasing level of air raids led to the instruction that all householders should put a bucket of water outside their doors, provided it did not obstruct the footpath and create a hazard in the blackout. In January 1941, the local Civil Defence Sub-controller appealed for fire-fighting groups to be established in every area of the town to deal with the threat of incendiary bombs. 'It is the positive duty of every householder to join such a party', he wrote to the *Herald*. 'There is no doubt whatsoever that a fire party of, say, one man and two women with a bucket of sand and a stirrup pump, who are able to reach an incendiary bomb can do more than the fire service who might take some time to arrive.'

There was a good response. Many of those volunteering were women aged over 60, but, with an acute manpower shortage, no one was rejected. The area was divided into patrol districts. Each patrol consisted of three people and took place in two shifts from 10 p.m. till 2 a.m. and from 2 a.m. till 6 a.m. At first they were instructed not to use whistles to raise the alarm or to enter premises that were on fire. Since this rendered them completely ineffective, the orders were soon amended. The volunteers could use a whistle as long as it wasn't a police whistle and enter premises if they had a letter of authorisation from the Fire Officer. Lists were compiled of the infirm and elderly and people were delegated to be responsible for their safety.

The volunteers had to provide their own equipment: pumps, axes, goggles were 2s a pair and helmets, 18s 6d. They were only required to be at their posts if the ARP Controller advised them of a possible raid. Otherwise, they were to wait at home during the hours they were on duty, fully clothed and prepared for action. When on patrol they were forbidden to play wirelesses or gramophones, but, in a touch of Dogberry, one could sleep if the other two remained awake.

On 8 April 1941, a Heinkel bomber took off from an airfield at Tours on a mission to bomb Coventry. Joining the four-man crew was Wolfgang Dieter Muller, who was reporting on the raid for the German media.

As it moved in for the strike at 1.45 a.m., the Heinkel was shot down by an RAF night-fighter. Four of the crew evacuated the plane, but the navigator was unable to escape and perished on impact.

Auxiliary Fireman Ted Williamson was on fire watch on the roof of the Midland Electricity Board in Guild Street and saw the plane descending in flames to the North East. Realising that the brigade was bound to be called out, he asked a friend to stand in for him and dashed down to await the alarm.

The Auxiliary Fire Service (AFS) was indeed called out. At Little Hill Farm near Wellesbourne they found a large crater full of burning wreckage. The body of Wolfgang Dieter Muller, whose parachute had failed to open, lay in the next field. The three surviving crew members were taken prisoner by the Home Guard.

On 14 November on a night of brilliant moonlight came the devastating raid that destroyed much of Coventry. The flames of the burning city could be seen from Stratford.

Bill Steele was attending his youth club at Shottery School. As they sat round the fire and chatted, the bombs started falling on Coventry. Each time a big one landed, all the windows rattled, although it was over twenty miles away. Then the big anti-aircraft guns opened up with the same effect. The boys said 'Blow this for a tale! Let's get out of it!' So they put on their coats and scarves and put out all the lights and went up to the corner of Quiney's Road:

> We could hear the bombers going over, droning, and flashes of course going on all over the place, and then we could see those shells... apparently they were these big anti-aircraft guns, and there must have been enough heat in the propulsion somewhere to make 'em glow, which we could actually see them going up! And on one occasion one actually hit something – phew! I always remember that evening.

At 8 p.m. that evening the Stratford Fire Brigade was sent over to Coventry. When they arrived, they found that the bombing had burst most of the hydrants and there was no water.

The AFS followed on to do its bit, training their hoses on a large warehouse. The roof had already collapsed 'All of a sudden there was Bang! Bang! Bang!' recalled Auxiliary Fireman Fred Wincote. 'We couldn't make it out.' It transpired that building was a store for corned beef and the sound was the tins exploding.

The main danger came from collapsing buildings. A traumatic moment came when the main means of transport – 'the Flying Bedstead' – was lost in this way. Fortunately no one was near it at the time. In no time most of the hoses were buried. Only three were taken back to Stratford – and they were all punctured – so they concentrated on rescuing people. Other volunteers went to Coventry on special trains, to pick up wounded and traumatised people and bring them back to Stratford Hospital.

By morning Coventry was awash with water from the burst hydrants. Even the canals were overflowing. At noon, as the firemen were preparing to return to Stratford, to their amazement, an old gentleman emerged from a cellar. They had not bothered to check it because they thought it impossible that anyone could have survived there on that dreadful night. He was carrying a bottle of whisky and gave them all a drink.

None of the volunteers was hurt in the hazardous operation, but in the words of Beatrice Morgan, whose husband Cecil was an auxiliary firemen, they were as 'black as coal, as if they had been dumped in the river and put up a chimney. Almost speechless, they were. They came home and couldn't speak.' Two men suffered breakdowns from what they had gone through.

The bombing of Coventry was a traumatic experience for Stratford people and not just because of their proximity. Many people had relations in the city. Mr and Mrs Betteridge of Glencoe, Arden Street lost their only surviving daughter, their son-in-law and their three grandchildren. Ethel Betteridge had served at F.J. Spencer's, the chemists, until she married Jack Witcombe, who worked for Messrs Walker &

Atkinson, the seed merchants and played hockey and tennis in the town. When he moved to a job in Coventry they bought a house in Earlsdon. When he did not turn up for work the day after the raid, his brothers went round to see whether all was well and found that the house had been swept away and the family buried alive in the cellar.

A trickle of refugees from the bombing began to arrive at Stratford, although the numbers were not as great as expected. Some had been sent out of the way of the relief work, some had hitched a lift over; some had come by bus, train or car. Most had gone to the police for help to find digs.

The ladies of the British Legion and the local Relieving Officer borrowed palliasses and blankets, prepared tea and sandwiches and stoked the fires at a temporary hostel that had been established for eighty people at the Grammar School. A mother and father and their eleven children were given a dormitory to themselves. One young lad was so exhausted that he went to sleep standing up and fell over, but he was quickly rolled up in a blanket near the fire. A honeymoon couple had to share a room with several others, but they were discreetly placed in a corner. A soldier who had been immobilising time bombs, sat near the radiator. He was taking his family, who had been made homeless by the bombing, to stay with relations. Two tiny tots who were dubbed 'the babes in the wood' were sleeping in an improvised cot in an upturned table.

Three helpers sat up all night in case they were needed. Morning brought a light breakfast, the filling of babies' bottles – and departure. Some wanted to pay for their primitive accommodation. A Scotsman who had slept on the floor positively insisted on contributing to the funds. In the cold light of day, many who had fled their homes resolved to return. 'Please can you tell me when there's a bus back to Coventry?' was a frequent question.

The Billeting Officer fixed up those who were genuinely homeless. The family with eleven children proved something of a problem and were shared out between six different houses, but eventually a cottage was found for them in Wellesbourne.

As a result of the influx, the basis for deciding the number of people a house should accommodate was changed from one per room to three per two rooms. Children under the age of 10 counted as half a person. In early December, Mr Davies, the Billeting Officer, estimated that there were some 4,000 evacuees in Stratford, of whom only 500 were registered. These included 160 adults and seventy-one children from London; thirty-one adults and fifty-six children from Birmingham; eighteen adults and ten children from Coventry and forty adults and twenty-four children from the south coast. In addition there were 103 unaccompanied children, who included fifty-four deaf and dumb children who had been billeted in the Youth Hostel at Shottery.

'We have been able to carry on without using compulsory powers', the amiable Mr Davies announced with justifiable pride.

The Maternity Home on Rother Street continued to receive pregnant women from the blitzed cities. Sixteen-year-old Susan Buggins was moved by their desperation.

> Poor haggard ladies came from Coventry, Birmingham, London, Liverpool – anywhere else that was bombed, and they came there for a four week's rest to have their babies, and, oh, dear, the poor things. Their faces were so drawn with pregnancy and fear and lack of food and comfort.

The Stratford Fire Brigade was stretched to the limit during the Blitz, going into action as far afield as Coventry, Birmingham, Swansea, Cardiff, Avonmouth, Bath, Exeter, Nuneaton and London.

At Bristol the Germans had bombed the docks. The Stratford AFS had to pull down the blazing oil tanks on the quayside, which were liable to explode at any moment.

The Stratford Auxiliary Fire Service, 1943. (Image courtesy of the Shakespeare Birthplace Trust Records Office)

Volunteers were requested. 'What about you, Fred?' asked the Chief Fireman, in the timeless tradition of service volunteering. So Fred Wincote went up the turntable ladder. 'They put the water on when you got to the top.'

The Stratford firemen were billeted at the Fishponds Asylum. The irony of this did not escape them, but there were advantages:

> We went in, what would it be, about midday. Then we had a meal, wash up. Then they put us in a big room, mattresses on the floor and they gave us like baskets to drop our stuff in. They said 'Put your name, what brigade you are'. They gave us the papers and put them away and said 'Your clothes will be clean when you come back: the inmates, they clean them.' Of course, you got ever so messy, black, horrible.

The Auxiliary firemen were called out to some 100 plane crashes. At some lives were saved. On his return to Stratford after one such crash, a senior officer upbraided Fred Wincote for not wearing his tunic:

> I said, 'Wait a minute. You haven't asked what happened to it.' He says, 'What happened to it then?' I said, 'It's in holes – I have been at a plane crash and the petrol tank exploded' and I says, 'Look at my eyebrows, look at my eyebrows, look at me. I got no eyebrows, no eyelashes.' He said, 'I thought your eyes looked a bit red.' I said, 'Ah, that's a plane crash. Don't start something.' 'Oh', he said, 'I'm very sorry.' I said, 'Yes, you want to approach me more pleasantly than you did.' Of course, you see, the petrol coming burnt holes in my tunic, petrol all around the face, eyelashes gone, eyebrows. All I had got was a bit of hair.

Few, if any, who served in the war would see horrific sights on such a consistent basis as the firemen. The Stratford AFS was called out after the Germans bombed the factory in the Tylesley area of Birmingham that was making wings for Mosquito aircraft:

> Some of them was working nights. They went into the shelter just outside their factory and the bombing hit the factory on the corner, burst the central heating pipes and that flowed into the whatsit in the shelter… concrete over the top and the water went in there and they were all drowned. We had to pump that out. You can imagine what it was like.

Stratford's greatest moment of airborne danger came on the morning of 13 September 1941 when a Procter Percival flew low over the town. Its course was followed by hundreds of people. Leading Aircraftsman Sidney Hines was walking down Grove Road and watched its progress. 'It made a number of steep bank turns and side slips, losing quite a bit of height in this way. The pilot came down rather low in one of these banks and the plane seemed to straighten out, lift a little and then crashed.' It hit the air-raid shelter on the road island at Evesham Place. Fortunately it was unoccupied. The plane burst into flames and clouds of black smoke rolled over the town. Sidney ran to the spot but was driven back by the fierce heat. The two-man crew, both aged twenty, was killed on impact. Beatrice Morgan saw the lorry arrive to pick up the bodies, which looked 'just like charred logs'. They were buried in the cemetery and a memorial service was held at the Guild Chapel.

Despite the destruction wrought on the neighbouring industrial centres, Stratford remained relatively unscathed by the bombing. The alert sounded ninety-seven times and a total of nine high explosive devices, an oil bomb and some 100 incendiaries fell on the town, all on the outlying areas as German bombers dropped their cargoes rather than face the flak over Birmingham and Coventry. Apart from broken windows and tiles, no damage was done by this mini-Blitz, but it had its farcical moments. When bombs fell near the Maidenhead Road, a searcher found freshly turned earth and diagnosed an unexploded bomb. The occupants of nearby houses were evacuated and the area roped off. At dawn the owner returned from a night in an air-raid shelter. 'Unexploded bomb, my foot!' he exclaimed, 'That's where I dug up an apple tree yesterday.'

It was almost miraculous that no one in Stratford was killed. On the night of their twenty-fourth wedding anniversary, Mr and Mrs Batchelor and their family stood at their gate at 56b Maidenhead Road, watching the searchlights and listening to the planes going over. When the all-clear sounded they went back inside the house. A few minutes later they heard a whistling sound and an explosion shook the house. The lights went out and 'there was panic and fear all round'. They went outside and found that the bomb had dropped exactly where they had been standing. It had sunk deep into the soft ground and the explosion had pushed earth up, burying the gate. The gas and water pipes were leaking. Everyone, including the ARP Warden, reckoned they had heard the whistling of a second bomb, but there had been no explosion. William Batchelor, the son, was worried because the family was crowding round the crater, peering into it. The Air Raid team arrived after about half an hour and set out in a line to comb the orchard for the unexploded bomb. They were unsuccessful but one of them fell into a bath that Mr Batchelor had sunk into the ground for his geese. William's mother spent the rest of the night at his aunt's in Great William Street, while the rest of the family went into their homemade air-raid shelter. At 3 a.m. the bomb went off. They could hear the clods of earth falling all around them. 'That's the house gone', said his father stoically, but when they emerged it was still standing. The bomb had exploded in a neighbouring field and caused no damage whatsoever.

*The ARP Rescue
Squad.* (Image
courtesy of the
Shakespeare
Birthplace Trust
Records Office)

*Rother Street
Maternity Home,
1941.* (Image
courtesy of the
Shakespeare
Birthplace Trust
Records Office)

'To the Satisfaction of the Bods'

In 1941, the Government finally decided not to relocate to Stratford and released the accommodation it was holding for other war use. Most of the hotels were taken over by the services. The Falcon, Red Horse and Shakespeare accommodated the RAF's Number 9 Initial Training Wing: the Boat Clubhouse was sequestrated as a recreation area and the Masonic Hall on Great William Street as a Morse training centre. Shottery Hall was taken over as a convalescent home for army wounded and the Union Club for wounded from the RAF.

The Canadian Salvation Army established a Forces Club at the Alveston Manor Hotel. During the course of the war, 20,700 Canadian servicemen and women stayed there. Many of these were aircrews from the No. 22 Operational Training Wing based at Wellesbourne and Atherstone.

At the Shakespeare, it was agreed that the cellars should be locked, barred, bolted and sealed 'to the satisfaction of the bods'. A blacksmith was called in to do the job, but some smart boys could almost smell the liquor behind the barrier. With the aid of hacksaws and other instruments they forced an entry and made merry over the next few weeks. The depredations only came to light after a 'bod' who had lost his trousers found some empty bottles in a bedroom. The remaining liquor was transferred to a secure warehouse in London.

Malta

The entry of Italy into the war meant that the British Mediterranean island of Malta was severely threatened and likely to fall. The colony was subjected to ferocious air raids. Captain Lawrence Stokes-Roberts was stationed on the island in the early days of 1941 and enjoyed watching the dive-bombing. The Stukas came in one by one, dropping almost vertically from 12,000ft to 200ft before releasing their bomb. The aim of the pilots was so accurate that if you were not on the target you were perfectly safe.

With Teutonic efficiency, there were three raids a day, coming regularly at 9.10 a.m., 12.30 p.m. and (the worst) at 6.15 p.m. Exactly six minutes after the sirens sounded, the planes would arrive and it was all over in half an hour.

The Germans and Italians had virtual control of the air because the siege meant that the British planes were grounded for lack of fuel. Food supplies were an even bigger problem than the raids. Prices on the black market spiralled to fantastic levels. An egg cost 3s 6d. Cotton was 18s 6d a reel, a needle 2s 6d. Sugar was about 15s a pound and meat over £1 a pound. Everything and anything was stolen, so many locals kept chickens, rabbits and even goats in their bedrooms. Left in the farmyard they would simply disappear.

Early in 1942, Capt Stokes-Roberts suffered a severe injury to his foot. The subsequent surgery incapacitated him for further active service, so he became organiser of DNSA, the overseas branch of ENSA, the forces' entertainments arm. He found himself organising every kind of show from community singing to *Macbeth*.

Sub-Lieutenant Peter Morris, aged 22, from Albany Road, was a pilot with the Fleet Air Arm on the beleaguered island. His main task was to mount torpedo attacks on Axis shipping with his slow-moving Gladiator biplane. From the air he witnessed the destruction wrought by enemy bombing:

> One had only to fly over Malta to realise what a tough time the G.C. island had had. It was 'pock-marked' from bombs everywhere one looked and there were many big bomb craters. The food problem was acute. Careful rations were handed out every day. There was no wood and few amenities. Yet everybody 'kept their end up.'

For the island to survive, the siege had to be broken. On 11 August 1942, Flight Sgt Elliot Roberts was on the hanger crew for a fighter squadron on an aircraft carrier that was part of a strongly escorted convoy to Malta, as part of Operation Pedestal, which was intended to lift the siege. Axis spies watched the fleet leave Gibraltar. Seventy miles south of Majorca the alarms sounded and the aircraft left the flight deck to combat an air attack. The aircraft carrier HMS *Eagle* was close to the ship on which Roberts was serving when she was torpedoed:

> It all happened very quickly. I heard the explosion and saw columns of water and smoke shoot into the air. When these had cleared I saw that the *Eagle* had heeled over to an angle of 45 degrees. Then she rapidly sank. 900 survivors were picked up and transferred to another warship.

Among the survivors was CPO Hugh Dale.

That evening the convoy suffered a heavy air attack by Ju88 dive-bombers. Most of them were shot down. All they achieved was a 'near-miss' on a merchantman.

Next day there were attacks from dawn to dusk. The worst time came at six o'clock that evening off the coast of Sicily. Torpedoes were being fired and dive-bombers constantly attacking. In the midst of it all, an aircraft in Roberts' squadron crashed in flames on the deck of his ship, but the pilot managed to crawl out.

Soon after, Roberts had his most frightening moment. Probably due to a blast, a petrol valve burst and flooded his hanger. One spark and things would have been, as he put it, 'rather difficult', but 'you don't have time to get excited, or anything like that. You get a bit short-tempered and find yourself snapping out at all sorts of things.'

Once within the protective zone of Malta, the seriously depleted escort turned back, leaving the merchantmen to run for harbour. Although the arrival of the convoy lifted the siege, the process had been immensely costly. Although it was not publicly revealed at the time, as well as the *Eagle*, two cruisers, a destroyer and ten out of the fifteen merchantmen had been sunk.

The Cruel Sea

The war at sea was less restricted by the censor than the land war. Whether this was because it was not static and the enemy was an equal party to the available information is unclear, but certainly more graphic accounts appear from Stratfordians at sea than elsewhere.

In 1940, Alan Sutton, who had got married the year before, left the Borough Treasurer's office to join the Royal Navy as an Ordinary Seaman. He had never been to sea before, 'but it happened just to fit me. I was the same as everyone, scared to death the first time you go to sea, but I wasn't seasick...' After twelve months, he applied for a commission and went through the training and selection boards.

The ship on which Elliot Roberts, now a Flight Sergeant, was serving conveyed the first ANZAC troops to the Middle East. Subsequently she took the first South African troops from Simons Town. On a visit to Cape Town, he was invited out to dinner by a soldier he had met casually and met a lass who worked in the post office at Durban. She came to England to marry him in 1941 and got a job in Stratford Post Office, where her 'charm of manner' captivated people.

After disembarking its human cargo in Egypt, Elliot's ship was torpedoed in the Mediterranean, but he survived.

On leaving the Grammar School at the age of 16 in 1940, Malcolm Kennard joined the Merchant Marine. On 23 February 1941, the ship on which he was serving was caught in the sights of a periscope in the Atlantic. What happened next is described in the U-boat Captain's logbook:

> A lone merchantman is spotted at 303 degrees. I opt for a submerged attack, so I get to a good firing position. At 18.00 the first torpedo is launched. It's a dud, but a second torpedo sends the 'SS Temple Moat', a cargo merchant ship of 3,146 BRT in ballast to the bottom.

On 23 April 1941, his parents, Mr and Mrs Percy Kennard of Rother Street, received a letter stating that Malcolm's ship had been lost at sea:

> Although we now feel there is little chance of her still being afloat, we have not given up hope for the safety of the crew. There have been numerous cases of crews being taken prisoner and landed in enemy territory, from which they have only been able to communicate with their homes after several weeks' captivity.

In this case the hope was forlorn, but it was not so for Lt-Col J.M. Crawford who was serving aboard the armed merchant ship, *Avila Star*, as acting doctor when she hit by a torpedo in the Atlantic in August 1942:

> The crash came... I turned on my private electric light, independent of dynamos, took my first-aid medical bag, and, as I left the cabin, the 'abandon ship' went. I sought my boat, met no one, jumped in it as it passed the rail and reached the

water. I spoke to the figure next to me – the little purser. We were in the stern, and I remarked 'All's well'.

Figures came sliding down ropes, and I flashed the torch for them to see when to let go, as we rose and fell on the swell. At that second, No. 2 torpedo hit the ship down below us and with a roar our boat and ourselves rose in the air.

I did not see anything but flew upwards and then fell down head first into a soft white light. Then I found myself feet downwards and swam up.

Being brain-clear, I wiped over my mouth, nose and eyes before drawing in air, for I was covered in thick oil, so I didn't even taste it, and was not sick. I came up some distance away from the ship, and hearing and seeing nothing, struck out, afraid of being sucked down. Cap and torch were gone. I swam quite a bit, till tired, and rested, and called and whistled.

I could see the ship was sinking and was down far. I sank in a hollow of the swell, and when the swell raised me – no ship!

After a time he saw two lights far away. As they were rising and falling, he realised they were boats. As he started out for them, he realised that one of his legs was badly hurt and one of his eyes closed. He had to let go of the haversack containing his medical equipment. He let his leg hang down and did a dog paddle to the boat, which he hailed and was pulled in. 'Things were a bit dreamy, but I lay there.'

After three-and-a-half days they were picked up by a Portuguese ship and treated with 'wonderful kindness'. Lieutenant-Colonel Crawford was put, 'after much washing' in the ship's doctor's cabin. 'Total injuries', he wrote: 'Left eye closed, cut lip, three teeth gone, broken right leg and right foot, scraped left leg and masses of bruises.'

When they reached Ponto Delgado in the Azores, they were taken ashore and sent to a nursing home. When he wrote to his wife in Shottery Road, Lt-Col Crawford was already on crutches:

Alas! For the Captain, the purser and many others, and the old Avila.

Apprentice J.C. Passey, aged eighteen, also found himself on the hazardous business of manning a merchant ship. At about five o'clock on the afternoon of 5 November 1941, he was in his cabin when there was a loud whoosh. His shipmate asked what it was and he replied that he thought it was wind coming through the porthole. It fact a German raider, which he thought was a pocket battleship, had come up on the port side and fired two shells into the middle of the convoy. The aged cruiser escort, *Jervis Bay*, out-gunned and out-manoeuvred, turned and opened fire in an attempt to hold off the enemy. The merchant ships scattered, but the wind was too strong to enable them to put up a smoke screen.

Four shells from the raider, which was firing three shells simultaneously, hit the *Jervis Bay* and her bridge burst into flame. She continued firing, but was soon ablaze from stem to stern. The raider sank three merchant ships at the rear of the convoy before darkness fell. One shell hit a ship just 50 yards away from Passey's:

We could see gun flashes on the horizon, about ten miles away, and at about 8 o'clock three star shells went up from the raider. We thought it was all up with us, and went all out (about 11 knots).

After a tense night, dawn found them alone on the sea, with not another ship in sight. Three days later they came up with five British ships with an escort. Five other ships joined them in the course of that day and they arrived safely in port six days later.

The 17-year-old boy seaman Raymond Timms was serving aboard the cruiser HMS *Dunedin* when she left Portsmouth for the South Atlantic in April 1941.

Her movements were governed by the intelligence gained through the breaking of the German Enigma Code. Together with HMS *Eagle* she was drafted onto the search for the German tanker *Lotheringen* that had been supplying the doomed pocket battleship, *Bismarck*. She was spotted by a Swordfish aircraft from the *Eagle* that disabled her with a torpedo and captured by the *Dunedin* soon after. A prize crew was put aboard to steam her to Bermuda.

The *Dunedin* spent the next few months sailing hundreds of miles over the South Atlantic, calling at Freetown several times, St Helena and Bathurst. In November, the Admiralty learned from the Enigma decrypts that the Germans were planning a mass attack on shipping near Cape Town, involving four U-boats, the armed merchant raider, *Atlantis* and the supply ship, *Python*. On 22 November, it was reported that the *Atlantis* had been sunk. That afternoon, U-124, on her way to rendezvous with the *Python* near St Paul's Rocks, just south of the Equator, sighted the *Dunedin* sailing on a north-westerly course. Captain Jochen Mohr steered a course to the west to lie in wait, but a lookout on the *Dunedin* spotted the periscope at about 12.50 p.m. and the ship changed course. This took her further away from the U-boat, which was still proceeding westwards. Captain Mohr saw HMS *Dunedin* disappearing into the distance, at least 4,000 yards away, steaming at 17 knots and taking continuous evasive action. Nevertheless, he fired three torpedoes and, incredibly, two of them hit their target within seconds of each other at around 13.26 GMT. The first struck amidships, wrecking the main wireless office and sending the ship lurching to starboard. The second caused even greater damage, blowing off the starboard screw. The order was given to abandon ship. Men jumped over the side to the Carling rafts or onto any available debris.

Captain Mohr moved in for the kill and fired a fourth torpedo. Despite the easier target from close range, it missed. Seventeen minutes after the first torpedo had struck, the *Dunedin* turned on her beam-ends and sank. Shortly afterwards, the U-124 surfaced and circled the survivors who numbered up to 250 – half the ship's complement. As a spontaneous gesture of defiance, they sang *There'll always be an England*. After ten minutes, the U-boat dived and left them alone on the sea. In the fierce tropical heat their numbers dwindled rapidly. Some died of injuries, some went insane, some drowned, some were killed by sharks. After seventy-eight hours of agony the seventy-two survivors were picked up by the SS *Nishmara*, a US merchantman. A further five died on the passage to Trinidad.

Whether Raymond Timms died when the ship sank or whether he perished on the open sea is not known. He was recorded as 'missing believed killed' on 17 December.

Norman Bennett had become an Engine Room Artificer on submarines. Early in 1942, he travelled to New York as one of the forty-two crew members who were to pick up the US submarine P514, which was transferred to the Royal Navy in March. She had been built in 1918 and was therefore obsolete, but it was intended to use her as a training ship for the Royal Canadian Navy so her new crew sailed her northwards to the fishing port of Argentia on the southern coast of Newfoundland. On the evening of 20 June, HMS P514 embarked on the short voyage around the Avalon Peninsular to St John's. She was escorted by a corvette, HMS *Primrose*. Earlier that day, the minesweeper, HMCS *Georgian* had left St John's as an escort to a convoy of six ships bound for Sidney on Cape Breton. Due to engine trouble on one of the ships, the convoy was soon off schedule. Thus the Captain of the *Georgian* was unaware of the scheduled presence of friendly ships, but he had received warnings that two U-boats might be in the area. At 4.25 a.m. on 21 June, with visibility down to about 400 yards, HMS P514 was travelling on the surface and crossed the bow of the *Georgian*. When she failed to respond to a challenge from a blue night lamp, the minesweeper promptly rammed and sank her. An immediate search of the area was launched, but no survivors were found. The body of a British sailor was seen floating in the water, but it sank before it could be rescued. The Captain of the *Georgian* was exonerated at a Public Enquiry because HMS P514 had failed to respond to signals.

The body in the water was that of Norman Bennett. It was washed ashore four months later and found on a beach by a 20-year-old Canadian girl. His wallet still contained photographs of his two young children.

In November 1942, the ship on which Dennis Wickstead was serving as Third Officer was hit by a torpedo 700 miles out in the Atlantic. Three of her crew were killed. As the ship was sinking, two lifeboats were boarded and launched. The Second Officer stayed behind on deck to cut Dennis's boat away, but this brave man received fatal injuries when he jumped. The submarine, which turned out to be Italian, surfaced and pulled alongside. The survivors requested medical attention for a severely injured crew member. The Italians said that they were unable to help him, but they gave them three bottles of brandy, thirty gallons of water and a compass. The Italian First Officer was so upset at their plight that he burst into tears.

The two boats were separated soon after the submarine had dived. Dennis never saw the second boat or any of its crew again. After rowing 300 miles for nine grim days, Dennis and his twenty-three companions were picked up by a Vichy French sloop which was escorting a convoy. They were landed at Dakar and taken to an internment camp at Sebikotane, where their chief worry was a shortage of food. Rations consisted chiefly of mutton, pumpkin and macaroni:

> We heard the news of the American landing and the reported Darlan agreement, but the authorities firmly refused to release us. Suddenly one day, I was called down to the orderly room, where the officer said 'You are liberated.'

Fortuitously the Vichy French authorities, under threat of invasion, had made a pact with the allies and he was released after only four weeks:

> It seemed as though a great load had been taken off their minds. They rushed to the camp, took us off to their houses and gave us food and cigarettes. They entertained us royally.
>
> For the first time in many months, radios were tuned in to British bulletins. In the train on the way to the frontier crowds appeared all the way, bringing us food and beer. The joy and the relief of our boys cannot be imagined.

Frederick Pope proved an exemplary Petty Officer in his revived naval career. He was mentioned in dispatches on 6 June 1941, after his ship, HMS *Firedrake*, an 'F' class destroyer, had been in action against the Italian fleet in the Mediterranean.

On the afternoon of 16 December 1941, *Firedrake* was acting as escort leader to Convoy ON153 bound for Canada. A hurricane was raging. The air was filled with spray and the sea was a foaming white. At about 17:00 hours, the ASDIC operator picked up a contact and tracked it to about five miles south of the convoy. At 20:10 hours, the destroyer was struck by a torpedo fired by U-boat U211 and broke in two. The bow section sank immediately. The stern stayed precariously afloat with thirty-five men aboard. Rockets were fired and the other ships in the convoy steamed towards the hulk, which narrowly escaped destruction when a corvette mistook it for a U-boat. At 00:40 hours, it sank, leaving the men struggling in the water. Twenty-seven were rescued. Frederick Pope was among the 168 who perished.

CPO Hugh Dale had transferred to a cruiser on the Russian convoys. That too was torpedoed and so was the ship that picked him up, but he was about to experience naval victory rather than humiliation. He was serving aboard the battleship HMS *Duke of York* that was part of the squadron that sank the German pocket battleship *Scharnhorst* in the closing week of 1943:

At about 4.30 p.m. on Boxing Day, the Commander over the loudspeaker system told us that we should be opening fire very soon. At this even though the office was a hive of industry… there seemed to be a silence that could be felt. From the time of the Commanders last warning until the actual opening fire seemed an eternity. It felt as though we were never going to open fire. Yet maybe it was only twenty minutes, the longest I have ever spent. But upon feeling the ship shake to our first salvoes, there seemed to be a feeling of security, of safety, that we were now making a fight of it.

In the office we knew everything that was going on in the Fleet, the *Scharnhorst* altering course, destroyers attacking and all those other things that happen at high speed.

The three-hour battle took place in the total darkness of an Arctic winter afternoon.

Telegraphist Dennis Hastrop, aged eighteen, was also serving in what Hugh Dale called 'the office'. He lived round the corner from the Dales at 113 Shottery Road. An ex-KES boy, he had been in the Navy only a year.

Global Conflict

By the summer of 1941, there were only three old boys of the Grammar School at university. Most were going straight into the forces. One such was Richard Spender, who had deferred his Bracegirdle Exhibition in Modern History at St Catherine's Society, Oxford, to take up a commission with the Royal Ulster Rifles.

At KES Grammar School, he was a popular figure, CSM in the school corps, a keen oarsman and boxer, a good Rugby forward and amateur actor. He was regarded as a promising poet, a talent he pursued during his service career, publishing in a variety of journals. *The Times Literary Supplement* carried his poem, 'The Young Soldier':

> I am young
> With my proud young body
> I have run over the smiling threshold of life…

The global nature of the conflict was spreading Stratfordians across the world to many latitudes and climes. Private Colin Hughes was in the joint British and Norwegian force that made a spectacular raid on the Lofoten Islands in the Arctic on 4 March 1941. By contrast, Leading Aircraftsman B. Thompson found himself stationed at an airport on the edge of the jungle 'somewhere in Africa'. One evening he went to the cinema and was amazed that the newsreel showed Cllr. Waldron and his macebearers 'doing their stuff' at the Mop of 1938. 'I was disappointed', he added, 'that the picture did not depict a bloke… who tried to pick my pocket. Anyway, I hope he is out of hospital by now.'

In February 1940, Robert Lysons' Battalion embarked round the Cape for Egypt. 'We have crossed the line and are in tropical waters', he wrote to his parents, giving an amusing account of the traditional ceremony. Later he revealed that he was undergoing strenuous training. On 16 April 1941, by now promoted to Corporal, he took part in a successful seaborne raid on Bardia behind the Axis lines. He was one of sixty-seven soldiers who returned to the wrong beach and could not be picked up. His anxious parents received the news that he had been posted missing, but on 4 July, they received two cheerful letters from him in an Italian prisoner-of-war camp. He had had no kit with him when captured and had a five weeks' growth of beard. Conditions in the camp were tolerable and improving. Macaroni was the staple food, but Gorgonzola was occasionally sent in from outside.

Gunner Tom Barr had participated in Wavell's rout of Marshall Graziani's army in Libya after the Italian entry into the war. A more serious business came with the arrival of Major General Erwin Rommel and his *Afrika Korps*. Tom was on patrol with a mobile gun at Sidi Rezegh on 21 November 1941 when it was surrounded by German tanks and armoured vehicles. A shell exploded near his foot and his gun was put out of action. After surrendering he was taken to a dressing station in an Italian light car. He was deeply impressed by the humanity of the nuns who attended his wounds.

Stratfordian L-Cpl Bill Winter had joined the Worcestershire Regiment and was posted to the Middle East in March 1941. He saw service against the Italians in the Abyssinia and was part of Wavell's advance into Tripolitania. He was wounded early in 1942 while on patrol, but got back to Tobruk just before the nine-month siege. While there, he formed a friendship with Corporal Philip Robilliard, a Guernseyman. Both were captured when the garrison surrendered as was the Dunkirk veteran, Fred Ryman, who had been promoted to Lance Corporal during the siege.

Bill Winter's account of events reveals why Rommel was regarded with an admiration bordering on veneration by members of the Eighth Army. He ordered that all the captured Allied prisoners be assembled and addressed them, telling them that they had fought well and their failure to win was not their fault.

The Germans treated their captives strictly but well. Any search of their possessions was always for military objects – pay books, badges, maps and so forth, but Bill Winter considered that 'the Italians did search you so much as loot you. Rings, wallets, cigarette cases, all were taken and never returned.'

With their companions, Bill Winter and Philip Robilliard were held at Benghazi waiting for transport to the Italian mainland. They hoped that an Allied counterattack might release them, but after eight weeks they were taken across and spent some highly disagreeable months in different camps.

Also captured at Tobruk was Pte Frederick Coleman of 15 Glebe Road. Educated at the Church of England School, he had joined the Grenadier Guards in 1938 and had later served as a paratrooper in the Long Range Desert Group. He managed to escape three days after his capture and rejoined his unit.

Driver Harold Dornborough embarked on the long voyage around the Cape in June 1941, having got married two days before. He arrived in North Africa on 25 November. In January 1942, he was wounded in the leg during an encounter with Axis tanks and armoured cars at Agedabia. Two of his mates, who had also been captured, carried him to a German medical officer for treatment. From the dressing station they were sent via Sirte and Misurata to Tripoli. On the way they were strafed by the RAF, which made the Italian guards so angry that he thought they were going to shoot him. When they got to Sirte, however, the Italians were so pleased to have taken some prisoners after their previous debacles that they fed them on macaroni and tomato puree washed down with wine. He learned that they were being taken to Naples, where the guards assured him that he would be well looked after.

After embarking from Tripoli to the Italian mainland, they were placed on a train to Naples, which had been badly knocked about by the RAF. A daylight raid took place while they were still on the train. The German AA guns opened up and there was a dogfight over the city. He spent the whole of his captivity in hospital at Caserta.

The Warwickshire Yeomanry had fought its way with its horses through Iraq and was now battling in Syria. Lance Corporal R.F. Spender was involved in the capture of a Syrian village. He was ordered to destroy the telephone link with a nearby town. He did this by removing the 'one and only' phone and cutting through the wires on the telegraph poles:

This was effective, but I had reckoned without the local 'Wog' populace, who gave a hand… When we left about three hours later they had stripped the poles of wire for miles and were going out on donkeys and camels to complete the job.

Wings for Victory: an RAF Bomber is put on display outside the Shakespeare Memorial Theatre. (Image courtesy of the Shakespeare Birthplace Trust Records Office)

Per Ardua ad Astra

The RAF was striking back at Germany. Its increasing power was reflected in Stratford by the placing of a symbolic bomber on the car park in front of the theatre. Later one of the first power operated gun turrets was put on display.

Some nights the bombers from Wellesbourne seemed to skim the roofs of Stratford because they were so low. Lillian Booker got little sleep on the night before her wedding, 'with these planes soaring, just clearing the rooftops, going out'.

In February 1941, 21-year-old Sergeant Pilot Howard Foott-Hewitt of 130 Evesham Road, was reported missing. His plane was last seen over the coast of Holland. He had spent his honeymoon in Stratford two months before. His 23-year-old brother, Edward, was also a sergeant pilot. Neither his wife nor his mother had heard anything of him for a year. All they knew was that he was somewhere in the Middle East. On 15 March the mother was listening to the radio and heard it announced that he had been awarded the Distinguished Flying Medal for his brilliant work in the Albanian campaign. He was a pilot of deadly efficiency, with at least thirteen kills to his credit. When he was attacked by five Italian fighters while on a solo flight over Tepelini, he shot down three before breaking off the engagement, his ammunition exhausted. That month he had already shot down four enemy planes.

Pilot Officer Bruce Organ had left his theatre company to join the RAF in 1940 and began operational flying with Bomber Command in the late summer of 1941. In September, he was reported missing, but to the relief of everyone who knew this popular figure, the news was received two weeks later that he was a PoW. His Hampden bomber had been shot down over Holland.

The time that families waited for news of their loved ones was shortening. The family of Sergeant Observer Jeffrey Longford, who had been shot down over Germany in late November, heard that he was a PoW just thirteen days later.

The narrowest escape achieved by any Stratfordian in the war was probably that of Fl-Lt Charles Brayshaw, the 22-year-old only son of Mr and Mrs W.H. Brayshaw of 6 Hathaway Hamlet in Shottery. On a mission in September 1943, he had just cleared the English coast in his Hawker Typhoon when his engine cut out. He was too low to bail out, so he jettisoned the cockpit doors and 'ditched' the plane into the water at 140mph. It skidded momentarily on the surface before sinking. The impact pitched him forwards and he was knocked unconscious. His breathing apparatus saved his life for, when he came to, he found himself strapped in the cockpit as his plane lay eighteen feet down on the bottom of the English Channel. He quickly unfastened his straps and tried to release the gas that would inflate his Mae West, but its buoyancy floated him to the surface before he could do so. He had 'ditched' amidst a small inshore fishing fleet. 'We thought he had gone down for good', said one of the fishermen, 'but suddenly a head bobbed up in the middle of the pool.' They hauled him out and the only after-effects were a cut between the eyes and the feeling that he had 'just about swallowed half the English Channel.' After a day in hospital, he was released for a short leave.

Charles Brayshaw was awarded the DFC on 20 February 1944. 'This officer', reads the citation, 'has made telling attacks on enemy railway sidings, shipping and airfields, often in the face of severe opposition…. He has destroyed one enemy aircraft.' Next day he was killed in action. On a sortie over Villers-sur-Mer, his Typhoon was hit by flak and crashed into the sea north of Cabourg.

'Don't Stare at Them'

The air war took its toll on many who survived it. One of the many plane crashes to which the Stratford AFS was called out was at Wellesbourne. It was so cold that the foam they were using to extinguish the fire froze on the aircraft and on their axes. Despite this they got the rear gunner, a Canadian, out and he was taken to hospital. Fred Wincote, who was part of the rescue team, was interested to know how he was and visited him:

> He was a very friendly chap and I went to see him most days. There was only one rule enforced and that was that he was not allowed to look in the mirror because of the horrible burns he had sustained. Then one day… I went to visit and a nurse said I wasn't to go into the ward, but the sister wanted to see me. She told me that the rescued man had seen himself in the mirror and promptly committed suicide.

In 1944, Bob Stroud, a merchant seaman from Liverpool, got a weekend off to visit his brother in Stratford who had just been called up for the RAF. They were taking a stroll along the banks of the Avon when they saw a number of couples coming towards them. 'Don't stare at them', said the brother, 'but try to get a good look at them as we pass.'

> The men were all in RAF officers' uniform. Their companions were really attractive young ladies, good-looking and smartly dressed – and they were all laughing and joking. As they approached us, I realised the men were all burned facially. Their skin was brown and wrinkled, their ears shrivelled. One had no top lip. Another had one bright pink cheek where a graft had been done – and, of course, they had no eyebrows.
>
> My brother said that their escorts were volunteers who were trying to help them get their lives back after the plane crashes.

The Far East

Japan's entry into the war in December 1941 was heralded by the sinking of the battleships *Prince of Wales* and *Repulse* off the coast of Malaya.

Nineteen-year-old Ordinary Telegraphist, Joe Birch, of 6 Knight's Lane, Tiddington, was one of the survivors of this disaster; *The Prince of Wales* was the first ship on which he had served. He had joined the Navy a year before, having been employed at the County Council offices in Warwick. He too had been a member of the Stratford branch of the St John's Ambulance Brigade and, with his two brothers, had played in the Salvation Army Band since early childhood.

The sinking of the two capital ships presaged the biggest debacle in British military history: the fall of Singapore in February 1942. A number of Stratfordians were taken prisoner. Aircraftsman First Class Fred Scruby was among the prisoners taken on Java. He had been posted to the island only a few weeks before.

In Sumatra, Leading Aircraftman Anthony Claridge of 65 Albany Road, a nursing orderly, was captured but then left to his fate 'in the heart of the worst jungle in the world'. One of his companions, Norman Graham from Newcastle, was given up to die when he went down with malaria, dysentery and 'the dreadful disease', beri-beri. Claridge, at great risk to himself, sold all his personal possessions except his last pair of shorts and used the money to bribe the natives to get food for him and at least six other sufferers, even going hungry himself. With his expert medical knowledge he gradually brought them to almost full recovery. After suffering 'indescribable hardships on various hell islands, they were eventually recaptured and sent to the notorious Changi Camp on Singapore Island.

The family of Gunner Alfred Tutt of 31 Ely Street, who before joining the army had worked at Hewitt's Nurseries on the Banbury road, heard that he was in Japanese hands in October 1942. For others, the long anxious wait to hear the fate of their loved ones was to be even more prolonged. In July 1943, the vintner Chris Rookes received a postcard from his brother dated 20 June 1942 and covered in Japanese markings. It bore the laconic message 'I am quite well. Best wishes – Wilfred.'

After this the postcards trickled in, all with laconic and optimistic messages. All followed the same formula. 'I am quite well' wrote Gunner John Seeney, to his parents at 11 John Street, 'and getting plenty of food. Hope to see you again soon.' Gunner Tutt's parents got a card in December 1943, saying that he was in good health and working for pay. Fred Scruby's card arrived at his parents' home at 9 Holtom Street early in 1944, saying that he was in a PoW camp in Java and quite well. Trooper Ronald Morris of the Royal Armoured Corps had joined the army before the war. He had been evacuated from Dunkirk and captured when Singapore fell. In July 1944, his mother at 63 West Street received a card saying that he too was well and working for pay. Only the war's end would fully reveal the cynical motives behind these cards and the desperate deprivations suffered by the prisoners of the Japanese, but what else could they put?

Joe Birch's respite was brief. On 4 March 1942, HMS *Anking*, the ship to which he had transferred, was sunk by Japanese cruisers as she escaped Singapore and all hands perished. On 19 March, a 'penitent form' was dedicated to his memory at the Salvation Army Barracks in Scholars Lane.

El Alamein

Fred Morris of 3 Kendall Avenue was an Accounts Clerk with Kendall's, the chemical manufacturers, and married with two children, Gill and Jimmy. He was called up in 1942. He was 39 years old and bespectacled. His experience destined him for the Pay Corps. Kendall's proved model employers, sending him regular 5/- postal orders during the time he was serving. On 17 June, he embarked on a ship on which there were 'lots of fags and tobacco'. After a leisurely stay at the Cape, he arrived in Egypt on 5 September. 'Jolly good sleeping places, but isn't it hot?' he wrote in his diary.

After the austerity of wartime Britain, Egypt seemed a veritable cornucopia. Fred went into Cairo, a 'smelly place', a week after his arrival and bought his wife Molly two pairs of stockings and a silk scarf and a necklet for his daughter Gill. A week later he sent Gill a pair of pyjamas. He was able to send commodities that were virtually unobtainable at home: packets of raisins, pairs of leather sandals and sweets. In return Molly sent him copies of the *Stratford Herald* and the *News of the World*.

Frequent excursions provided diversions from life in the departmental office. Fred visited the pyramids and took a bus to the statue of Ramases I at Memphis. 'What lousy looking villages', he commented. Amidst this interesting existence, he omits to mention that Rommel's *Afrika Corps* had advanced to within 150 miles of Cairo. If the worst occurred, even members of the Pay Corps might be sent to the front, so they were called to regular shooting practice on the 25 yard range. He turned out to be a good shot, once scoring eight bulls in ten shots, but he found 200 yards range 'much more difficult'.

The Warwickshire Yeomanry had been transferred to Egypt and exchanged its horseflesh for steel. Some horses were retained for pack duties, but most were taken to the remount depot in Palestine. 'There was never a dry eye when they took the horses from us', recalled one trooper. 'Every man was crying.' The tears were not just for the loss of the horses, but for their almost certain fate. Most were sold to local dealers and ended up being worked to death on the streets of Cairo and other places.

'C' Company was preparing for the coming decisive battle. Its nickname, the 'Swedeheads', was amply borne out by the Sergeant's instructions to the troopers on laying mines. 'It's quite easy: you put 'em down in rows, like turnips.'

The Regiment went into action with tanks for the first time as part of the 8th Armoured Division at the opening of the Battle of El Alamein on 21 October 1942. It spent four days fighting round the Miteiriya Ridge. After a brief rest, they prepared for action again on 1 November. General Montgomery had warned that he expected heavy casualties.

The attack began early next morning. Eight hundred guns let loose a terrific barrage. The Yeomanry's 44 tanks moved up in the dark and swept past the advancing infantry. There was some delay while the sappers made a gap through a newly-laid minefield. The enemy gunners were well dug in and the tanks had to make the last 2,000 yards to their lines with little artillery support. Every so often, one went up in flames and the crew scrambled out. Aerials were shot away and messages had to be sent by runners. The fight continued for over three hours, during which, the Yeomanry accounted for all the enemy's anti-tank guns. At 10.30 a.m., the Colonel gave the order to withdraw. As they pulled back, they continued firing. The Regiment had taken a severe mauling. Only eleven of the tanks that went into the charge came out and only eight of these could both move and shoot.

On 13 November 1942, the bells of Holy Trinity sounded the glorious victory, a major turning of the War's tide. In the subsequent advance, the 8th Armoured Division over-ran the supply lines of the retreating Germans. 'At the moment', wrote Cpl Aubrey Jaggard, 'I am smoking a Jerry cigarette, of which I have several boxes, having just finished a dinner of Jerry bread, coffee and jam. They have tins labelled "Marmelade", and when you open them there is a red liquid inside, which is because they use beetroot instead of oranges, I believe.' The German bread was beautifully 'done up in airtight packages, 3ins thick', but it was made of rye and tasted like

> very stale Hovis. The other chaps won't touch it, but as I am off biscuits, I have been sampling it and it is not bad with bacon or jam. It is made for eating with German sausages, I think.
>
> It is very cold here at night, but still like English August in the day, with fleas, butterflies and birds. Our driver dug away a small pile of stones that he had been using for a pillow, and found one large scorpion, one medium centipede and one small lizard. He was quite upset.

During the advance, the Warwickshire Yeomanry remained true to its cultural heritage and put on a production of the *Merchant of Venice* on the back of trucks in the Western Desert. The lack of women entailed a reversion to an Elizabethan theatrical tradition. Paul Morgan dressed up in a female costume to play Portia.

Eighteen months after the battle, Fred Morris visited El Alamein. 'Bags of burnt out vehicles. Guns. Tanks and planes are still lying around.

Trooper Paul Morgan of 'C' Company, Warwickshire Yeomanry, on patrol in the desert. (Image courtesy of the Shakespeare Birthplace Trust Records Office)

'Wonder how they are'

Fred Morris's life was one of routine. He attended regular sessions of shooting practice. Once a month he was 'hellish busy' with the Pay Parade, but there were diversions. He went regularly to ENSA shows. These were variable in quality, but could include the very best like Emlyn Williams' 'very fine' performance in his own play, *Night must Fall.*

On Christmas Day Fred went to dinner in a large tent called a Shamiana that had been erected by the Royal Marines. It was made with large mats that bore colourful designs. They had a 'fine spread with cigs and cigars and beer'. After dinner there was 'a bit of a show':

> Native dancing girls. What a sight, practically naked as they only shuffle round doing suggestive body movements. Soon got fed up with it. Then came the Gulli Gulli men (Native conjurors). Not bad.

With many professional sportsmen serving in forces, teams could be of a high standard. In the summer of 1944, Fred attended a cricket match between the Army and the RAF in Alexandria. 'Smith of Essex is a fine bowler',[1] he recorded.

Loneliness was a problem for families divided by the war. Fred received a letter from Molly on 18 December. She was 'still feeling lonely'. Little Jimmy had got his first pair of trousers. 'Would love to see him', he wrote. Later she wrote that Jimmy wanted a baby sister. 'What oh!' thought Fred. 'I want what gets them too.'

'This is our wedding anniversary', he wrote on 5 September. 'What a life.' Once he had a very vivid dream that he was at home and heard Gill calling, so he dashed upstairs and found her on the landing. 'I was so frightened Daddy', she said.

'Just imagine', Fred wrote on 4 March 1944, 'my 40th birthday and so far from home. Wonder how they are?'

Illness was another problem in an unfamiliar climate. On New Year's Eve he went sick with what he called 'Gyppo gut'.

Notes

[1] Fred was right. Peter Smith took 1,697 wickets during his Essex career and won four caps for England.

SIX

'THROUGH AGONY AND DEATH'

The Wheels of Industry

On 14 July 1940 at 1.40 p.m., a German reconnaissance plane took photographs of Stratford from a great height. When military intelligence examined them, everything that appeared a strategic objective was marked and numbered. The bridges over the Avon and the gas works were recorded as potential targets. A section of the railway was shown as a marshalling yard and a building on the Banbury road described as a food depot. Most disturbingly, the Alcester Road School was reckoned to be a military camp and barracks.

Had the *Abwehr* possessed more knowledge of what went on in Stratford, they would have taken the place more seriously. Even before the war, the town had become a light engineering centre. These workshops were rapidly converted to war work. Some of what they were turning out was so vital to the war effort that had the Germans known of it, they would certainly have sought to drop a few well-placed bombs on the town.

In the well-equipped workshops of Wright Engineering, in Mulberry Street, delicate work proceeded for the Ministry of Aircraft Production. The lathes and the sawing, drilling and planing plants machined hundreds of thousands of parts with exceptional accuracy to within a two-thousandth of an inch. Firmaments were manufactured for Lancaster, Stirling and Mosquito aeroplanes and, later in the war, the new jet fighters. Other parts went into tanks and other armoured vehicles. Fittings were made for an ingenious device that checked the weight of bullets at the rate of seventy per minute and automatically rejected any that were incorrect. The drums for barrage balloons were machined and accessories for the shell-fitting plant manufactured.

Round the corner in Arden Street, Messrs Balls Brothers (Engineers) Ltd were making fabric for barrage balloons and parachute material. Their foundries maintained an enormous output of castings in grey iron, aluminium alloys and gun metal, the major proportion of which was for machine tools, jigs and press tools. During the course of the war, productivity rose by 60 per cent, although the workforce remained at pre-war levels. The staff made the increase possible by working longer hours.

In peacetime the foundry at the Royal Label Factory in College Lane produced road signs that went all over the world. Now it was converted to the production of sand castings for the Admiralty, the Ministry of Aircraft Production and the Ministry of Supply. A special staff, composed mainly of women, was recruited and trained. Not one of the 9,799,000 castings produced in the gas-fired furnaces was rejected. They were made in ten different alloys. Many of the 400,000 aluminium castings were used in the assembly of Halifax bombers, Beaufighters and Seafires. During the course of the war, no less than 19 million holes were drilled at the foundry. No discrepancy in the stated quantities of weekly dispatches was ever reported.

Messrs Howard Clayton-Wright of Tiddington Road was fulfilling defence contracts of considerable magnitude and secrecy. Products were sent as far afield as Russia and Burma. Over two million of one part was produced for the Admiralty. The company made the Harrisflex bearings on which the engines of most British aircraft were mounted. Other work for the Ministry of Aircraft Production included the manufacture of oil seals and tens of thousands of gaskets for fuel tanks, exhaust systems and undercarriages. Anti-vibration mountings were supplied for the protection of instruments in aircraft cockpits and for use on intercommunicating systems on warships. The Clayton-Wright designed recuperator rings were used on 17- and 23-pounder guns and were eventually adopted as standard.

Another Stratford company vital to the war effort was Messrs T.N. Waldron Ltd of Great William Street, whose owner had been Mayor at the outbreak of the war. The firm's work for the Admiralty was of such importance that its nature could not even be revealed at the end of the war. In addition parts for many different types of aircraft were made. At the peak of production, 40 tons of steel were being used on a single order and the company was licensed to procure as much as 30 tons of rolled brass at a time.

The works staff of the Wildmoor Engineering Company of Guild Street included a 'bright and breezy lad' of 71, who assisted in the assembly of throttle parts for four-engined bombers. Ingrams Garage on the Birmingham road was no less active, manufacturing over a million sten gun parts. The Aluminium Service Co. in Windsor Street was making die-castings for aircraft carburettors. Many orders for tank parts and gearbox castings were also fulfilled.

The German Blitz on manufacturing industry had been anticipated. In June 1940, the Coventry Repetition Company, which specialised in the mass production of small parts for aircraft, took over 'commodious' premises behind Guyver's Garage in Rother Street. A wide range of machinery was brought from Coventry. A hardening shop and testing house were erected. Skilled operatives moved to Stratford to train eighty-five workers to fill the 4,600 piecework hours per week needed to maintain production schedules. Mr R. Rotherham, the manager, was delighted with the result, reckoning that the majority of the trainees were more than equal to the job. He considered that women were just as good as men in many aspects of the work.

Another Coventry firm, Messrs John Harris Ltd, took over the Warwickshire County Garage on Waterside which was used for screwing ground-thread for aeroplanes and naval craft. To keep the machinery fully occupied the staff worked double shifts and at the peak of production were turning out 17,000 taps per week.

The machine-tool company, Messrs R.O. Gray, moved its combination lathes and heavy milling machines from Park Royal in north-west London to part of the old cattle market site at Bridge Foot. The move was undertaken at astonishing speed and Mr Gray expressed his gratitude to the Town Council for its help. At the new plant, propeller hubs were manufactured for Spitfire and Hurricane fighters and engine and gearbox parts for tank engines produced.

When war broke out, the Ministry of Food took over a half-built garage on the Birmingham Rod owned by the local entrepreneur Tommy Bird. It was used as a warehouse to store flour and sugar, but, after the Blitz on Coventry, it was taken over by the Ministry of Aircraft Production as a site for rebuilding the Kestrel engines of Miles Master trainers. The manufacturer, Messrs Alvis Ltd, sent Reginald Warner to Stratford as Foreman of Works to organise the relocation. It was a tough task. The building was a mere shell. Mr Warner recalled that there was

No glass in the windows, just a roof and four walls – no toilets. There was electricity and if you wanted water it was a lead pipe sticking out of the ground, but it didn't take long before the Ministry started sending things.

After a 'wonderful crane' made by the Ipswich firm of Ransome & Rapier arrived, 'we could lift the engines about'. Despite the difficulties, the workforce completed 100 engines in the first three months. 'Tell him we did it for Britain', was Reginald's response when the managing-director conveyed his congratulations. 'Everyone was patriotic when the war was on'.

Later the Merlin 20 and Bristol Pegasus engines of Lancaster and Wellington bombers were repaired there. Sometimes the engines were removed from the plane and taken to the factory by lorry. On other occasions, the engineers had to dismantle them *in situ* and salvage what they could.

Reginald Warner covered thousands of miles, many of them in the blackout, scouring aerodromes for spare parts in a new Morris 12 van that he was issued with by the RAF. It was painted in military grey. It was no easy task. Often he could see the parts that he wanted from the Maintenance Units on the shelves, but 'red tape' meant that he couldn't acquire them. Once, when the Corporal in charge was called away, he leapt the counter and took what he required 'because the war had to carry on'.

The relocated factory was a very busy place. Over 300 people – including seventy women – worked there on three eight-hour shifts. They were mostly recruited locally. At their peak, they turned out thirty-two engines a week. They were trained by Alvis's highly-skilled operatives. As demand grew, the floor space was expanded to six times its original size. A canteen and a sports and social club were provided. The Hippodrome in Wood Street was commandeered as a store. 'Everything to do with aircraft was stored there, cowlings and radiators and old cones'.

The work was vital to the war effort. The only other factory doing the same work was Morris Motors at Cowley. By the end of the war, more than 3,300 engines had been repaired. For obvious reasons, most Stratfordians had at best a vague idea of this huge industrial output. When young David Warner's teacher asked him what his dad did, he told her that he was a manager at Alvis. 'She looked completely nonplussed... She didn't even know there was an aircraft factory on the Birmingham road.'

India

The Dunkirk veteran Tony Hawkins married Vera Dyson at Holy Trinity in March 1941. It was during the prohibited season of Lent, but Tony had a forty-eight-hour leave so the vicar, Canon Noel Prentice agreed to marry them by special license. The ceremony reflected wartime austerity. Church bells were forbidden. There were no hymns because an organist was unobtainable and no white dress was available. The couple had no money, although Vera had got 'a bit of a bottom draw, which girls used to do in those days'.

On her 21st birthday in August, Vera was due for call-up. 'Please don't go in the services', said Tony, 'because I don't want you not to be here if I get leave', so she left Freeman, Hardy and Willis and got a job in a reserved occupation with Newton and Newey, the nurserymen on the Clopton road. Ironically, soon after, Tony's bridging unit was drafted to India, sailing from Dumfries 'as if they were going to America, to avoid those things with pimples on, and submarines and then they veered off to go to Bombay'.

Lance-Corporal Horace Davies of 102 Shottery Road had served in the Army in India since 1934. In 1942, he was transferred to the Military Police and was in Calcutta when the Japanese bombed the city on Christmas Eve. Civil unrest was in the air and the Military Police were involved in street fighting during which trams were overturned.

In January 1942, Chuck Taylor, aged 19, was called up into the 8th Battalion of the Worcestershire Regiment. He was pleased to be seconded into the infantry, where his

Home Guard training would stand him in good stead. He was posted to Cleethorpes, where his platoon was billeted in evacuated houses. It was the depth of winter and there were no fires, so it was 'blasted cold'. After further training at Richmond, they were kitted out with tropical gear and told they were going abroad. They assumed that this meant North Africa, although, as always, the location was not revealed. In January 1943, they embarked from Liverpool. The shipboard routine consisted of physical training, weapon training, lectures (especially on the medical dangers of the East!) and deck games:

> We went out by convoy and got to Gibraltar and half the convoy turned left and we kept going, and I thought, Christ, where the hell are we going?

They took on water at Freetown and went on to Durban where the ship's entry into the port was greeted by the famous 'Lady in White', the soprano, Perla Sielde Gibson, who greeted each arriving ship with patriotic songs sung through a megaphone. Chuck was deeply moved by the sound of her voice as it carried over the water and remembered it for the rest of his life.

After disembarking, Chuck found himself encamped on the racecourse. Several of his comrades were drafted to North Africa and newcomers joined them. The infantryman at this time could find himself wearing several cap badges in a short period. Chuck spent just four weeks with the 1st Battalion North Staffordshire Regiment before being posted to the 7th Battalion of the Leicestershire Regiment, which had arrived in Durban on 5 November. Two days later, they re-embarked aboard the Union Castle liner, *Capetown Castle*. He still had no idea of their destination. One day an old soldier stood next to him on deck and said 'Gateway to India, that's where we're going.' Sure enough, they arrived at Bombay and from thence travelled to Delhi, where they stayed for about six weeks.

The social system under the Raj was highly oppressive for 'other ranks' who were mainly confined to barracks. They weren't allowed to mix with the white women working for the army – 'and they didn't want to mix with you. All they wanted was officers. They didn't mix with ordinary privates.'

In Delhi, Chuck met six old soldiers who had been involved in the heavy fighting in Burma. The war had meant that their return home had been indefinitely postponed. One said he had been in India for thirteen years, 'Christ!' thought Chuck. 'I was due to go home', the soldier continued, 'that was a nine-year tour of duty and the war started and they couldn't get us back.'

'How are you ever going to get back?' asked Chuck. 'We'll wait for a boat and go across the Pacific to Canada and they are going to ship us across Canada and back to England.' Chuck never found out whether they made it, but was 'frightened to death' at the prospect of sharing their fate.

Tony Hawkins had arrived in Bombay. One very hot day, it was noticed that the electrical line on a nearby pole was malfunctioning. It was not his job to repair it, but he swarmed up it. When he reached the top, his tepee fell off, exposing him to the fierce sun. He suffered heatstroke and fell off the pole, severely injuring himself. At the hospital, Dr Pateliokov, a Russian émigré, diagnosed that he was suffering from Potts fracture (torn internal ligaments and a fractured fibula). After the long process of recovery, he was told he was C3, 'which means home to England'. Although many would have jumped at the chance, he was anxious to rejoin his unit that was preparing to transfer to the Burma front. 'I don't want to go before my mates', he replied. 'We've been together from the first.'

'There's only one way I can stop you being sent home', Dr Pateliokov told him, 'and that's if I keep you on to help me in the hospital'. This fulfilled his sense of duty, so, he spent the rest of the war as Dr Pateliokov's assistant, administrating injections and rendering all possible help to the 'marvellous' man he had grown to admire.

'C' Company, Home Guard, on exercise. (Image courtesy of the Shakespeare Birthplace Trust Records Office)

The Yanks are coming

With the German invasion of Russia, the Luftwaffe turned its attention eastwards and the mass bombing of Britain ceased, but, in retaliation for the RAF's bombing in Germany, 'Baedeker Raids' were launched, attacking places mentioned in the famous guidebooks that were of less strategic importance and therefore more vulnerable. Naturally, Stratfordians feared their town might be a prime target. The whispers of the year before began again. 'Have you heard that Haw Haw says they will raid Stratford on Friday?' When Friday passed the raid was transferred to Saturday. There was even a choice rumour that the Germans would bomb the tulip beds in New Place Gardens, which could hardly be considered a strategic target. As always no one had ever heard the broadcast personally. They had always been told about it by someone else. That it was highly unlikely that Lord Haw Haw would reveal German plans in advance seems to have escaped the rumourmongers.

The relaxation of the invasion scare was symbolised by the announcement in June 1943 that church bells could be rung again. Nevertheless, the Home Guard, by now an efficient fighting force, remained on full alert. Hundreds of men in Stratford were content to spend their spare time crawling through undergrowth to surprise a farmhouse where 'paratroopers' had landed, or in setting up road blocks to the annoyance of the local populace.

The birthday of 1942 demonstrated the note of cautious optimism about the progress of the war that was starting to permeate conversation. The fourteen flags of the Allied Nations were unfurled in Bridge Street. It was something of a dampener that six of them were still occupied by the Nazis, but it was a source of great satisfaction to see the Stars and Stripes fluttering in the breeze. The pleasure was not entirely strategic. An influx of American sightseers was anticipated: all in uniform! A Hospitality Committee was formed to greet them. The hope was fulfilled on 30 August when over 100 officers and men from the US Army visited the town. In November, a *Herald* reporter was amazed to see 45 American Negroes sitting on the riverbank singing *Way Down upon the Swanee River*. 'Not a sight or a sound to be forgotten.'

An American military band plays in Stratford. (Image courtesy of the Shakespeare Birthplace Trust Records Office)

Tommy Booker married Lillian Grace in May 1942 and the couple departed for a brief honeymoon in London. On the train home she met the Establishment Officer from the Treasury, who was on the way to Stratford to tell her section that they must vacate the White Swan for the Welcombe because the American Red Cross was going to take it over as a rehabilitation centre for wounded US officers.

The new influx had a salutary effect on the dormant tourist industry. The Birthplace was visited by 3,723 Americans in 1942 as against four in 1941. Local children learnt to use the catchphrase 'Got any gum, chum?' when they encountered GIs. The Americans were nothing if not generous, depositing unobtainable items like cocoa powder and orange juice at the Town Hall for children to collect. At Christmas, local children were invited to what Daphne Tizzard recalled as 'lovely parties' at the White Swan.

The potential for trouble in the local pubs was further increased as the home-based soldiers of various nationalities found a new set of better-paid rivals arriving to play court to the local women. There was often great tension at dances at the Town Hall and the Corn Exchange. The Green Dragon was another favoured battleground and the landlady, who was nicknamed 'Old Mrs Popery', would push the Americans out of one door and the British out of another. It was no use threatening troublemakers with the police. Most of the active force had been called up and been replaced by elderly 'Specials', who wisely kept out of harm's way. There was only one force of law-and-order respected by the soldiers, as Mary Hewins recalled:

> We didn't go out on Saturdays cos it so rough. We could hear it from the school. They'd be trouble at the Dragon – a dreadful commotion – then all of a sudden – whistles! The military police was there! Red Caps jumping out of army wagons. There was different regiments at the Long Marston Camp. They all went to the pub on their way back to camp. There were big fights. We couldn't get to sleep at home sometimes.

'The Americans came with the nylons and this that and the other', recalled Lillian Booker. 'All sorts of affairs were going on. It was wartime. What do you expect?'

One evening an American came down Kendall Avenue and knocked on a door. 'Do you mind if I have my watch?' he asked the boy who opened it. 'Where was it?' 'Up in the bedroom'. The conversation was conducted in loud voices, so most of the neighbours heard it.

A number of local girls married the strangers in their midst, including the Czechs and Canadians. Several of Beatrice Morgan's friends married Americans. They were

> so smart in their uniforms and seemed to be so well off... and the girls thought it was like that back home. Well it wasn't... I know some of them were very disillusioned when they went and found that their husbands lived in a bad place where there was no facilities... They stuck it out for a while and then came back to Stratford.

Some of them stayed on and were 'alright', however.

On the Buses

The problems in the pubs were as nothing to those on the Stratford Blue, whose buses had to take the boys back to their camps. 'They were awful, they were', said bus conductress Rosemary McAteer of the members of the Pioneer Corps they ferried to and fro to Long Marston. 'We used to take them back in the evening and had to sort them out occasionally.'

Another task was to take the Irish labourers back to the Atherstone aerodrome:

> You'd have perhaps 70-odd on the bus, but if you issued 40 tickets you were lucky, because one would buy six tickets and they would be passed down the bus and there were too many to argue about it.

The clippies had to wear skirts, which Rosemary did not think was a good idea on double-decker buses. One night as she was walking down the bus, an Irishman pulled up her skirt and shouted 'She's blue ones on tonight':

> I hit him on the head with my [ticket] punch and I split his head open. They were going to throw me through the window... I didn't let them see I was terrified. I just said I wouldn't collect any more tickets and stood on the back of the bus.
>
> I was up before the manager the next day. Of course the police were involved because he had to go to hospital to have stitches in his head. I told them what happened and the police chief said he fully agreed with what I'd done and he told the Manager that from then on he would have to arrange for either a man to travel on the bus, or to make it a contract bus, so it was made a contract bus. We still had to travel on it, because a double-decker in those days wasn't allowed out without a conductor... I was 25 then. I knew how to handle myself, I suppose.

'Worst of all', she considered, 'were the Canadian aircrews from Wellesbourne, especially the flyers. Some of them were so rude.' As a young girl with a job to do, she can be forgiven for not realising that these young men who had volunteered to come from afar could be dead next day, but she could deal with them:

> I would stand at the top of the bus. It was a front door loader and there were two steps down and, as they went to go, I put my foot out and tripped them into the ditch and word got around. No fooling with me!

Any Chance of a Game?

The thoughts of the military were turning to invasion. Michael Long of Manor Road had joined the 60th Rifles in 1942 and was commissioned later that year. At the end of 1943, he was transferred for training to the Glider Pilot Regiment in preparation for an airborne assault at a place as yet unknown.

As the fear of German invasion disappeared, thoughts turned to the post-war world. In February 1943, the Mayor called a meeting to discuss the Beveridge Report, which would lead to the foundation of the National Health Service.

Another sign of renewed optimism was the return of organised sport, although it was on an *ad hoc* basis. All the local sporting clubs had closed soon after the outbreak of war, but in 1943, Paul Bartlett, an enthusiastic footballer, erected a pair of goalposts on the Recreation Ground:

I got to know the Squadron Leader at Long Marston and also the Royal Engineers and I pitched them my story about not having this, that, and the other.

Paul told them that he wanted to provide a facility for the chaps coming home on leave and in no time he had two complete sets of football kit and six footballs:

However come twelve o'clock on Saturday, I never knew whether I'd got a team or whether I hadn't, because they used to come to my house and say they were home, any chance of a game? And from twelve o'clock till two o'clock I was scratting about trying to make up [a team], but then the Army and the Air Force bailed in again by saying, 'Well, if you're short of a bloke, just give me a ring and we will come out' and they used to send a lorry with half a dozen blokes...

A German prisoner of war football team. (Image courtesy of the Shakespeare Birthplace Trust Records Office)

Soon there were regular fixtures against teams from the Royal Engineers, the Pioneer Corps and the RAF.

The increasing numbers of German and Italian prisoners of war in the area started to organise football matches among themselves. Paul wondered what the reaction would be if he challenged them to a fixture, but the local players had no objections:

> In fact they got on very well with them. The War was forgotten. There was no carving up on the pitch or anything like that and the most surprising thing was that there were professional footballers from Germany and Italy and there were some brilliant footballers who played for their country taken prisoner of war and we had the privilege of playing against that type of player. The only difficulty for them was, whereas they were used to a good football ground, we played on the Rec, which was always flooded.

Shortages

The Nazi occupation of most of Europe and the U-Boat campaign led to grave shortages of most commodities. If victory were to be won, everything had to be conserved. Early in the war, two huge silos were built: a grain store by Lucy's Mill and a meat store behind the station. A tea store was erected on the Evesham road.

Shortages inevitably led to queues. This harmless activity earned the ire of the local Women's Council. Mrs S. Nichols was scathing about it. 'During the hours spent in queues, women, many of them from blitzed areas, talked, stories go round, often exaggerated, and people imagine all sorts of things might happen.' Mrs Muriel Waldron said the queues were for such 'luxuries' as cigarettes, cakes and tomatoes. Her butcher had told her that boys queued for items like sausages and then resold them with a mark-up. The shopkeepers contributed to the problem by posting such notices as 'Tomatoes will be served at 3.30 this afternoon.' Miss Hastings said that one local shop had ingeniously got round this by posting a notice saying that the first six people in any queue would not be served. Several ladies said that people should grow more of their own food.

The discussion brought a riposte to the *Herald* from Mrs Margaret Jones, an inveterate queuer, who pointed out that they had no fruit for their children and that their husbands were out from early morning till late at night. 'We have to pack lunches for them.' As for growing their own food, did the ladies of the Women's Council realise that many people in Stratford were evacuees and had no gardens?

In the same issue, James Barnard from Manchester, a regular Festivalgoer since 1921, voiced another grievance – profiteering. His lameness necessitated that he be driven about a good deal. A local taxi driver whose services he had often used, told him that he had increased his charges by 300 per cent. 'I told him that this was extortionate and that I would stay indoors, or limp my way along rather than pay his demands. Fortunately I obtained a much fairer and better deal elsewhere...'

The longest queues were for cigarettes and tobacco and it was anticipated that the shortage was likely to become more acute. Even when the smoker obtained his packet of fags, he could still be in trouble because of a shortage of matches. When a man walked into a tobacconist's and asked for six boxes, the assistant gaped at him in incredulity.

Unknown food items appeared. 'All sorts of funny fish were on display in Mr Kinman's shop, including whale meat and snook.' Hughes, the Bull Street butchers, made faggots once a week. They were not part of the meat ration, so people took their basins and queued.

Those in more strenuous jobs got extra rations. 'We got twelve ounces of cheese a week instead of the normal two or three ...' recalled Vera Hawkins, working in the market garden, 'because we were laborious workers.'

The Mayor of Stratford, Cllr Roderick Baker, receives his ration book, 1941. (Image courtesy of the Shakespeare Birthplace Trust Records Office)

Even beer was in short supply. There were complaints that many publicans locked the front door and admitted their regulars round the back, or that they simply served until the beer ran out and then shut. In June 1941, Flower's introduced a rationing scheme and asked their tenants to reserve a proportion of their beer for each period of opening.

Like most other employers, Flower's faced a problem of labour shortages. To plug the skills gap, they hired maltsters from Guinness's brewery in neutral Dublin. They were housed in a large caravan parked in Justin's Avenue. They proved good workers and kept the vital supplies flowing.

With beer as with everything else, priority was given to the war effort. By the end of the War, the brewery was supplying over 150 British and American service camps and depots, forty aerodromes, fifty canteens at munitions factories, twenty Home Guard and National Fire Service canteens, as well as Government construction camps and searchlight and anti-aircraft stations. Regular supplies of malt were dispatched to the Middle East for brewing purposes and monthly rations of bottled beer sent off to the fighting forces on many fronts. It was no wonder that ale was in short supply in the pubs.

The boys of the Grammar School also had their problems. It was impossible to obtain rugby boots or shirts in the school colours. An appeal went out to old boys to look in their bottom draws and send in whatever they found.

Inevitably there was a thriving black market. In its very nature this was undercover, surreptitious and little spoken-of. The *Herald* did reveal, however, that much of it was supplied by gangs who stole goods in transit. The contraband would be marketed through people in a position to make public contact. One such was the day guard at the Alvis store at the Hippodrome, a cockney. This exotic character had once been a member of the Music Hall troupe, Fred Karno's Army, and had taught Charlie Chaplin how to roller-skate. He was reputed to be a serial polygamist.

A 'Dig for Victory' shop window display. (Image courtesy of the Shakespeare Birthplace Trust Records Office)

Then there were 'under the counter' activities, in which regular customers received special favours from the shopkeepers. W.R. Batchelor had to stand to one side if a stranger came into the tobacconists in Bridge Street. Once he had been served and left, the goods were handed over.

A wartime institution, a British Restaurant, accommodating 130 diners, opened in the Corn Exchange on 12 November 1941. It provided a three-course meal and a cup of tea for 1/3*d*, but it was no gourmet's paradise. It was only open between noon and 2 p.m. and there was no lingering over the pudding. Patrons served themselves at a cafeteria and were expected to take no longer than quarter of an hour to eat up and depart. Nevertheless, it did over 500 covers on the first day. Later it served suppers for a mere 8*d*.

The theme of 'Dig for Victory' was taken up in no uncertain terms. Sheep reappeared on the Recreation Ground and part of the rugby ground at Pearcecroft was ploughed up. The humble pet rabbit was transformed into a food item, kept by many people in cages in the back yard. A Domestic Livestock Club formed to encourage sound breeding drew ninety entries at its rabbit and poultry show in 1942.

A fine example was set by the boys of the Hugh Clopton School in Alcester Road, where the playing fields were converted into a market garden and orchard. Tons of fresh produce flowed forth, including a number of varieties that would then have been regarded as exotic. In 1942, they produced 6cwts of beet; 1½ cwt of carrots; 1¾cwts of parsnips; 2cwts of turnips; 2cwt of kohl rabi; ¾ kale; 200 head of broccoli; 1¼cwts of purple sprouting; ½cwt of white sprouting; 80 cabbages; 100 Savoy cabbages; 3cwt of Brussels sprouts; 200 lettuces; 1½cwts of peas; 60lbs of runner beans; 20lbs of broad beans; 3 quarts of haricot beans; 200 cucumbers; 6cwts of ripe tomatoes; 2cwts of green tomatoes; ½cwt of endives; 40lbs of salsify; 2cwts of rhubarb and over 8 tons of potatoes.

Sometimes a returning soldier brought goodies from places where rationing was unknown. When Horace Davies returned after ten years in India in 1944, he brought supplies of tea and oranges.

The acute shortage of new vehicles meant that whatever was available was cannibalised for spare parts. Repair work became an urgent part of the activities at Archer's, the agricultural machinery manufacturers on the Birmingham road. The workers were proud that they always had the vehicles completed in time for the harvest.

Prisoners of War provided a useful source of agricultural labour under terms permitted in the Geneva Convention. Mary Hewins loved to see them go by. 'Oh and they were handsome, a lot of the German prisoners, fair hair, bright cheeks, only young chaps.... They used to wave to me and all, as they went up the Alcester road in lorries back to their camp. They waved and laughed. I think they were happy to be caught.'

Bob Bullard

With so many people in uniform, an ugly aspect of the Great War re-manifested itself. A wife, her husband and a young friend were sneered at in Wood Street and called 'scum' for not being in the War. The boy was under age, but his father and three brothers were in the forces. The husband had been all through the last war and was earning less than £5 a week doing essential war work for eleven hours a day. All three were evacuees who had been bombed out of their homes. They had slept for three months in a shelter before coming to Stratford.

One who bore such disapprobation like a battle honour was Bob Bullard, who had no intention of 'finding work of national importance', which he regarded as contributing to the war effort that he strenuously opposed. As a result he began to make regular court appearances. On 11 November 1941, he again failed to attend for medical examination and was later sentenced to nine months in prison for failing to obey the Court Order. On 3 November 1942, he was summoned to undertake agricultural work. 'I do not think it ought to be necessary to tell you', he told the Warwickshire War Agricultural Committee, 'I shall not be there on Monday.'

After this the Tribunal gave up on him. Instead he was summoned before the local magistrates where he got a sympathetic hearing. Stanley Warden, the solicitor appearing for the Ministry of Labour, told the bench that it was an unpleasant duty to prosecute a fellow townsman. A moral debate of high quality and mutual respect followed, with Bullard rehearsing classic pacifist arguments. 'To my mind', he told the court, 'there is no difference between doing work which I am ordered to do for the more efficient prosecution of the war and going into the Army.'

When the Chairman of the Bench, Cllr Trevor Matthews, asked him what work he was doing, he replied that he was helping his father in the fruit and veg trade.

When Cllr Matthews responded 'You don't mind helping in your father's trade, but not in anybody else's business?' Bullard replied that he was doing that before the war and because the state declared war, it did not therefore become war work:

Cllr Matthews: You see a difference between growing veg and selling them. You are prepared to benefit by the sacrifices other people are making, but are not prepared to contribute in any way.
Bullard: If I were prepared to help the war effort I would join up.
Cllr Matthews: You are helping the war effort. The only way not to help the war effort is to stay in bed. Is your attitude that you are willing to work for your present firm in distributing food for the nation, but you are not willing to assist in the production of food?

Bullard: I will admit it is a very thin point.

Cllr Matthews: And you would rather go to prison than solve that small point? If everybody carried out your line of argument we should all be in prison.

Bullard: There would not be a war then, would there?

Cllr Matthews: Is there the slightest chance that you are prepared to change your present attitude?

Bullard: I do not think so.

Cllr Matthews: The bench wants to be helpful if it can. Instead of acting as a neutral and helping neither side you are definitely helping the enemy.

Bullard: I do not want to help the Germans.

Cllr Matthews: But you are taking up the labour and time of other people...

Bullard: I am not doing it just to save my own skin...

Cllr Matthews: No, I don't think you are.

Councillor Matthews had probed severely, but not demolished, Bullard's case. The Court had no choice but to sentence him to a further three months in prison. When he was released from Stafford Gaol, he found that the most people in Stratford crossed the road to avoid him. A quarter century after the war, there were still those who snubbed him.

PoWs

Things were not too bad for Bertha Gover during her first year on the Polish estate, but the local inhabitants were suffering under the occupation. The Germans would round up the Poles for forced labour when they went to church and she had seen them with waiting with fixed bayonets and lorries at the bottom of the street. On the Feast of Corpus Christi in 1940, she warned three girls not to go to church, but they said it was a Day of Obligation. They did not return. She also saw the Nazis rounding up Jews.

Eventually an incautious remark about England made her captors suspicious and they kept a careful watch on her before arresting her in December 1940. She was sent to a crowded criminal prison where the diet consisted chiefly of bread, barley soup and ersatz black coffee. Fortunately, she was able to get a message through the Red Cross to her friends in England and they sent her food parcels.

Later Bertha was sent to an internment camp in a convent in Germany. It was also a lunatic asylum and the nuns were shielding 100 mentally ill people from the Nazis as well as looking after the 400 detainees. It was a great improvement on the prison. The nuns were very kind. There was plenty of fresh fruit and vegetables and the prisoners were allowed to go for occasional walks outside the walls under the supervision of a policeman.

At the chateau in France, Gertrude Bliss also enjoyed over a year of comparative freedom, but in September 1941, the Germans arrived at 6 a.m. and told her to pack up a few belongings before taking her to an internment camp at Vittel in the Vosges. Again she was comparatively well off. The 'camp' was in a large hotel situated in a park in which the internees were allowed to walk. The prisoners were treated well if they obeyed orders. She was put in charge of the hotel kitchen, which had several electric cookers. As a reward for taking on this responsibility, she was allowed to go for a walk outside the camp accompanied by German guards on about six occasions.

The food was very poor. Parcels from the Red Cross and food sent in by the local populace saved their lives. Apart from a few weeks at Christmas in 1942 when transport was difficult, the weekly Red Cross parcel never failed to arrive.

The internees had no contact with the outside world except through the Red Cross. It was not until eighteen months after the German invasion that Gertrude's mother in Stratford learnt of her whereabouts.

There were many nationalities interned at the camp. Very few were 100 per cent British, but there were many children of men who had married French women during the Great War who were British subjects.

When orders came for the deportation of the Polish Jews in the camp, some, knowing well their almost certain fate, committed suicide by various means. Apart from such awful incidents and the knowledge that the dreaded Gestapo had agents in the camp, life was fairly calm.

On 16 April 1942, the Lancaster bomber of W.O. Roy Salmon of Dale Avenue was attacked by a German fighter over the Champagne region of France. The rear gunner brought down the enemy plane, but was severely wounded and subsequently died. When the order was given to evacuate the stricken plane, Roy's flying boots were torn off by the slipstream as he sat on the hatch while preparing to parachute. He descended into a river and then stumbled into a bog. When a German search party found him, he felt it was no use arguing with an enemy who was pressing the muzzle of a gun against his ribs. After his capture, he was not allowed to wash for a week. Battered and bruised, he was locked in a guardroom with his companion's blood-soaked flying kit on the floor. He was then conveyed by public transport to a reception camp for PoWs in an obvious gesture to impress the civilian population. Before interrogation, he was put in a room with closed windows in which the heat had been turned up to 50°C which took 'all the stuffing' out of him. He was then conveyed to the PoW camp at Fallingbostel. This became a 'reprisal camp' on 10 January 1943 when the palliasses, tables and forms were taken away because the Germans said that their prisoners in Tunisia had been treated in the same way.

The first member of the Stratford Air Training Corps to win his wings was Ray Hartwell of 175 Evesham Road, whose family were in the building trade. In August 1943 when he was 22, the Stirling bomber he was piloting over Berlin was set ablaze by a German fighter. The crew baled out and were taken prisoner.

Edward Howell was proving a troublesome prisoner. He was beaten up after he refused to be inoculated, not trusting its purpose. He was given the task of filling petrol cans destined for the Russian front and filled them with water rather than petrol, so contributing in his small way to the German defeat at Stalingrad. When his activities were discovered early in 1943, he was banished to a *Strafe* [punishment] camp near Breslau.

Many prisoners used their ample spare time to enhance their future careers. Warrant Officer E.G. Evans gave lectures on accountancy and became head of the educational bureau in his camp that was formed to help for his fellow prisoners enhance their prospects after the war. He was no slouch himself. In December 1942, the Institute of Industrial Administration informed his wife that he had passed its Part C exam with distinction and that he had been elected an Associate Member.

Sergeant Air-Gunner Ronald Worrall from the Evesham Road was taking a course on bookkeeping and learning shorthand. In an obvious move, he started to learn German, but found that he was pressed for time with all his other activities. He had written home to apply for membership of the Caterpillar Club, an organisation for those who had bailed out when their plane was shot down, so giving his family an indication of the manner of his capture.

Bill Winter was having a miserable time. The Italian camps were filthy and the guards brutal. One camp was condemned by the Red Cross. It was sited in a bog and conditions were extremely unhealthy. The food was so terrible that, without the regular Red Cross parcels, the prisoners could barely have survived. He eventually found himself in a camp where he was obliged to do farm work. The prisoners were promised double rations as it was heavy work. They got the heavy work, but not the double rations. When they protested and laid down tools, the Italians stopped all rations until work resumed. He lost 3st 4lbs in ten weeks. At least the Italian peasants were sympathetic. They hated the war and blamed Mussolini bitterly for having plunged them into it.

The terrible food was a common theme for all PoWs. From camps from Poland to Italy, the message was the same: without the regular Red Cross parcels they would barely have survived.

Despite the promises of his desert captors that he would be well looked after, Harold Dornborough found the food and medical attention at Caserta Hospital very poor. Respite came early in 1943, when the Red Cross organised an exchange of wounded and disabled British and Italians prisoners. Harold and Gunner Tom Barr were thrilled to be transferred to the repatriation centre at Lucca. On the long train journey to Lisbon, they passed through France. Despite the presence of their German guards, wherever they stopped the peasants would ask them to come back soon.

After long months of captivity, Lisbon seemed very heaven. Nurses from their hospital ship were waiting on the platform as the train pulled in and gave them packets of cigarettes and the first English newspapers they had seen in months. They were taken to a café for cups of tea and then driven to lunch at the English Club. On their way to the ship, they sang war songs and 'She'll be coming round the mountain...' to the nurses.

Things were getting bad in Bertha Gover's nunnery. The internees had been crowded into another building to make room for refugees from the bombing in Berlin. Bread was in short supply and most of the available food went to the army. In October 1943, she was told she was going to be repatriated via Lisbon and was taken to Berlin where she witnessed an RAF bombing raid. On her journey across Germany the huge numbers of forced labourers amazed her. 'Hitler has filled the whole place with foreigners.' On her return to Stratford she told the *Herald* that she was convinced that the Germans were beginning to realise that they were beaten.

The Great Escape

The amenities at the Stalag Luft III for aircrews at Sagan in Poland were regarded as superior to those of the average camp. Pilot Officer Ray Hartwell was there at Christmas, 1943. Decorations were created from odds and ends like the labels from salmon and meat tins and a lantern out of a Red Cross box. Their food parcels were 'first class' and they sat down to a seven-course Christmas dinner, washed down by homemade raisin wine and beer provided by the Germans. They slept it off in the afternoon, but woke to attend 'an excellent show' in the evening.

The show was a panto, *Little Red Riding Hood*, put on by Bruce Organ, who had used his thespian experience to good effect, playing the leading lady in Gaslight and producing an open-air production of *Midsummer Night's Dream* with costumes scrounged from the bemused Germans in Berlin. His tour-de-force came when he played Hamlet. This theatrical panache was put to great effect in the episode that became known as the Great Escape. From the supposedly escape-proof camp, three elaborate tunnels were dug that were dubbed 'Tom, Dick and Harry'. They had to be shored up with wood, so bed boards were utilised. As the tunnels grew longer and more wood was needed, many prisoners found themselves sleeping uncomfortably on beds that had little support. A skilled forgery department manufactured maps, papers and disguises.

The tunnel 'Tom' was discovered, but 'Harry' was completed. The mass escape was scheduled for the night of 24 March 1944. Lots were drawn for the 200 places. As cover, Bruce put on a roisterous production in the assembly hall. At the time, he may have thought that he had drawn 'the short straw', but events were to prove him fortunate.

On the designated night, the escapers assembled in hut 104. Unfortunately the tunnel emerged 10 yards short of its target in nearby woods and on the direct path of German patrols. It was not till 10 p.m. that a system was worked out to inform the escapers that the coast was clear. It was decided to close the escape at 5 a.m., but, at 4.45 a.m., a shot rang out. The tunnel had been discovered. Seventy-six prisoners had escaped. Only three made it home. Twenty-three lucky ones were soon recaptured and returned to the camp. This saved their lives because when Hitler heard about the escape, he ordered the execution of the other 50 recaptured prisoners. When the inmates of Stalag Luft III were told of this, their morale dropped to a new low, which was deepened when an urn containing the ashes of those who had been shot was brought to the camp. The prisoners built a memorial to them. It may have brought some retrospective comfort to know that the escapees had diverted thousands of police, Hitler Youth members and soldiers from the war effort.

The Greek Mutiny

Although Fred Morris was well away from the war, life was not without its dramas. On 6 April 1944, the camp's ammunition dump exploded:

> All the windows went west. Shook us all rigid. A wog came walking in later. Got all his clothes blown off him. A lot of wogs injured I think.

Fred wrote that it was 'something to do with the Greek mutiny'. Following Italy's capitulation, the Greek Monarchists and the Communists had each formed Governments-in-Exile. The Communists demanded that the King pledge that he would not return to Greece before a post-war plebiscite. This he refused to do. The five remaining ships of the Greek Navy, operating as a unit under Royal Navy command, were in harbour at Alexandria. The sailors mutinied in support of the Communist claims and were joined by a considerable number of Greek soldiers from Fred Clarke's camp. By the end of April, the British had suppressed the rebellion, arrested the ringleaders and interned 20,000 Greek servicemen.[1]

On 22 July, a Greek Court Martial passed death sentences on four members of the crew of the warship, *Saktouris*, who were regarded as leaders of the rebellion. 'Bags of panic', Fred Morris recorded a week later. One of the Greek mutineers under sentence of death had escaped. He does not record the poor man's fate, but if he got away from the perimeter he might have stood a chance. Alexandria possessed a considerable Greek population, some of whom might have been sympathetic to the mutineer's cause. On 23 September, Fred saw a wedding party going into a Greek church there, so he went in with two friends:

> Funny sort of ceremony. People wandered around the church. The pair wore crowns joined together, which are swapped over several times. They drink a glass of wine and walk round the table. I wanted to kiss the bride, as everyone seemed to queue up for it, but Jim got windy and went out, so Jack and I followed him. A lady at the door gave me a box of sugared almonds.

Disparaging as the terms were in which described the local population, like many other British soldiers, Fred began to realise that there was a local culture of interest and charm. 'Native holiday tomorrow, "Shem-el-Nessim"',[2] he recorded on 16 April 1944:

> Wogs singing all night. Bells ringing. Heard 3 natives (1 girl, 2 men) harmonizing a wog song in the night and it was a most haunting melody.

This benignity lapsed a few months later. He was on an open-top bus when 'a blasted wog' jumped onto the side and tried to snatch his 'specs':

> I twisted my head away and knocked my pipe out of my mouth, broke off a tooth and the pipe dropped on the lap of the lady next to me. I did cuss, but the bus had gone too far to stop.

In October, Fred's section was transferred to the Field Signals Unit bound for Southern Italy. Someone in the Unit was clearly demob happy. 'A hell of a stink this morning', wrote Fred on 21 October, 'some silly blighter slung a lot of s*** over the CO's door, so everyone is confined to camp'.

Moral Values

The perceived decline in moral values brought about by the war was revealed at a meeting of the Diocesan Council for Moral Welfare at the Town Hall on 18 May 1943. Miss Steele, an army welfare officer, expressed great concern about the many cases of marital infidelity: not only by husbands, but wives too. Numerous homes had been broken up and the war was doing disastrous things to individual lives. There had been a great increase in the number of children born to unmarried parents and to married people who had separated from their partners. Many of these were quite young and they should be regarded as casualties of the war.

One of the greatest problems was that adolescent girls were able to dress attractively and look like older women and could pick up men from the military camps quite easily. They were completely irresponsible and difficult to reason with. There had nothing in their education enabling them to handle such situations.

As a result, there had been a great increase in the incidence of venereal disease. Some people said that this was nothing to do with morals, but purely a health matter. Miss Steele had strong views on the issue:

> Are we going to accept that? Is it sufficient to combat venereal disease merely by use of prophylactics or to deal with the unmarried mother merely by encouraging contraceptives?

A practical demonstration of the scale of the problem came in July 1944 when the Ministry of Health approved the adaptation of the little-used first aid post in the Poor Law Institution as a VD clinic at a cost of £360. Although the new miracle drug of penicillin could be used in the treatment of sexually transmitted diseases, its virtual non-availability meant that ineffective traditional methods were used which did little to stem the epidemic. After the war, Captain Alfred Dixon of the US Army told the Men's Fellowship at the Birmingham Road Methodist Church that VD could be abolished everywhere if legislation could be passed ensuring the detection and treatment of all cases within a limited time.

Two cases illustrating Miss Steele's concerns came to court shortly after her talk. In November 1939, a 20-year-old factory girl, Margarita Fisher, met Ronald Jacques, a 25-year-old Private in the Northumberland Fusiliers, who was stationed locally. He told her he was single and a romance developed. In February 1940, he was posted elsewhere, but they continued to correspond. In December 1940, he came in uniform to her mother's house at 4 Park Road and told her he was being discharged from the army. His papers would be coming through and he would obtain work locally. On 26 September 1942, they went through a form of marriage at St James' Church and lived together at her mother's house until he was arrested on a charge of desertion.

There was more to follow. On 1 June 1943, in the Borough Police Court, he pleaded guilty to bigamy. Elizabeth Jacques, his real wife, who was four years older than he, told the court that she had married him on 19 March 1932. He was only 17. Three months later she gave birth to a son. The relationship had never been happy due to his womanising. They had lived together until September 1939, when he had joined the army. She had last seen him when he had a three-day leave in December 1940. A month later he was posted as a deserter and her allowance was stopped.

The prisoner asked her from the dock if she intended divorcing him, but the Clerk, Mr L.C. Haynes, said that had nothing to do with the case. A month later Miss Fisher told the Assize Court at Warwick that she wanted to continue living with him. Passing a sentence of six months imprisonment, the Commissioner, Sir Walter Monkton KC, declared that 'bigamy is prevalent and serious'.

In 1940, 17-year-old Edith Ingram of 9 Swincotes had started to go out with a Czech Cadet Officer. Before the war, Staff Sgt Josef Schnelle had been a medical student, but now he hoped to stay on in the army. They wanted to get married, but her parents refused their consent, so Edith applied to the magistrates for permission to marry him. The case was heard on 15 June 1940.

Edith's father told the court that they had refused consent because their daughter was too young to marry and did not know her own mind. They had nothing personal against Josef, but he would want to go back to his own country after the war and they would lose touch with their daughter. If the couple were prepared to wait until the New Year and were then of the same mind, he would willingly give his consent.

The Mayor, Cllr Roderick Baker, said that the Bench could quite understand the parents' apprehension about their daughter marrying a foreigner, but this was not a matter for the magistrates to consider. There was no reason why they should refuse the daughter's application and they hoped that the young couple would be happy and that the parents would forgive and forget and take them back into the home.

Two months later the couple were married at St James Church, Alveston, but the parents do not seem to have been present. Enid's case is interesting for a number of reasons. The magistrates clearly considered that it was better for the young couple to marry rather than to cohabit as they might well have done if permission had been refused. It is noteworthy from Mr Ingram's evidence that, by the middle of 1943, there was a general assumption that the war would be won, rather than the previous vague hope that it might be.

The decline of moral values was having an effect on the war effort. Sergeant Ted Eborall who had spent two years on active service in the Middle East with the Royal Artillery was given compassionate leave because of his wife's illness. It was what he described as 'a queer voyage home':

> Many of the men on the ship were also on compassionate leave. Most of them were not happy about it, since they were coming to deal with problems like wives who had left them, homes that had been destroyed, and loved ones who had been killed or vanished.

This social disorientation caused odd situations. In January 1945, a 15-year-old local girl, who is kept anonymous by subsequent events, met Alexander Innes, a 30-year-old Glaswegian at a dance. He was a soldier in the Royal Engineers stationed at Long Marston. He came from 'a good family' and had been a solicitor's clerk, a probationer constable and a commercial traveller. She took him home to meet her parents who assumed he was single. He stayed at her house quite frequently on weekend leave. One night at the pictures, the girl told him she would be 16 in the following September. He told her she looked older. One evening while they were walking in a meadow by the river she told him she loved him and they had sexual intercourse for the first time.

When Innes was demobbed in January 1946, he stayed at the girl's home for a fortnight and asked the mother if he could marry her. She told him that her daughter was too young, but spoke to the father, who would not hear of it. Perhaps in the hope that the issue would go away, they agreed to an engagement, but Innes said that he was only interested in marrying her.

Innes returned to Stratford at the beginning of March and the parents agreed that he could take her to Glasgow to meet his parents, but in fact they went to Aberdeen. Soon after he took the girl away again. As they were preparing to leave she saw his army pay book and realised that he was married with a child. Nevertheless she went away with him and they lived together as man and wife in Leeds. The parents heard nothing for some time, until they received a telegram from their daughter: 'RETURNING HOME THIS WEEKEND. DON'T WORRY.' When she did not appear, her two brothers went up to Glasgow to try and trace her. They made enquiries of the police who put out an arrest order and detained Innes on a charge of underage sex when he made a return visit to Glasgow.

In July, at Stratford Magistrates Court, Innes claimed that he was unaware that the girl was underage. He was committed to Warwick Assizes. Earlier that day the girl, who was now 16, was made the subject of a supervision order by the Juvenile Court as being in need of care and protection. It was the first time the parents had seen her since March.

At the November Assize, Innes' defence counsel told the court that this was a case that arose from 'war conditions'. There was no doubt that the couple would marry if it were possible. This did not prevent his client from receiving eight months imprisonment. Mr Justice Singleton said it would be a good thing if he kept away from the girl for some time.

Chindits

After he had been in India for a few months, Chuck Taylor's company was summoned on parade. The Medical Officer, who was nicknamed 'Basher', arrived and told them that they were all having an examination.

'Anyone who has had "a certain disease" that way', he said. 'Anybody who has had malaria that way: everybody who has had something else that way and everybody who is over thirty over there. Right, has anyone any complaints?'

'Of course', recalled Chuck. 'You never answered any questions like that in the Army.'

'So right', said the M.O., 'you are all A1 pluses'.
Another officer then took over. 'Right, you have been chosen for a special force and you all had to be A1 plus to go on it. Now, are you sure no-one has any complaints?'

No one said a word. 'So', he continued, 'you are going on jungle training and you are going to do what they call "long-range penetration" with Wingate.'

None of them had heard of Orde Wingate, but they were about to become part of his legendary 'Chindits', the 3rd Indian Army he organised for guerrilla warfare in the jungle behind the Japanese lines.

At the training camp, volunteers were called for to look after the mules that would provide the transport for the two Chindit columns. Chuck was used to horses – his father had been a carter on a farm in Tiddington – so he and his mate got themselves detailed to the Mule Transport Section. They had to travel eighty miles to the nearest railhead to collect a few animals at a time. The mules, which had been imported from Australia, varied tremendously in size. Some were not much bigger than Old English Sheepdogs: others were monsters the size of a Shire horse.

When the full complement of seventy-five mules was assembled, the muleteers had to train them to carry loads. Chuck really enjoyed this. He had been assigned a mule called Queenie, who was relatively docile, but some of the soldiers had great difficulty and received not a few injuries from hooves and teeth. A great deal of time was spent in practicing river-crossings. The mules could swim, but were often reluctant to do so.

When the training was over, the mules were operated upon to remove their voice boxes, lest their loud braying gave their position away. They were then moved up to an American Air Force base in Burma in stages. 'I have never seen such a shambles in my life as those Yanks', Chuck recalled. 'How we won the war I shall never know.'

There were some gliders that were standing on the runway. 'I hope by Christ', that we never go in them bloody things', said Chuck's mate. He was taking a risk with his language. The strictly evangelical Wingate put anyone heard swearing on a charge.

The hope was forlorn. It was announced that the Americans would fly them behind the enemy lines in the gliders and they would take the mules with them. Charlie watched the first contingent depart:

> The cables were hooked up to a Dakota and all of a sudden the…plane set off in a wink, just got into the air and snatched these nylon ropes, and they used to kind of stand still – you would see them standing still. They were straining and all of a sudden you would see the elastic in those ropes took it and away it went. Just imagine, fourteen men in one of those blasted things. They were only canvass, tube and canvass. If there was a mule in there, there wouldn't be as many men, but you fancy having a mule in there. They are some of the wickedest damn things you ever knew.

By 4 April, the entire brigade had been flown to a prepared landing strip dubbed 'Aberdeen'. 'Operation Thursday' as it was code-named, was the largest airborne landing in history to that point. After a spell on stronghold defence, 47 Column headed north-east into the jungle to harass the Japanese. Chuck found that the saddles to carry the loads were well designed. Queenie was transporting a Vickers Medium Machine-Gun. The column was supplied by hazardous parachuted airdrops.

'Through Agony and Death'

After nine months as an instructor at the GHQ School of Battle, Richard Spender volunteered for the Parachute Regiment in October 1942. Next month he sailed for Africa with the 2nd Battalion. During the night of 28 March 1943 he was killed leading his men against German machine-gun positions at Sedjenane in Tunisia. *Parachute Battalion*, his slim volume of his poems was published posthumously:

> To-day some silent valley of Tunisia
> Shall tremble at their stroke from sky unsheathed,
> And, with the night, perhaps some God looking down
> With dull, cold eyes, by the near stars, will see
> One lonely, grim battalion cut its way
> Through agony and death to fame's high crown,
> And wonderingly watch the friendless strength
> Of little men, who die that the great Truths shall live.

Lieutenant Jack Tompkins, son of the Borough Treasurer, won the Military Cross in Tunisia. He had gone to Birmingham University to study law, but had joined the machine-gun section of the 6th Cheshire Regiment. On 20 April 1943, his platoon came under heavy mortar fire at Point 130 near Endaville. Fearing for the safety of his guns, equipment and men, he moved to another position and engaged the enemy until his ammunition ran out. Point 130 was retained and no equipment lost.

Among the skills that Arthur Walton had gained with the Royal Engineers was the hazardous business of mine clearance. He was to prove his worth in the 1st Army's invasion of Algeria before going over the Atlas Mountains to link up with the 8th Army in the fight for Tunis.

The expulsion of the Germans from Africa was followed by the return of the allies to Europe with the invasion of Italy. Kenneth Smith from Greenhill Street, a corporal in the RAF Regiment, was killed while supervising the disembarkation of a vehicle from a landing craft on the beach near Reggio Calabria. He was operating the braking device when the vehicle skidded throwing him against the side of the ship. He died shortly afterwards.

Notes

[1] The American commentator, Robert Higson, considered that the incident marked the start of the Cold War.

[2] Shem-al-Nessim is the festival marking the first day of spring.

SEVEN

'YOUR FEET FELT LIKE LEAD'

'I congratulate you'

In the chaos following the Italian capitulation, many PoWs took the opportunity to escape. Robert Lysons left Camp 78 with a number of companions on 12 September 1943. They faced a dilemma: whether to make for Switzerland or the Allied lines, or to try to survive until the area was liberated. They decided on the latter, but when it became clear that the progress of the 8th Army was slower than they'd hoped, they made a dash for the lines and were recaptured on 30 November. Robert's parents heard nothing from him until February 1944, when they received a printed card stating that he was a PoW in Germany. A week later a card arrived from him apologising for causing them concern and acknowledging that they should have taken a different course of action, 'but it's wasteful to have regrets'.

Fred Ryman, who did not make an escape bid, was also transferred to a PoW camp in Germany.

On their Italian farm, Bill Winter and Philip Robilliard had made friends with a girl from a nearby village. When Italy showed signs of collapsing after the Sicily landings, she promised to help them escape when the time was right. When the Italian Government sought an armistice, she conveyed the news to them in an apple, cunningly hollowed out and pieced together again. At her home, civilian clothing, maps and food awaited them. The British lines to the south were still too far off, so they boarded a goods train heading north before spending a gruelling five days making their way through the Alps towards Switzerland. Bill was barefoot. His canvas shoes had long perished. Philip was in better shape. Before the war he had been a fisherman and he was tough.

Near the Swiss border, the two companions saw a German patrol barring their way and hid in a wood. A providential thunderstorm sent the patrol to cover and, well nigh exhausted, they slipped across what they hoped was the frontier. They had not gone far when a patrol consisting of an officer, three soldiers and an Alsatian dog, challenged them to halt in German. They froze. 'After all this trouble and hardship', thought Bill, 'we bump into a German patrol. Of all the rotten luck!'

The officer asked them who they were in German. 'Englander' replied Bill.
The officer stepped forward and stretched out his hand. 'I congratulate you', he said in English. 'You are in Swiss territory.' Bill passed out.

The exhausted but thankful pair were given first aid at the nearest sentry post. They were interned in Locarno and then in a camp on the shores of Lake Constance where they had the strange experience of watching the RAF bomb Friedrichshaven across the water while feeling perfectly secure.

Sleek-haired Romeos

The transition of Italy from enemy to ally posed the dilemma of what to do with its PoWs? The answer was to redefine them as 'co-operators'. Richard Reid of Beechwood House on the Alcester road was not happy with this. Whenever he walked through Stratford he saw 'our gallant soldiers' who had been wounded while fighting 'to rid the world of Hitler and his Nazi thugs and make the world fit for all to live in:

> They try to enjoy themselves on 10/- a week, and I'm sure they would (as the English Tommy puts up with lots of things) if they did not see, breathing the Stratford air, those Italians who were killing and wounding their fellow troops only a few months ago.

The Italians could do almost anything they pleased. They could go to the pictures and theatre and go boating. Bombed out Londoners were given second place to them when it came to housing and they had special reserved coaches on some trains. Worst of all, young English girls were 'fraternising with these sleek-haired Romeos':

> Any day now I expect a 'Salute the Italian Airman Week' in aid of those gallant airmen who sent a special request to Hitler asking him to permit them to take part in the bombing of London. The sooner a few divisions of these co-operators are sent to fight against the ideals they not so loyally tried to defend, the happier the English people will be.

The Picture House was indeed crowded with Italians. Hundreds stood in the queue, which snaked all the way down Greenhill Street and into Arden Street. Most didn't speak enough English to follow the films, but they went anyway.

At the Hospital, Auxiliary Nurse Marcelle Méliès was ordered to dress the wound of an Italian prisoner of war who had undergone the extremely painful experience of having a piece of shrapnel lodged in his penis. She assessed the amount of bandaging required but, when she started to do the task, she found it insufficient for obvious reasons.

The German PoWs remained in custody, but those who were deemed to be 'anti-Nazi' – sixty in all – were housed separately at Ettington Park.

Fearsome Battles

On the road to Rome, Arthur Walton was dealing with unexploded mines during the fearsome battles at Monte Cassino, regarded as some of the toughest of the war:

> We ended up digging up mines with our bayonets because the enemy started using 'pumpkin mines' which were made out of glass and paper, so the metal detectors were useless.

On Longstop Hill, scene of some of the fiercest fighting, he was severely wounded when a shell burst overhead, sending shrapnel through his stomach.

In August 1943, 34-year-old Pte Bill Mitchell left his pregnant wife and three young children at 54 West Street to sail for the Mediterranean. Before joining up he had worked for Messrs Smith and Unitt, the builders. This popular figure had played Rugby for the town and for many years been a scoutmaster and a trustee of the Methodist church. In January 1944, he participated in the Anzio landings and received severe shrapnel wounds to the neck and head during the German counter-attack. He was treated by stretcher-bearers, but in the confusion of retreat had to be left. It later emerged that he had died of his wounds. Two months later his wife gave birth to his child. It was not till November 1944 that his grave was found in the Military Cemetery.

On leaving Malvern College in 1941, Dick Stokes-Roberts joined the 'Young Soldiers' Battalion of his father's regiment, the Hampshires. He was later commissioned into the Grenadier Guards and died on 22 June 1944, during the breakout from the Anzio beachhead. He was awarded a posthumous Military Cross.

Second Front

Recognition of the major contribution being made by the Russians towards the defeat of Hitler came in November 1944 when the employees of Messrs N.C. Joseph raised £150, which was matched by the directors, to endow two beds in the hospital at Stalingrad.

A Stratford branch of the Communist Party made its sole appearance in the local press on 17 September 1943 when the *Herald* reported that it had passed an inevitable resolution calling for a Second Front against the Germans.

For the troops allocated to the Normandy invasion, there had been a long wait on the home front. 'D' Company had been moved around about every three months. Many of its members had been transferred to other regiments to serve in Africa or the Far East and some had become officers. They were replaced by men from other regiments, so although there were still quite a few Stratfordians in its ranks, it was no longer a purely Stratford Company.

Jack Hall had always been left behind during the transfers, but now he was to return to the France he had left four years before. The ex-builders, Joe Pitts and Don Clark were now Royal Marine commandos. Joe's platoon had been training on an LCP (Landing Craft Personnel) at Invergordon.

'We had trained hard and were well disciplined', recalled Don. 'Paramount of all those things though was comradeship. Even during the practice landings we lost a few people.' After the training period, they went down to Portsmouth. On the night of 4 June 1944, they embarked aboard a LCVP (Landing Craft, Vehicle and Personnel):

> We went out to sea on the Tuesday, but it was too rough, so we returned to Portsmouth. Then the next day we had to go. They knew if we didn't go then, we would have to wait for a very long time before the tide was right again.

They arrived on Gold Beach in the half-light of dawn on 6 June 1944. The fearsome barrage from the warships in support of the invasion was still roaring overhead, but some shells were falling short, which increased the hazards faced by the troops:

> If anybody was shot down next to you as you were coming up from the landing craft, you didn't stop. You had to save yourself. Your feet felt like lead. You don't feel like you can move. You were scared. Everybody was. It was wicked, but there were thousands. I was just one of many.

Joe Pitts' LCVP arrived at Sword Beach at 7.25 a.m. His duty for the next three hours was to ferry troops from HMS *Ranpura* onto the beaches. They were shelled from Le Havre by the Germans. 'HMS *Belfast* was out by the cliffs trying to get them before they got us. They didn't get them all though.'

> We were trained for it. You've got a job to do and you just do it. We were with the people who we had gone through training with. There was a great sense of camaraderie.

Don Clark's platoon fought its way to Port-en-Besin, where they linked up with the Americans. He was given the task of escorting German prisoners back to Mulberry Harbour on Gold Beach. When they paused on the sands, he got out his cigarettes, which he made sure were always kept dry:

> This German looked at me, so I asked if he wanted one. I passed the packet round, but they didn't take one each. They broke them in two and shared them. It just goes to show what type of people they were. They were only our age. If we hadn't been fighting as enemies we would probably have been friends.

For six weeks, the Royal Warwicks suffered greatly in the fierce fighting in the Normandy fields. An anonymous correspondent with 'D' Company provided a graphic picture of what Waldron's Warriors were up against:

> Every yard of the country and all main and secondary roads were mined and booby-trapped. Men who paused to rest for a few minutes, leaning against the high-banked hedgerows, were killed by box mines placed in the hedges. Infantry casualties were numerous. Every orchard had its well-placed enemy mortar pits, Spandaus (machine-guns) covered all approaches and German snipers strapped themselves to the high branches of trees clothed in heavy, almost tropical foliage.

There were 800 casualties. The nature of the battlefield meant that some three quarters of these were in the rifle companies of the infantry Battalion. 'D' Company took so many casualties in the Falaise pocket that it was disbanded. The remnants were fed into other units as reinforcements. Waldron's Warriors were no more.

There was only one officer in the infantry Battalion who wasn't killed or wounded. Norman Watson had attained the rank of Captain and served as ADC to General Steele. Before the invasion he was on the staff of Brigade HQ, but had been transferred to active service. He was killed in the second phase of the invasion in early July.

Corporal Gordon Mucklow began his army career in the Warwicks, but was transferred to the Duke of Cornwall's Light Infantry through a bureaucratic error. He was involved in the heavy fighting around Caen, destroying two tanks with his PIAT mortar. He was about to tackle a third when a burst of shrapnel hit his loader who fell dead over him. He was lucky to escape with his sight. His glasses were smashed, an eardrum perforated by the blast and he was severely wounded in his left arm and hand. He spent nineteen weeks in a Scottish hospital before being discharged from the forces. It was hoped that he would make a full recovery and arrangements were made for him to reopen his grocery business in Chapel Street. He was later awarded the Military Medal.

The 4th Battalion, the King's Shropshire Light Infantry (4th KSLI) had become part of the 11th Armoured Division which had trained specifically for the Normandy campaign. Now its moment had come. Charlie Baldwin had been promoted to a Platoon Sergeant with 'C' Company. When the Battalion embarked from Tilbury, the dockers were on strike and refused to load their transports so they had to do it themselves. They sailed through the Straits of Dover and lay off the Isle of Wight to await the arrival of ships carrying the rest of the division. They landed near Arromanches on D-Day plus 2. On the beach, Charlie picked up a mussel shell. He carried it with him through the rest of the war. The regiment advanced to relieve the forces holding Pegasus Bridge, where the first airborne landings had taken place.

The Warwickshire Yeomanry, by now equipped with Churchill tanks, was involved in the invasion. In July, Major H.N. Hopkins of Merrienmeet, Tiddington Road, the Second-in-Command, took the surrender of fifty-six men in German uniforms. 'Pale and emaciated-looking after living for weeks in holes in the soil of Normandy, a batch of enemy soldiers ran from a wood shouting "No shoot. We Pole and Czech."'

In the immediate aftermath of D-Day, news came to Gertrude Bliss's internment camp that English prisoners were to be repatriated. They were examined by an English doctor and on 13 July, they were taken to the railway station to embark for Lisbon. After remaining on the train for many hours, they were told that they could not proceed because the Allies had blown up the tracks.

They finally set off on 24 July. The fighting in Normandy meant that they had to follow a circuitous route via Lyons, Avignon, Toulon and Perpignan. Time and again the train had to go back because the track had disappeared or bridges had been destroyed. There were air raids en route, but the train was not hit. The journey across Spain was an ordeal. They were not allowed to leave the train when it stopped and the heat was overpowering.

Even after they arrived in Lisbon after a journey of nine days, their troubles were not over. Nine hundred passengers were embarked aboard the Swedish liner, *Drottningholm*. Their happiness at the prospect of a speedy return was baulked when the ship did not sail. The fourteen Germans who were being exchanged for the British had not arrived. After four days of waiting it was decided to leave fourteen Britons behind in recompense. Miss Bliss got back to Stratford on 10 August, but her luggage went astray. Despite her ordeals she expressed a desire to return to France as soon as possible.

Anxiety about the potential fate of the prisoners still in the hands of the Germans and Japanese led to the formation of a self-help group in Stratford, the PoW Relatives Association.

Doodlebugs

After D-Day, the fear of air raids on the Midlands was all but over. A 'dim-out' of lights was introduced in place of the 'black-out'. On 15 November, the Civil Defence Control Centre was stood down from the continuous vigil it had maintained since 24 August 1939. The Home Guard was disbanded, but the enthusiastic volunteers of the 4th Warwickshire Battalion were rewarded with a final parade and march-past at which the Foreign Minister and local MP, Anthony Eden, took the salute.

Yet the work of the Stratford AFS was far from over. A week after D-Day, the first V1 flying bombs, universally known as 'doodlebugs', fell on London and the brigade was sent to the capital in response to the new crisis – some 2,500 V1s found their target. The effect on the nerves of the civilian population was devastating. Fred Wincote soon learnt that the danger moment was when the engine cut out. 'If you could count to five, you were alright.'

Once he was walking down a London street when a flying bomb was going over. 'This poor woman sat there, screaming like hell, she was.' He put his hand on her shoulder, 'Madam, don't worry about that one. That's gone far away.'

'Aren't you calm', she replied. 'Yes. I have been through it, love.'

The V2 rockets were a different matter. They soared fifty miles into the stratosphere at speeds of up to 3,500 miles per hour. There was no defence against them. The programme had been delayed when the Allied armies had captured their uncompleted launch sites in Northern France, so it was not till Saturday, 8 September 1944 that the first one was launched from a mobile site in Holland. It fell on a Woolworth's store that was crowded with schoolchildren and many were killed. At first it was thought that a gas main had exploded.

The Stratford AFS had been given a weekend's leave, but Fred saw the devastating effects on their return to London. 'They were huge things, they were. One of the fins had blown off. It was buried about 2ft deep… They are hot when they come through the air and it had bent it... It was about 6ft high and square.' Later he saw one in Trafalgar Square. 'Stood on its tail end. It was 30ft high.'

It was only with the capture of the launch sites that the bombardment ceased.

Into Belgium

The 11th Armoured Division had survived twenty-three days of fierce fighting in Normandy and was now preparing for the breakout. Charlie Baldwin had obtained some war trophies: four postcards taken from captured members of the SS. One carried the words of the *Horst Wessel Lied,* another commemorated the first national Hitler Youth Rally at Potsdam: the other two were from the Nurenberg Rally in 1934.

On 26 August, General Montgomery authorised a thrust northwards towards Antwerp. It was vital to capture the port intact. There followed the most spectacular week of the entire campaign in North-West Europe. Amiens was taken in a rapid swoop. The surprise was complete. Villagers opening their shutters to discover what the noise was all about could not believe it when they saw British tanks. The speed of the advance bewildered the Germans. On several occasions their lorries joined the fast-moving convoy, under the impression that it was one of theirs. A number of prisoners surrendered to Charlie Baldwin, shouting 'Tommy good: Ruskie bad!'

By 2 September, the 4th KSLI had advanced beyond Lens. Vimy Ridge was liberated in half an hour at the cost of one man who sprained his ankle when he fell down a shell hole: in contrast to the 130,000 Canadian and British soldiers who had perished there in the Great War.

Next day the Battalion advanced into Belgium. The liberation triggered off wild celebrations. It was a Sunday, so crowds lined the streets in every town and village, cheering, waving flags, singing and dancing, pressing wine and flowers on every vehicle. It was also a day of retribution. Women who had formed liaisons with Germans had their heads shaved and the houses of collaborators were fired.

There was no time to stop. The Battalion sped on at 25mph well into the night, halting just twenty miles from Antwerp. Next day, the armoured columns advanced into the city. Two miles from the centre, the tanks were fired on by Germans snipers from the upper floors of houses. The Shropshires were given the task of clearing the streets, which only infantry could do. They descended from their TCVs (troop-carrying vehicles) and advanced on foot. Charlie Baldwin's company was ordered to take the Central Park, which not only housed the German headquarters, but was the hub of the city's road system. Its possession was the key to the city. Their progress was 'like a madhouse with civilians thrusting flowers, fruit, anything they could lay their hands on at us, also kisses, etc.' As they approached the park, 'all hell let loose:

> Machine-gun and rifle fire stopped us in our tracks. Needless to say, all the civilians disappeared in a second. Where they went to, I do not know. We dived off the pavement for cover behind shrubs and trees. Our bren gunner, Smith A.E., was seriously wounded and lay on the pavement. I turned and said 'Smithy has had it' when he opened his eyes and said 'I have not.' To prove it, thirty years later on, my front door bell rang and who should be there but Smith A.E.!

In conjunction with 'A' Company, 'C' Company captured the German command bunkers and spent the night in the park. The prisoners they had taken were locked in the lions' cages (which were fortuitously devoid of animals) at the famous zoo, which was nearby.

Next day, the KSLI was ordered to seize the road bridge over the Albert Canal at Merxem. Again, the happy crowds hindered their progress. As they crossed over some allotments, they came under heavy fire from the other side of the canal. When they got to within 50 yards of it, the Germans blew up the bridge. 'C' Company remained pinned down in the allotments until nightfall when they were able to withdraw. The men were exhausted. Charlie Baldwin hoped that they would get a rest next day, 'but no such luck'. The four companies were ordered across the canal by boat. 'C' Company occupied a paper factory. Charlie saw two or three German tanks supported by infantry pass the entrance archway:

> We placed a Piat into position waiting for a tank to come past. We fired twice and there was a loud explosion so we got the hell out of it as soon as possible as we were in a yard in the open. I remember seeing a German in the Archway when one of our lads fired and hit him in the arms, making him spin round like a top. Then about half a dozen of our lads joined in and that was the end of the German. We made towards a high wall where the German tanks were coming round behind. I threw a grenade over the wall which caused a few shouts to go up.

The company was taking heavy casualties and withdrew to a clothing factory on the canal bank. At three o'clock next day they were ordered into the boats:

> The barrage that was put down in preparation for our withdrawal did the trick... We got into the boats and rowed like hell using rifles and anything else we could lay our hands on to get to the other side.

The Merxem operation was an expensive error of judgement. Twenty-one men had died. After just one day's rest, the KSLI was on the move again, thrusting eastwards through Mechelen and Leuven.

In its rapid advance, the 11th Armoured Division had by-passed many towns and areas held by the Germans. Now these had to mopped up. Trooper Kenneth Westwood of 39 Bordon Place, had landed with his tank regiment on D-Day. By late September he was in northern France. His tank and another one were sent out to locate and destroy an anti-tank gun that was causing problems further down the road. As they rounded a corner to go up a hill, they realised that the gun had been moved forward to meet them. They were caught in its blast. As they bailed out, they came under mortar fire. One of the tank crew was hit in the stomach. They scrambled for the nearest ditch and got there just in time as machine-guns opened up on all sides. Ken Westward started to crawl back towards his own lines, with the wounded man clinging to his feet. He managed to get within 20 yards of the other tank, which had also been hit and was lying on its side in a ditch, when a German jumped out of the hedge about 20 yards behind them:

> He hit me in the arm and my friend in the back and foot. Then something hit my hand – whether it was shrapnel or a bullet I don't know – but it pretty well knocked my thumb clean off. There was no other course but to surrender.

Five other members of the tank crews were captured and taken off. Kenneth's comrade had died and was left lying in the ditch. Kenneth was taken to an advanced field-dressing station, and then by ambulance to a town some twelve miles away. It was getting dark and the Germans were moving up reinforcements and supplies, for the most part on horse-drawn vehicles. Their chronic shortage of petrol was reflected in the fact that he only saw three motor vehicles on the entire journey. His wounds were dressed at a field station and he spent the night there with about thirty wounded

Germans. Next day, he was moved up to a military hospital in Belgium where his hand was operated upon. He was placed on a ward with several other British prisoners. The orderlies were very attentive and always at the patients' beck and call. Kenneth felt he was treated very fairly by the Germans, although he uttered the usual complaint. 'Horrible was too mild a term to describe the food – black bread, a butter substitute of white grease, sausage, soup and a concoction called tea that tastes like mint and was clear in colour.' The Belgian civilians working in the hospital slipped into the ward periodically to tell the prisoners about the progress of the British army.

Excitement was intense next day (which was Kenneth's 21st birthday). They were told that British troops were only 30km away and heading in their direction. That evening, advanced parties entered the town and shortly afterwards an Allied soldier arrived in the ward. He turned out to be a Pole who understood very little English, but grasped the fact that they wanted some English cigarettes:

> When I awoke the following day, I found myself and bed floating along the corridor, borne by six men of the Belgian Marquis. I was taken to another ward where there were five other British soldiers. And, not only that, we had four Belgian nurses to look after us. Incidentally, the civilians who had been informing us of the British advance had all been officers in the Belgian army. They had donned their uniforms and very smart they were.
>
> Then the visitors came – the whole town I should imagine. They brought us every kind of luxury – flowers, butter, eggs, milk, cream, sugar, cake, bread, tomatoes, pears, apples and mountains of grapes. They brought a barber in, too, to give us a much needed shave.

That night the Germans counter-attacked and broke through the British lines. The released prisoners spent a sleepless night with continuous firing around the hospital. The Germans were driven back next day and things quietened down. It was decided to move the patients to a hospital in England, which they reached three days later. He had been wounded, captured, operated on, freed and brought home – all in a week!

The 7th Battalion of the Royal Warwickshire Regiment was involved in the drive into Belgium. Private William Colwell's unit came under heavy fire at a lunatic asylum at Venrij. He was sent forward to assess the possibility of evacuating some of the 1,700 inmates and found himself dodging the bullets of two snipers. He concluded that it would be impossible as the enemy was constantly shelling the only road. He was outraged that the Germans appeared to be 'deliberately firing on those defenceless people. While I was there a sniper killed one patient and injured another who had wandered out in the grounds.'

Corporal W.F. Dyson of the Royal Corps of Signals returned to his home in Evesham Road after the war with an extraordinary trophy: a complete set of booklets and maps issued by the German General Staff in preparation for the invasion of Britain. He was given them by a Belgian officer who had found them in a chateau hurriedly vacated by high-ranking German officers.

On 17 September came the last Allied defeat of the war: the disastrous airborne assault on the Rhine bridges at Arnhem. Michael Long piloted his glider in the first wave of the assault by the 1st Airborne Division. He landed at Wolfheze, a small village five miles west of the city:

> The gliders were down before the parachutists, so I watched the first drop from the ground. Most colourful – especially some of the language.

Among those flung into this cauldron was 25-year-old Sgt Edward Wilkes of 67 Clopton Road. He had worked in the brewery offices before joining the Parachute

Regiment two years before. He was wounded in the battle and cared for by Dutch civilians until the RAMC took over. The Germans gallantly allowed the medics to withdraw before taking the men prisoner.

Another taken prisoner was Michael Long:

> My 'battle' lasted from the Sunday until the Wednesday, when I had an argument with a man at rather short range – and lost...
>
> It was the Dutch people though who were the real sufferers. Many of them having a battle actually fought over them – some houses were German in the morning, British in the afternoon and German again in the evening.

With the opening up of the Swiss frontier in late autumn, Allied internees were repatriated. Among them were Bill Winter and his friend Philip Robilliard. Bill was back in Stratford in the first week in November, but Philip had to wait till the end of the war for the liberation of his native Guernsey.

In November, Sgt Sam Dalton of 36 Park Road, arrived at a Dutch town with his Battalion of the Gordon Highlanders. They had received reports that the place was clear of the enemy, but on the way in they were greeted with 88mm shells and mortar bombs. They had no sooner got their platoons into position for an assault when three Spandaus opened up from the windows of nearby houses. Sam dashed forward with his Piat mortar and fired a couple of rounds into one house. Half the wall was blown away and no more was heard from the Spandau. 'You can judge of our surprise', he recalled, 'when a few minutes after a couple of Germans came walking down the road. They were obviously on a recce patrol. We let them pass us and then opened up with the Bren. They ran round in circles screaming their heads off. A stretcher-bearer dashed out and got hold of them, treated their wounds and brought them back.'

Private W.H. Conway of 2 Days Court, Bull Street, who had joined the Worcestershire Regiment in 1940, was robbed of both his legs by an exploding mortar bomb at Elst on the Dutch-German border.

The Long March

Sgt Wilkes had been placed in 8C Camp at Sagan, next to Stalag Luft III, where Bruce Organ and Ray Hartwell were incarcerated. Conditions were sparse. Each prisoner was given a chunk of black bread a day and soup which was 'more like paste for putting on wall paper.' The vital Red Cross parcels didn't get through too well after D-Day. The prisoners were restricted to a third of a parcel per week.

As the Red Army advanced on the Eastern Front, the Germans prepared to move the PoWs. This was an odd decision. They were of little immediate military use, so it would have made more sense just to leave them, but on 29 January, the inmates of Stalag Luft III embarked on a long march westwards to Leuckenwalde in eastern Germany. The 17,000 inhabitants of 8C Camp remained where they were for the next ten days. They were following the news on a smuggled radio set and indulged in hopes that they would be liberated by the Russians, but, on 8 February, they were ordered to begin their march. Only the hospital cases were left behind.

The march took a month amidst the winter snows. Every 20 yards along the column there was a guard – the shortage of manpower meant that many were over fifty. They had expressionless and dreary faces. The only food the prisoners were given each day was a loaf of black bread between twelve. If they attempted to pull root crops from the frozen fields, the guards forced them back into line with their rifle butts. Thousands dropped out en route, many to die. At night they were sometimes housed in barns and managed to get hold of raw potatoes.

After a long and horrendous march of some 380 miles, the column arrived, in a desperate state, at 9B Camp near Frankfurt-am-Main. It was full of Serbs who generously shared their Red Cross parcels with the new arrivals.

The inmates of Edward Howell's *Straffe Stalag* were marched westwards from Breslau, crossing the Carpathian Mountains into Bohemia. Many died or suffered from chronic frostbite. The local people – Czechs and Poles – tried to give them food, but the Germans beat back even the women.

In February 1945, Flight Sgt Denzil Wheeler of Albany Road was reported missing after his plane was shot down over Northern Italy. He had crash-landed and, with his wireless operator, spent 13 days in a haystack, obtaining food from local farms. Italian Fascists betrayed them to the Germans and he became the last Stratfordian of the war to be taken prisoner.

Endgame

Operation 'Veritable' was planned at the close of 1944. The intention was to clear the country between the rivers Maas and Rhine of the enemy. The attack was delayed as the British divisions paused to wait the outcome of the German offensive in the Ardennes ('the Battle of the Bulge'). The Americans held firm. Relief was not required, so the advance resumed on 8 February 1945.

German resistance was strong to the last. The 4th KSLI was caught up in fierce fighting in the Reichwald Forest, the last natural barrier before the Rhine. Heavy mortar fire had taken its toll of the attackers and a German gun had 'brewed up' a Sherman tank. Sergeant Baldwin, his Company Commander, six men and another sergeant had to finish the assault on their own. Strong resistance was focussed around a farmhouse, which the little party encircled. They managed to silence the gun that had destroyed the Sherman and Sgt Baldwin flushed seventeen Germans out of a trench in the front garden. When a self-propelled gun fired at them at close range, they took cover in a trench near the house. Sergeant Baldwin had crawled out to bring in two wounded men when a shell struck the corner of the house and burst over the trench. He returned to find that many of the assault force were casualties, including the Company Commander. Their Bren gun had been put out of action by shrapnel, the wireless set was shattered and its operator wounded.

Another section arrived out of the woods to bring the numbers in the slit trench up to eight again. Not realising this, the enemy decided to press home their apparent advantage. A German appeared above the trench not 3 yards from Sgt Baldwin. He felt something being pressed into his hand by a private and realised it was a ready-primed grenade. The German poked an 'ugly-looking Schmeisser' at the men in the trench and called upon them to surrender. Baldwin lobbed his grenade. It killed the German and two others behind him instantly. Another three Germans were killed by grenades before, with suicidal courage, a German officer jumped into the dug-out between Baldwin and the disarmed Bren gunner. The gunner shouted to get the officer's attention as Baldwin grabbed a rifle. He fired it at the German from point-blank range – and missed, so he floored him by 'smacking him up the clock'.

The Company Sergeant Major was a casualty of the skirmish, so Sgt Baldwin was promoted in his stead. He was later awarded the Military Medal.

On the night of the 2 March 1945, Sgt Frederick Davis of Luddington Road, commanding No. 9 platoon of 'A' Company of the Herefordshire Regiment was ordered to force a gap in the German front line southeast of Uden in the southern Netherlands to enable the rest of the Company to pass through to consolidate the position. There was no cover and the advancing troops were silhouetted in the moonlight. On approaching the objective, they came under intensive small arms, spandau and mortar fire. The whole leading section became casualties. Sergeant Davis moved about organising return fire and personally attending to the wounded. This undoubtedly saved a number of lives for it was impossible to evacuate them until later. He then reconnoitred the enemy position, standing in full view no more than 80 yards from their lines. Leaving the platoon under the command of another sergeant, he returned to brief the CO. On the basis of his information, the enemy position was captured in a company attack without further casualties. Sergeant Davis was awarded the Military Medal.

The Forgotten Army

Not for nothing did General Slim's 14th Army, fighting the Japanese in Burma, become known as 'the forgotten army'. It was natural that public attention, after the threat of invasion and the Blitz, should be concentrated on the conflict nearer home, but news from the Far East filtered into the public arena through news reports and letters home.

In the deep jungle, where every man was totally dependent on the support of others, discipline was fierce. The extreme punishment was to leave a soldier behind to face certain death, but this was probably more of a threat than an actuality because Chuck Taylor never heard of such a case. He did claim that a man was lashed on one occasion, which would have been contrary to Army regulations, but never revealed whether he had seen it, or it was hearsay.

The Chindits faced two enemies, the Japanese and the jungle. Chuck had the misfortune to be the simultaneous victim of both when he was attacked by ants during a Japanese air attack! The affects of the bites went unrecorded, but he was wounded by the strafing but had to soldier on until he could be flown out.

Back in India, Chuck was issued with a casualty note which bore the Chindit symbol of the Cinthe, the mythical beast, half lion, half flying-griffin, which guarded Burmese temples. 'You have taken your full share in the achievement about which the whole world is talking – an achievement which has hit the Jap where it hurts most – in the guts.'

The note carried a warning against talking to anyone about any detail of the campaign. 'Get well quick', it admonished. 'Special Force needs YOU back.'

Chuck was indeed back, but not with the Chindits. The 7th Leicesters had taken a mauling in and from the jungle, so the Battalion was withdrawn and the survivors were transferred to the 2nd Battalion. Recovered from his wounds, Chuck flew several missions on board Dakotas, dropping the supplies that were the Chindits' lifeline.

In December 1944, Captain Ronald Lysons, the brother of the PoW in Italy, an acting Company CO with the Royal Sussex Regiment, was involved in a two-day struggle with the Japanese in the railway corridor south of Myitkyina in North Burma. It was decided to advance from 'Sussex' stream and secure 'Bridge's' stream, 350 yards away, which was held by the enemy. Heavy British shelling had pitted the ground and covered it with dead trees and foliage, making it 'a veritable no-man's land'. Supplies and ammunition were to be brought up by a soldier on four mules.

A road linked the two streams. Captain Lysons' 'D' Company was to advance on the right of it and 'C' company on the left. 'A' Company was to follow up closely. The advance was immediately pinned down by medium machine-guns to the left, right and centre and by sniper fire. They could see no enemy. Pushing forward, they passed over a series of unoccupied enemy bunkers. They reached their objective and established a perimeter astride the stream, digging in with their bare hands and a few entrenching tools, only to discover that they were on the verge of disaster. 'C' Company had been forced back just 10 yards from the stream and had withdrawn behind the support Battalion's perimeter. The enemy had slid surreptitiously back into their bunkers and their fire had pinned down 'A' Company. Worst of all, the muleteer with the vital supplies had been unable to get through. They were cut off with no food and little ammunition. They were ordered to spend the night in their precarious position. Relief would be attempted at Battalion strength next morning.

The night was extremely cold. They had neither rations nor sleep and they were subjected to spasmodic firing from small arms, grenades and mortars. One NCO was killed, but they accounted for three of the enemy. Next morning, the Battalion made three attempts to get through, but each time was driven back. Captain Lysons realised that the only hope was for the company to fight its way back to the British lines. That afternoon they made three attempts from different points, but each time they ran into heavy machine-gun and sniper fire. The telephone lines they had laid had been cut by the enemy, but they could still communicate with the Battalion through signals to the forward artillery observation post. They were ordered to attempt another escape that night. At 1.20 a.m. when clouds had shielded the moon, they set out, using a compass bearing. Captain Lysons gave his men strict orders not to fire. They moved forward, carrying their casualties with them, hoping that the sound of the heavy dew dripping from the trees would cover any noise. As they passed the enemy bunkers, they could hear Japanese soldiers snoring just 2 yards away. The leading group had regained the trenches and all seemed well for the centre and rear when they heard the sound of a bolt being drawn back and they were engulfed in grenade and machine-gun fire. Despite this, all the men eventually crawled into their own lines. It had taken them an hour to cover the last 150 yards. The last man came in at 4.20 a.m. They had suffered only seven casualties during this daring escapade, but even then they were not safe, for the Japanese bombardment continued. When this eventually died down at 6 a.m., they were rewarded with the whole Battalion's breakfast.

During his abortive expedition, Capt Lysons had been shot at by two machine-guns and had two grenades thrown at him from 10 yards range. A sniper killed a man standing next to him. He had run into an enemy bunker, which he found occupied and had two more grenades thrown at him before the thrower was killed. Yet he received not so much as a scratch during the whole adventure.

Liberation

With their advance into occupied territory, the Allied forces experienced the genuine joy felt by the liberated peoples. Captain W. Badger, of 38 West Street, serving with the Central Mediterranean Forces, was in charge of a unit that freed a Greek village. At the Mayor's house, they were greeted by his wife, 'a stately rosy-faced dame' who wrapped a Greek flag round the neck of each soldier and kissed him. When her husband arrived, they went indoors to talk. Apples, nuts and wine were set before them. The wine in question was probably Retsina for Captain Badger described it as tasting and smelling like turpentine. Local dignitaries joined the party while outside a great crowd gathered. A public holiday was declared. Captain Badger had to stuff down more apples. They just couldn't eat fast enough to please the Mayor, so he and his family peeled and cored them and cut them into quarters, offering them to the soldiers on the point of a knife. Later they were each given three eggs fried in olive oil with two slices of brown bread. After he had finished them, Captain Badger had a fourth egg pressed upon him. To their amazement, a plate of roast mutton chops arrived and they were given two each. When they had struggled through that, two more were pressed upon them. Captain Badger declined through the interpreter, but the Mayor would take no refusal:

> Then came more apples and we drank the health of everybody present and also of Winston Churchill. Eventually, very reluctantly, they let us go. But that was not all. They loaded us up with nuts and then brought a big basket of apples decorated with flowers and evergreens for us to take away. We found ourselves confronted by a large crowd with plates of cakes and nuts and wreaths of flowers and evergreens...

Thus we rode out of the village and you couldn't see the carrier for people and greenery. When they left us, about half a mile from the village, the carrier still looked like a harvest festival. What a day!

Peace at Last

On its drive into Lower Saxony, the 4th KSLI was under orders to advance to the Baltic with maximum speed to secure territory before the Red Army could occupy it. En route the concentration camp of Bergen-Belsen was passed, but the stop was brief. Charlie Baldwin was vaguely aware of the function of the place. Typhoid was rife, so they did not enter the camp.

At Edward Wilkes' PoW camp near Frankfurt, conditions had deteriorated even further. Many of the men were so emaciated that they could hardly turn over in their beds. In early April, the guards beat a hasty retreat, putting out the PoW signs as they went, so that the camp was liable to be bombed or shelled by the Allies. On Easter Monday, the first American tanks appeared and were met at the gate by the Camp Commandant and Padre with a white flag. Among the prisoners there was not the elation that might have been expected. The dreadful experience had taken too great a toll. Food was brought up, but it was 'too rich for us. We couldn't take it.'

The German guards fled the PoW camp at Leuckenwalde in front of the advancing Red Army on 21 April. The Russians arrived next day and proved very efficient and overwhelmingly friendly, but the prisoners' final evacuation was delayed due to the Russian desire to conform to the terms of the Yalta Agreement. During the delay they did everything possible for them. The repatriation took place on 20 May. The Russians organised a ceremony before driving the prisoners to the River Elbe, where they crossed the bridge and were taken by American lorries to Halle.

Edward Howell was released from captivity in Nurenberg by the US Army in the closing days of the war. He had received no new clothes since 1942 and arrived back in England wearing an American jacket and Serbian trousers.

Lieutenant Dennis Flower, released from his PoW camp, was on a plane flying home on 7 May when he heard the official announcement that the war in Europe was over. News of the German surrender came to Stratford at 9 p.m. that evening. Within an hour, the streets were transformed. The flags, banners, streamers and bunting that had greeted the Coronation reappeared and the flags of the four main Allied powers – the UK, USA, USSR and China – flew in Bridge Street. Two days later street parties took place in many parts of the town. To celebrate the peace, Flowers brewed a special victory ale called 'Stingo'.

Despite the genuine and joyful spontaneity of the VE-Day celebrations, there were bitter complaints about the failure of the Town Council to organise any kind of event to mark the great occasion. There was no excuse. It had been apparent for weeks that the war was drawing to its close.

In one area of activity the Town Council was less lethargic. Even before the war was over, it was considering ways to deal with social problems amidst the austerity to come. In February 1945 it ordered fifty of the temporary factory-built homes that were to be universally known as prefabs and selected a site off the Clopton Road. German PoWs were used to erect them.

Flensburg

Just as a Stratfordian – Edgar Cranmer – had had a ringside seat at the closing stages of the epic drama of the Great War, so did another – Charlie Baldwin – in the Second

Street party in Avon Crescent. (Image courtesy of the Shakespeare Birthplace Trust Records Office)

Street party in Scholars Lane. (Image courtesy of the Shakespeare Birthplace Trust Records Office)

Street party in Shakespeare Street. (Image courtesy of the Shakespeare Birthplace Trust Records Office)

World War. The 4th KSLI had advanced to the Baltic at Flensburg and established itself in a German army camp.

Hitler had committed suicide on 30 April. Regarding himself as betrayed by Goering and Himmler, he had nominated the Commander-in-Chief of the Navy, Grand Admiral Karl Doenitz, as his successor. The new *Fuhrer* arrived in Flensburg on the same day as the 4th KISI The town had escaped the war relatively unscathed. Doenitz had obtained copies of the demarcation lines that the four Allied powers had agreed for the administration of post-war Germany and, in a remarkable operation, had organised the sea-borne evacuation of some two million people from the proposed Russian Zone, where he felt they would be subject to atrocities, to the proposed British Zone. Thus the entire area was crammed with refugees. The troops of the 4th KSLI, like all the occupying forces were obliged to follow a strict policy of non-fraternisation with the Germans. The German troops were still armed, so the men of the Shropshires were only allowed out of the camp in pairs and had to carry their rifles with them.

Doenitz wasted no time in establishing a Government. It was housed in the Torpedo School at nearby Muewik and was mainly drawn from the middle ranks of Hitler's administration and included as many members as possible who were comparatively untainted by Nazism. Even Albert Speer, a former Nazi Cabinet Minister and a member of Hitler's inner circle, who was appointed Minister of Economics and Production, could present himself as a moderate face of the old regime. A military command headquarters was established under Generaloberst Alfred Jodl.

After VE-Day, the small area around Flensberg-Muerwik became an enclave in an otherwise totally occupied country. Armed German soldiers marched through the streets and stood guard outside the offices and residences of members of the Government. The Reich's war flag with its central swastika flew over Doenitz's headquarters. Allied officers who had business there observed the diplomatic niceties. Every day, Doenitz drove the 500 yards to a Cabinet meeting in a grand Mercedes limousine that had been part of Hitler's fleet of cars.

The Doenitz Government represented a dilemma for the occupying authorities. Whereas in the First World War, it had been the politicians who had signed the armistice, in the Second it was the military establishment represented by Jodl. Hitler had come to power through a process that was at least tenuously legitimate, so Doenitz could claim legitimacy as his successor. The situation might even be useful to the Allies in legitimising their own status as occupying powers. The Russians even offered Doenitz a return to Berlin, although this was quickly rescinded.

It was in Doenitz's interest to play for time and hope that he could establish his Government as a recognised means towards reconstruction and reconciliation. On the other hand, it was clear that his writ scarcely extended beyond the boundaries of Flensberg. Amidst this uncertainty the American Major-General Lowell W. Rooks arrived in Flensberg on 12 May to establish a Control Commission with the British Brigadier R.L.S. Foord. They were to be joined by the Soviet General Nikolai Trusov. Rooks set up his headquarters on the SS *Patria*, a ship belonging to the Hamburg-America Line. The die was cast for the Doenitz Government. On 19 May, the Allied Commander, Major-General Eisenhower, ordered it dissolved. Four days later, British troops moved in to round up the German soldiers. The atmosphere in the town changed from cautious optimism to sullen quiet.

Doetitz and his acolytes were ordered to report on board the *Patria* at 10 a.m. The military men were in uniform. They were taken to the bar where Rooks told them they were under arrest. Sergeant Major Charlie Baldwin was part of the guard that escorted Doenitz, Jodl, Speer and others into captivity.

Charlie Baldwin remained with the 4th KSLI in Flensberg until he was demobbed. On 6 June, the annual drumhead service was held to commemorate the Battalion's collective award of the *Croix de Guerre* for its gallantry in action in the Great War. On 12 August, General Montgomery presented Charlie with his Military Medal at the newly-dubbed 'Drury Lane Theatre' in Hamburg. 'Monty' asked him whether he intended to stay on in the army. 'No, sir. I've had enough', replied the Sergeant Major. He wanted to get home to Rene.

Belsen

The ending of the war brought a full revelation of the horrors perpetrated by the Nazis. In early May, Sister D. Rider found herself nursing the victims in the concentration camp at Belsen. The survivors were being evacuated from the original camp (Camp 1) to the former German Army camp (Camp 2). Even for the nursing staff, admission to Camp 1 – 'the dreadful camp you may have seen pictures of', she wrote home – was by permit only. Inside there were still 1,500 women and 'goodness knows how many men'. Medical students and Red Cross workers were doing 'an excellent work', feeding them and sorting the living from the dead. Polish internees were trying to nurse them. At the liberation there were 200 deaths a week. This had now dwindled to eight. The place was reeking with typhus. The huts were so small that, although there were 200 people where there were previously 1,000, they were lying side by side with only walking space between their feet:

> They cooked, ate and slept in the same room and were dragged out when they died. They are still dying, two to nine a day, and are buried in the big pit, where there are already some 3,000 bodies, just a sprinkling of sand over them.

Sister Rider was working in Camp 2. The inmates – mostly women – were suffering from typhus, dysentery or famine. Before their arrival they were stripped, scrubbed and put on a stretcher with three blankets. On her first day on duty, she had to wash down an inmate. 'I had never washed a skeleton before', she wrote. Every day before she went on duty she was sprayed all over with louse powder.

In Camp 2 there were eleven squares with eight 'houses' on each. There were around 700 people on each square. Because of the shortage of beds, many patients were lying on palliasses on the floor.

On Sister Rider's square the patients were still dying at the rate of four a day. They received little medical treatment. 'Apparently it's not much use,' she explained in her letter home, 'the main treatment being the correct diet.' If proper food was given to them, they swelled up and it killed them, so they were put on the 'No. 1 diet', consisting of an intake of milk, water and rice water every two hours. Even the liberation had not ensured that the horrors were entirely over. There had been no water in the camp for drinking, washing-up or washing bedpans for the previous four days. 'You can imagine the smell.' There had been no news from the outside world since her arrival and she wondered how Stratford had received the news of the peace. 'Did all the church bells ring at home? 'I went over to the baby and children's ward today', she added. 'Poor little marasmus-looking things. What is their future?'

Burma

At Fort Dufferin near Mandalay, Cpl Joe Charles of 1 Clopton Road, who in civilian life had been a cold storage operator at the brewery, and an officer were driving up rations to a forward company. It was so well camouflaged that he drove on past them for two miles. Close to the Japanese positions, five light machine-guns opened fire. Thirty-six bullets hit the jeep. One volley burst amongst six grenades that Joe had placed under the driving seat. They owed their lives to a fragment of his mess tin that prevented the firing pin from detonating the grenades. The officer was wounded in the leg in another burst that passed over Joe's lap. Joe drove him back to the British lines and organised treatment before returning to the forward position.

The last Stratfordian to be killed in the war was 20-year-old Sub-Lt Roy Keeley, the son of Mrs H. Keeley of 12 Ely Street, a pilot in the Fleet Air Arm. He was trapped in the cockpit when his plane overturned as he was taking off from an aircraft carrier. He was pulled out, but died of his injuries two days later. His elder brother, Sgt Donald Keeley, an air-gunner, had been killed in March 1944 at the age of 22 and was buried in Germany.

The 2nd Leicesters had been earmarked for 'Operation Zipper' – the invasion of Malaya, but the Japanese surrendered before this could take place. Chuck Taylor found himself on internal security duties. With the volatility of India under the atmosphere of impending partition, the troops were in constant demand.

In the House of my Father

News of the final ending of the Second World War came at midnight on 13 August. On hearing the joyful tidings, people gathered at the Fountain outside the American Red Cross Club in the White Swan. Some had dressed, but others appeared in their pyjamas and dressing gowns.

Someone started a bonfire in the street. A dash of petrol every now and then sent the flames soaring high. Fireworks thrown among the embers exploded intermittently, hurling clouds of sparks into the sky. Eight-year-old Mion Hetherington was puzzled when the residents of the American Hostel at the White Swan rushed into the street and flung suitcases full of clothing onto the flames, shouting 'We're going home! We're going home!' 'What are soldiers doing with suitcases' she thought, 'and what are they going to wear?' A piano appeared and set the crowds singing. It was soon joined by an accordion and a big bass drum. American army trucks gave joyrides to all and sundry. With blaring horns they roared through the streets and into the countryside beyond, making sleep impossible for those who had not joined the celebrations. Half of the Festival Company formed one load.

Next evening, the Town Council, conscious of the criticisms of its inertia at the time of the VE celebrations, organised a dance in Bridge Street. At the outset, only half a dozen couples took the floor, but the Palais Glide soon set hundreds of feet in motion.

At 8.30 p.m., the Mayor, Cllr Roderick Baker, spoke to the crowd through a microphone and called for three cheers for all who had served the nation so well during the long years of war. Half an hour later, the large crowd fell silent as the King's broadcast to the nation was relayed. At the end, three hearty cheers were given for His Majesty.

The joy and thankfulness at final victory was heartfelt. Next day street parties were thrown in many parts of the town and in the evening there was more dancing in Bridge Street.

At the Mayor's Church Parade to give thanks for the peace on the following Sunday, the sword-of-honour was carried by W.O. Roy Salmon. He was released from captivity on 16 April: three years to the day since his capture.

For most people the ending of the war brought unrestrained joy, but for others it meant the end of the hope that had been draining slowly away for years. Philip Tyler's parents finally accepted that he would never return and sent his savings off to the two hospitals as he had requested.

A major priority with the ending of the war with Japan was the safety of the thousands of allied prisoners. On 30 August, in Changi Camp, Anthony Claridge looked up and saw six paratroopers descending onto the airfield, half a mile away. They were paramedics from the 44th Indian Airborne Division. When they arrived at the camp, he asked the first man where he came from. Pat came the answer, 'Stratford-upon-Avon.' It was Pte Wally Brooks of 27 Great William Street who became the first man to land on Singapore Island after the Japanese surrender. When he parachuted down he had no idea whether the Japanese had ceased firing or not. For the first time in over three years the surviving prisoners could contact their families and the newly-released Alfred Tutt wrote home to say that he was well.

In the autumn the PoWs started to arrive home. Anthony Claridge returned in late October. Others had not been so fortunate. Mr and Mrs George Scruby at 9 Holtom Street heard that their son Fred had died on 12 October 1944, aged 22.

Hopes that the end of the war would see the relaxation of austerity were soon thwarted. If anything the reverse was the case. Bread rationing had never been introduced during the war, although supplies were restricted, but on 20 July 1946, people received their coupons to collect their loaves.

On 28 January 1946, the first of a series of 'Welcome Home' parties was held at the Town Hall for returning servicemen and women. It consisted of a 'substantial' meal and a 'first-class' concert party. No alcohol was served. The cost was borne out of the rates. The progress of demobilisation was slow and the final party was not held until May 1948.

Alan Sutton, who had joined the Navy as an Ordinary Seaman, had risen to the rank of Lieutenant Commander. He rejoined the Borough Treasurer's office, but found that the war had completely changed his attitudes. He had grown used to being addressed as 'Sir', but Henry Tompkins continued to address him by his surname as he had before the war. 'I wasn't going to be dictated to by a Treasurer or anybody else... and told him what he could do with his job.'

Chuck Taylor did not return from India until a year after the war in the east was over, 'so people had got used to it by the time we got back'. There were celebrations at Tiddington for the returning servicemen, but he did not join them:

You had 2½ years in the jungle, nobody to talk to only your mates. It kind of clammed you up somehow, so it took me a long time to get over that. It took me a fortnight to get out of the house. It gradually came back of course.

There was a proposal to give a cash grant to the returning heroes, but the 'upper class' of the village opposed this and suggested presenting a book instead:

They said that all that cash would enable them to do was to go drinking in the pub – my mother, being outspoken, told them what she thought about them.

W.H. Conway had shown no self-pity since losing both his legs. Equipped with false legs, he taught himself to walk again and got a job as a cellulose fitter at the Royal Label Factory. He began to court a Bidford lass, Winifred Cooper, and they were hoping to get married soon.

The Town Council's efforts in the housing sphere were substantial. Despite their nominal independence, the councillors were overwhelming politically Conservative. Yet in the post-war era, municipal endeavour was the order of the hour. On 31 July 1946, the keys of the first council house to be completed for seven years were handed to Mr R.H. Simmonds, BEM, who until he was demobbed a few weeks before was a Quartermaster Sergeant with the Warwickshire Yeomanry.

The situation was not helped by the fact that the Government was still holding over 500 bedrooms in the town. It was not until November 1946 that the first of the leading hotels requisitioned for war service was returned to civilian use. The Falcon was bought by the wine merchant Chris Rookes. When he took it over there was 'not a stick of furniture and the building was in a state to which only care-free service units could reduce it.'

Kate Higgins recalled that the Shakespeare was 'very knocked about':

This lovely oak staircase that went up from the front door was all belted about. You can imagine with RAF personnel marching about.

'My God', said Mr Higgins, the Manager. 'I don't think it's the old Tudor house that it was.'

Marcelle Méliès was one of a group of nurses from the Hospital who were invited to a party in the Officers' Mess of the Royal Engineers at Long Marston. There she met and later married the CO of the Demobilisation Section, Major David Bobroff and finally found nuptial bliss in England.

One who self-confessedly did well out of the war was Tommy Bird. A sickly youth, much in hospital in his native Birmingham, he had persuaded his doctors to collect the money to buy him a donkey cart on which he could deliver firewood. He came to Stratford in 1928 because he liked 'the look of the place' and had a big stall on the market when it was in Bridge Street. He then went into the scrap metal business on the site of the old brickworks up the Birmingham Road. During the war, he worked for the Government on clearing bombsites in Midlands cities. The war over, he handled vast quantities of surplus material.

The German prisoners of war continued to be the largest source of gang labour available to local agriculture. At Christmas in 1946, the sixty anti-Nazis at Ettington Park were invited to dinner by local families.

Repatriation of the prisoners began early in 1948. Rudolf Weichart and Fritz Waschau, two of the 'good Germans', were hopeful of returning home on 30 January, but instead found themselves before the Borough Magistrates for riding a bicycle without a rear light. The Chairman, Dr A.R. McWhinney, expressed regret that their repatriation had been delayed, but somewhat mean-spiritedly said that no allowance could be made and fined them 7s 6d each.

In 1949, the *Herald* dubbed the Ministry of Pensions 'the Government Department with a soul', following its decision to present cars to 1,500 disabled ex-servicemen. Three were from Stratford. On 29 April, W.H. Conway walked unaided upstairs to the ballroom at the Town Hall to receive the documents for a Ford 8, together with petrol coupons and a cheque for £11 5*s* to cover the first quarter's maintenance. A similar presentation was made to Mr E. Barr of 25 Percy Street, who was paralysed from the waist down.

The third car went to Teddy Barr of 29 Percy Street, who was probably a relation of the other recipient. He had enlisted in the Royal Berkshire Regiment in 1939 at the age of 18. He was severely wounded and spent three years in hospital, undergoing thirty-two operations, but he was always cheerful and in high spirits, never complaining. Before leaving Winnick Hospital in Warrington, he married his nurse, who came to Stratford with him. Sadly, his ordeal had so weakened him that he died at Stratford Hospital on 4 April 1949.

There were again moves to remember the fallen. A Cross of Sacrifice erected in the cemetery in 1949 by the Imperial War Graves Commission commemorated the 154 servicemen who had been killed in the locality. Ninety-four of them were Canadian aircrew out of Wellesbourne, who had mainly died in flying accidents. They were buried in a sunken garden lined with maple trees.

In the following year, Field Marshall Viscount Montgomery unveiled a memorial at Holy Trinity. Among the ninety-four men commemorated was Richard Spender, the young poet who had gone so gladly to war. Let his words represent an epitaph to the people of this small town who, whatever their strengths and failings, had given so much in fighting for what they perceived as a righteous cause in two terrible wars:

'Who dies? Who dies?' We who have read
Let us shut the book gently. 'Who dies?'
A thousand, thousand voices told me -
Taking me by the elbow and leading me
Gently and whispering down the aisle –
'He laid me on His shoulder and brought me
(Yes, even me) rejoicing Home.'
    I am amongst my own people
And in the House of my Father.

INDEX